EGIMENT

THE 5

Now the

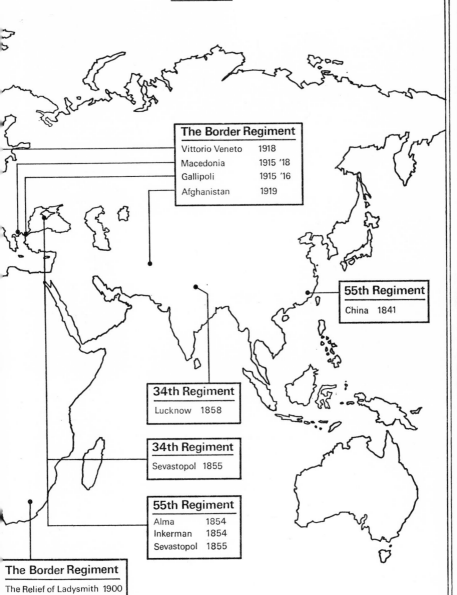

The Border Regiment

Vittorio Veneto	1918
Macedonia	1915 '18
Gallipoli	1915 '16
Afghanistan	1919

55th Regiment

China	1841

34th Regiment

Lucknow	1858

34th Regiment

Sevastopol	1855

55th Regiment

Alma	1854
Inkerman	1854
Sevastopol	1855

The Border Regiment

The Relief of Ladysmith	1900
South Africa	1899–1902

Tried and Valiant

The Queen's Colour (*top*) and
The Regimental Colour of the
4th Battalion, The Border Regiment

Tried
and Valiant

THE HISTORY OF THE BORDER REGIMENT

(The 34th and 55th Regiments of Foot)
1702 - 1959

DOUGLAS SUTHERLAND

LEO COOPER · LONDON

First published in Great Britain, 1972, by
LEO COOPER LTD,
196 Shaftesbury Avenue, London WC2H 8JL

Copyright © 1972 by
The Trustees of the Border Regiment Museum

Foreword Copyright © 1972
Major-General V. Blomfield

ISBN 0 85052 042 8

Printed in Great Britain at
The Compton Press
Salisbury

CONTENTS

ILLUSTRATIONS 7
FOREWORD 9

PART I   THE EIGHTEENTH CENTURY

Chapter I   *page* 13
Chapter II   25
Chapter III   38
Chapter IV   44
Chapter V   53

PART II   THE NINETEENTH CENTURY

Chapter VI   63
Chapter VII   83
Chapter VIII   96
Chapter IX   112

PART III   THE TWENTIETH CENTURY

Chapter X   127
Chapter XI   145
Chapter XII   159
Chapter XIII   173
Chapter XIV   183
Chapter XV   193
Chapter XVI   196
Chapter XVII   216

Postscript 223

Appendix I   *The Regimental Music* 225
Appendix II   *The Badge* 227
Appendix III *Victoria Crosses* 229

Index 233

ILLUSTRATIONS

facing page

1	Sir Richard Steele	16
2	Private of the 34th Regiment	17
3/4	Two Officers of the 55th Regiment	17
5	The 34th Regiment at Fontenoy, 1745	32
6	The Battle of Brandywine, 1777	33
7	Private of the 34th Regiment	64
8	Drummer of the French 34e Regiment	64
9	Display of captured Colours, 1811	64
10	A Crimean Scene	65
11	55th Regiment at the Battle of Inkerman, 1854	65
12	Private Thomas Beach, winning the VC	80
13	The Storming of the Redan, 1855	80
14	A grim reminder of the Indian Mutiny, 1858	81
15	The Border Regiment at Spion Kop, 1900	112
16	Unpacking the Royal Gift, Orange Free State, 1900	112
17	Before landing at X Beach, Gallipoli, 1915	113
18	Men of the Regiment at Cape Helles	113
19	Sergeant Riley at Gheluvelt, 1914	128
20	Men of the Border Regiment, Thiepval Wood, 1916	128
21	Recruiting poster, 1922	129
22	Presentation of new colours by HM King George V, 1924	160
23	Officers relaxing in Shanghai, 1927	161
24	Boundary post, Tien Tsin, 1928	161
25/6	Day and night uniforms, Palestine, 1937–38	176
27	Boy Drummers of 1st Border	176

28   *Recruiting, 1940*   177

29   *Learning to use the Bren*   177

Between Pages 200 and 201

30   *Major Neill and Captain McCartney at Arnhem, 1944*

31   *Private O'Dowd at Arnhem*

32   *4th Border Regiment near Kohima, 1944*

33   *Muleteer Little*

34   *9th Border Regiment in Meiktila, 1945*

35   *9th Border Regiment occupy Pegu, 1945*

36   *Three former Colonels of the Regiment*

37   *Parading outside Carlisle Castle*

Foreword

BY MAJOR-GENERAL V. BLOMFIELD, C.B., D.S.O.

'THAT THE BORDER REGIMENT has never been found lacking is its finest epitaph'; so ends this book. The author, when he wrote that, was concluding a story, covering three centuries, which tells of the contribution made by the Regiment in our country's wars and of the triumphs of its soldiers, often despite the most appalling dangers and conditions.

As we follow the Regiment around the world and read of the changing pattern of warfare, of battles won and lost, of fateful decisions, of superb gallantry, so, at the same time, fitted into its historical background, is the life of the soldier since 1700.

For years, scant consideration was given to his welfare by those who sent him off to fight or to garrison Britain's possessions overseas. Years were spent in bad climates, in quite unsuitable clothing and with very meagre rations. Although some of the early pages make grim reading, there is a lighter side to the story. Humour is there and, typically British, it often appears at the most unlikely moments. Nevertheless, it is hard to understand how it was, even all those years ago, that so little was done for men from whom so much was demanded.

As the years went by and there was a regular standing Army, improvements were introduced and it is interesting to note that an early revolutionary change in both meals and recreation was initiated by the Regiment. From the Crimea onwards lessons were learned from the big campaigns and, whilst the horrors of War remained, the accompanying conditions were made more bearable.

Readers of the exploits of the Regiment throughout the pages of this History will be able to trace the golden thread of pride of Regiment. One can feel it was this which inspired gallant deeds and, perhaps more important, gave to one and all a sense of responsibility. Yet, at the start and indeed for many years, that loyalty was given to a simple number, 34 or 55.

The linking of the two regiments was, in due course, to bring the splendid support of 'The Two Counties', but one cannot meddle lightly with regimental traditions and affections and the threatened abolition of the magic numbers, 34 and 55, shocked the Regiments at the time. In fact, the numbers lived on and today's Army List shows regiments with the old numbers in brackets.

This History will be of absorbing interest throughout Cumberland and Westmorland and the Author's handling of this century's wars will be appreciated – the many battalions, changes of role, switches between theatres and the need to do justice to all presented a problem indeed.

One must, however, remember that since its earliest days, men have stood in the Border ranks who came from the length and breadth of the British Isles; so this History, so ably and so happily woven together by Mr. Douglas Sutherland, invites the interest of all.

I had the honour to be the last Colonel of The Border Regiment. A sad distinction it is true, but I know the tradition and spirit, of which you read in these pages, live on in The King's Own Royal Border Regiment (4, 34, 55) and I hope that all who enjoy this chronicle of years gone by will look with interest and affection on those who are following on.

PART I

The Eighteenth Century

CHAPTER I

THE BRITISH ARMY, as opposed to the English Army, came into being with the Restoration of Charles II. The dowry of Charles's queen, Catherine of Braganza, brought the territories of Bombay and Tangier to the British Crown and it was necessary to raise professional troops for their defence. It was also in the reign of Charles II that for the first time Scottish and English soldiers, later to be joined by regiments of Irish and Welsh, served together in the same army. The New Model Army included troops like General Monk's Coldstream Regiment, who elected to serve the Crown as a body of royal guards, and the Royal Scots, who left the service of the Dutch as mercenaries to become the First of Foot.

The establishment of the British Army, for the first time, provided men who wanted to adopt soldiering as a profession with an opportunity for doing so in their own country (instead of having to hire themselves out as mercenaries on the Continent), and the standard was high. Officered by the cadet sons of aristocratic families and the landowner class, the army drew its recruits from the sons of farmers and respectable tradesmen. Following the example long set by Scotland, where to carry arms was an honourable tradition, to be a soldier at first carried with it a considerable measure of prestige.

This admirable state of affairs was not, however, to last long. As the army expanded it ceased to be an elect force of dedicated professionals. Recruits grew scarcer and eventually demand exceeded supply so that the most degraded specimens were admitted into the ranks in order to keep up numbers. The result was that the local populace came to dread the quartering of soldiers in their district because of the increase in crimes of robbery and violence and rape which inevitably followed. By the end of the seventeenth century the reputation of the army was at such a low level that it was regarded as a suitable profession only for felons and worse.

With increasing commitment abroad, however, the need for a standing army continued to grow.

When the eighteenth century opened, Louis XIV was on the throne of France and his ambition to be ruler of all Europe was causing the ailing King William III of England the greatest anxiety. Treaty after treaty was violated by Louis, culminating in his securing the throne of Spain for his grandson, Philip, Duke of Anjou, thereby seriously upsetting the delicate balance of power on which peace in Europe depended. At the same time, he supported the exiled James II's claims to be the rightful King of England and there were many who would have liked to have seen him on the throne instead of the Dutch interloper. James had already tried to regain his throne through the support of the Irish and had been decisively defeated at the Battle of the Boyne. Now there were signs that the Scots might support another attempt.

In 1702 William, as head of the European alliance against France, decided that he must once again go to war to limit Louis' territorial ambitions and to this end it became necessary greatly to augment the strength of the army.

According to the custom of the times, a custom which was to be continued for many years, the task of raising new regiments was deputed to commanding officers, who were paid a lump sum to cover recruitment expenses and the payment of bounties. These officers in turn delegated their responsibility for actual recruitment to junior officers, each of whom were allotted an area in which to operate. Because of the low esteem in which the army was held, persuading men to join the colours was an extremely difficult task and all manner of nefarious methods were used to trick likely candidates into enlistment. It was common practice to get a man so drunk that it was easy to slip the king's shilling into his pocket so that, when he recovered his senses, he was well and truly hooked. There were even cases of abduction similar to the press-ganging of sailors.

Amongst others charged with the raising of new regiments to fight Louis of France was Robert, Lord Lucas, a lieutenant-colonel in Sir John Jacob's Regiment, the Thirteenth Light Infantry. His authority was dated 12th February, 1702 and his recruitment area extended from Norfolk to Essex. He set up temporary headquarters at Norwich and Colchester and appointed as his deputies Lieutenant-

Colonel Thomas Dare, Major Garth and Captains Kitson, Shadwell, Parsons, Lechire, Pardon, Steele and Cecill, each of whom were charged with the raising of one company.

Little is known about any save one of these men, who might be described as the fathers of the regiment. The exception is Captain Steele, who became better known to posterity as Richard Steele, essayist, playwright and wit, who founded both the *Tatler* and the *Spectator* and was eventually knighted for his services, not with the sword but the pen.

The county of Norfolk in particular proved fertile recruiting ground. It was a county where communications were extremely bad at a time when communications throughout the country were far from good. Many of the little villages on the Norfolk Broads were completely cut off from the outside world, scarcely having a visitor from one year's end to the next. These circumstances assisted the recruiting parties in that the young men of these isolated communities were anxious to see something of the world outside and, at the same time, were probably more ignorant of the harshness of the life they were undertaking than a town-bred boy. The result was that the regiment very rapidly attained its full complement of nine companies, each of three officers and sixty-six N.C.O.s and men. Shortly afterwards the strength of the Regiment was raised to twelve companies.

Rapidly though the warrant of King William had been executed, the Regiment was not fully formed at the time of his death. Queen Anne came to the throne on the 8th March, 1702, and it was to her that the oath of allegiance was taken. The Regiment was gazetted as the 34th Regiment of Foot.

It is likely that the new 34th Foot had recruits of a higher physical and mental standard than was general throughout the country for the reasons given above. They were at least healthy country lads. Other regiments were not so lucky. There was no such procedure as a medical examination in those days and recruiting parties were grateful for any specimens they could lay their hands on. Thus we find, a few years before, Lord Lucas's own regiment advertising the reward of a guinea for the apprehension of a deserter from the 13th Light Infantry, who could be readily distinguished by 'six toes on his left foot, on his left hand two little fingers growing together and the little toe on his left foot always sticking out of his shoes'.

The lads from East Anglia must soon have discovered that they had substituted one impossibly hard way of life for another. An agricultural worker earned about a shilling a day out of which he was expected to house, feed and clothe his family. He rose early and bedded late and often was driven to the stealing of food from the pigs it was his job to feed. If he was caught poaching a rabbit or a pheasant, the penalty was a long term of imprisonment. It was a life, however, which compared favourably with that of a soldier.

The foot soldier's pay was fixed at the sum of eightpence a day after the Restoration and remained unchanged, regardless of such factors as the rising cost of living, until 1783. This princely sum was divided into sixpence for 'subsistence', which was paid to the man's Company Commander and twopence, which was retained by the Regiment to pay for clothing and various stoppages. Of the sixpence, fourpence was allocated to the innkeeper or owner of the billet where the soldier was accommodated and the remainder given to the soldier himself, after the deduction of such items as laundry. Thus the man might be lucky if he retained twopence for himself at the end of the week.

One of the great financial inducements dangled in front of the prospective recruit was that he would be entitled to a share of the spoils of war but it was a hope that was seldom realised. Peculation was rife in the upper echelons of the army and any booty was generally distributed long before it reached the level of the rankers.

The 34th Regiment of Foot did not have long to learn the ropes before they were required for operational duty. The War of the Spanish Succession, in which England was now involved, was fought on many fronts and the demands on manpower were heavy. Soon after the regiment was formed and even before it had reached its full strength, Lord Lucas was ordered to send five companies to Landguard Fort, Sheerness and Tilbury to replace companies of the Buffs, who had been ordered to join the expedition to Spain. The remaining companies were sent to relieve the Foot Guards on duty at the Tower of London, of which Lord Lucas was the Lieutenant-Governor.

We have a glimpse of life at Landguard Fort, through the eyes

1.　Sir Richard Steele (*National Portrait Gallery*)

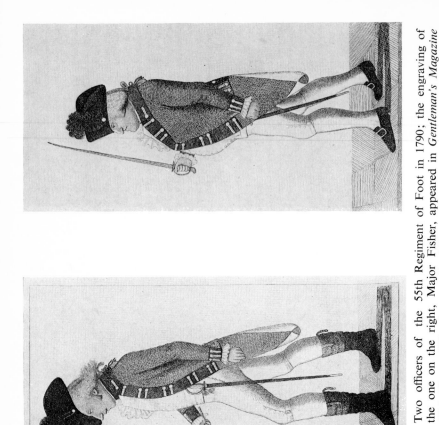

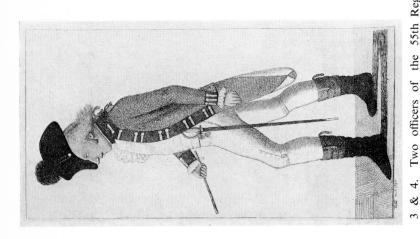

3 & 4. Two officers of the 55th Regiment of Foot in 1790; the engraving of the one on the right, Major Fisher, appeared in *Gentleman's Magazine* (Vol. 72, p. 478) where, whilst billeted in Edinburgh, they are quoted as conducting themselves with such propriety.

2. Private of the 34th Regiment about 1760. (*Courtesy of the Lord Chamberlain*).

of Captain Richard Steele. The summer was spent turning his ploughmen into soldiers but, with the winter approaching, Dick Steele, who was a first-class regimental officer, felt constrained to write to the 'Q' authorities about the conditions his men had to endure:

> The Governor of this garrison, Colonel Jones, before he went to Town, where he is at present, directed Mr. Hubbard, your officer here, to represent the ill-condition the barracks and all parts of this garrison are in, as to our windows and tiling. There are sick men here of the Company (whereof I am Captain) lying in their beds exposed to all the injuries of the weather. I have at present two sergeants, two corporals and nine sentinels so that they cannot do duty, which, if I cannot attribute to this cause, I may say that I do not expect the continuance of other men's health if the remedy be deferred until the winter advances further upon us. I hope my duty has not pressed me beyond the rules to you in giving you this trouble.
>
> I am, Gentlemen,
> Your most obedient and humble servant,
> Richd. Steele.

Before the year was out, three hundred men were drafted to the West Indies to make up the strength of the Sixth Foot and the remainder were marched back to Chelmsford for a further recruiting drive. The following year they started the long march northwards, stopping for a time at Hull and Berwick, before taking up their quarters in Carlisle Castle, which was to be their depot for the next two hundred and fifty years – an unbroken association which is almost unique in the annals of the British Army.

In many ways the Regiment was lucky to be given the occupancy of Carlisle Castle. Because Parliament was loath to grant any money for the upkeep of the Army at home, there were no army barracks built for their accommodation. Compared with the Navy, whom Parliament and the country regarded with pride, the Army was the Cinderella service and treated as an unfortunate necessity. In peacetime their upkeep was considered to be the personal responsibility of the Monarch. The consequence was that, to save expense, troops were quartered wherever possible in the many royal castles which were scattered up and down the country. Thus such ancient fortresses as Dover, Carlisle, Chester and the Tower of London, have a long history of military occupancy.

There were obvious advantages in having a permanent home instead of being quartered in different parts of the country. The disadvantages were that most of the royal castles were quite unfitted for human habitation. Their great stone-walled rooms were cold and damp, their general layout often unsuitable and the sanitary arrangements primitive. All these snags were to be found in Carlisle Castle, which had been occupied alternately by the Scots and the English during its long history, dating from the twelfth century, with both sides regarding it as a point of military advantage more than a home.

It was here that the lads from East Anglia first set about learning the business of war. For two years they were left to learn the intricate manoeuvres required by the military practice of the day and the handling of arms, which were new to them. Lord Lucas did not live to lead the troops he had raised into action. He died on the 31st January, 1705 and was succeeded by Lieutenant-Colonel Hans Hamilton. Four months later the regiment embarked for service on the Continent. By this time the war had spread from the Netherlands to Italy, Germany, Portugal and Spain and the Duke of Marlborough was hard put to it to decide which front required his most urgent attention. When the 34th were taken aboard the fleet commanded by Sir Cloudesley Shovell, it was not decided whether they were to assist in the driving of the French out of Italy, to make an attempt on Sicily, or to land on the coast of Spain. In the event they did none of these things but landed at Lisbon to join the force commanded by the brilliant if somewhat eccentric Earl of Peterborough. They rested there for a month before sailing for Gibraltar, which had been captured by Sir George Rooke the previous year. It was only after they had been there for some time that it was decided to use them in Spain after all.

Accordingly, as autumn approached, they set sail once again and this time landed in the Bay of Altea in Valencia. With this show of arms by Peterborough's troops, many Catalonians and Valencians decided to throw off their allegiance to the House of Bourbon and join forces with the British. Encouraged by this unexpected increase of his force, Peterborough decided that he would undertake the siege of Barcelona.

It was a brave undertaking. In 1697 the French had brought a force of thirty thousand men against the town and had given up the attempt after losing twelve thousand. The Earl of Peterborough could only muster a force of seven thousand and suffered from an understandable lack of enthusiasm for the enterprise by his allies, notably the Dutch, who positively refused to take part in what their commander considered to be a suicidal venture. For three weeks Peterborough sat in front of the heavily fortified town before coming to the conclusion that the odds were too great. Reluctantly he ordered his cannon to be taken back aboard the fleet. When the defenders of Barcelona saw this evidence of imminent departure, they went wild with joy and threw themselves into an orgy of celebration. At midnight the unpredictable Peterborough changed his mind. Instead of retiring he advanced a light force under cover of darkness right up to the walls of the city. Amongst the leading troops were the grenadiers of the 34th, who were given the task of storming the fortress of Montjuich on the west side of the town. The attack took place at daybreak and the surprised defenders were decisively overcome. The cannon were quickly brought back from the ships and, within a few hours, the victory was complete. It was an action which was to have an important influence on the whole campaign and the 34th had every reason to be proud of the part they played. After the battle was over, the local troops, who had joined with Peterborough's forces, ran riot through the town, looting the houses and shops of known Bourbon sympathisers. Peterborough, however, would not tolerate such conduct and ordered the 34th, together with other troops, to defend their erstwhile enemies against their countrymen. The 34th rescued the Governor and saved his garrison from the vengeance of the people, so learning early the virtue of humanity in war.

Thus Archduke Charles was able to write to Queen Anne 'But your Majesty's troops, entering into the town with the Earl of Peterborough, instead of seeking pillage (a practice common on such occasions) appeased the tumult and have saved the town, and even the lives of their enemies, with a discipline and generosity without example.'

The success in the capture of Barcelona led to the Allied troops taking over control of all Catalonia and most of Valencia. The 34th took little part in the mopping-up operations. Instead, they had the luck to be sent to the ancient town of Tortosa, which stands on the left bank of the Ebro near the point where it reaches the sea. They remained in this extremely pleasant station for several months before being called upon to take part in some minor operations with Peterborough's army.

In the meantime the Archduke Charles, who was now acknowledged as the King of Spain, had been left with his retinue in the newly conquered city. He made no attempt to repair the breaches in the defences or to organise a defence force, with the result that the French, smarting under their defeat, determined to re-take it. King Philip fitted out a powerful army, well supported by heavy artillery, and moved against Barcelona. At the same time a large French fleet appeared before the city.

The 34th, who were a hundred and twenty miles away, were immediately rushed to the aid of the endangered town. They made the journey by mule in the incredibly short time of two days – the 30th and 31st March – and on the 1st April mounted guard on the breached defences, including that of Montjuich which they had successfully stormed the previous year. They had not been in position for two hours before the French attacked the fort at a point where they had a mere hundred men in defence. A desperate battle ensued, but the 34th held their ground and the main French attack was blunted. King Charles, to his honour, proved himself a brave and resolute man in danger, rallying his tiny force and supporting his men by his presence wherever the battle was thickest.

For over a month the garrison held out against everything the superior forces of the French could do but gradually their numbers became more and more reduced through casualties and disease until there were scarcely a thousand men fit to man the defences. Just when it seemed inevitable that the French must mount a successful attack, the combined British and Dutch fleets arrived off the town with strong reinforcements. At once the enemy beat a hasty retreat, leaving behind them not only a vast amount of warlike material but all their sick and wounded. It was estimated that their total killed amounted to over five thousand. When they abandoned their siege they also abandoned Spain, returning by forced marches to France.

Had the Allies followed up their advantage it is likely that they would have had little difficulty in carrying out their first plan of advancing to take Madrid itself, but they were bedevilled with conflicting advice and Court formalities which postponed what could have been a triumphal march for King Charles until it was too late. Fresh French forces arrived in Spain and the Allies were obliged to withdraw from the outskirts of Madrid to Valencia.

The 34th had suffered severely, both in the desperate defence of Barcelona and from sickness which was rife in the bitter winter which followed. By the spring of 1707 they were so reduced in numbers that they were ordered to return to England to recruit, after having transferred to other regiments all their private soldiers who remained fit for duty. After long delays, caused, amongst other factors, by the crushing defeat of the British at Almanza, the officers and non-commissioned officers of the Regiment arrived back in England in the autumn. They were stationed in the home counties, where they undertook a vigorous recruiting campaign to fit themselves as soon as possible for further service.

It was not an easy task as recruits were becoming harder and harder to obtain. Previously a man enlisted 'by beat of drum' signed on for life. Now men were allowed to sign for as short a period as three years to encourage those adventurous spirits who wanted to experience the thrills of war without having to put up with the tedium of peacetime soldiering. George Farquhar, in his play, 'The Recruiting Officer', written in 1706, gives some idea of the lighter aspects of recruiting and the wiles of the recruiters. The play opens with Sergeant Kite addressing the throng in Shrewsbury market place:

If any gentlemen, soldiers or others, have a mind to serve Her Majesty and pull down the French King; if any 'prentices* have severe masters, any children have undutiful parents; if any servants have too little wages, or any husband too much wife, let them repair to the noble Sergeant Kite at the sign of the Raven in this good town of Shrewsbury and they shall receive present relief and entertainment.
Gentlemen, I don't beat my drum here to ensnare or inveigle any man; for you must know, gentlemen, that I am a man of honour! Besides, I don't beat up for common soldiers: no, I only 'list grenadiers – grenadiers, gentlemen . . . now, gentlemen, I have no more to say than this: here's a purse of gold and there's a tub of humming ale at my quarters; this is the Queen's money and the Queen's drink. She's a generous Queen and loves her subjects – I hope gentlemen you won't refuse the Queen's health?'

*Farquhar is incorrect here. To enlist apprenticed men was strictly forbidden.

To this the crowd shouts: 'No! No!' and off they go after Kite and his drummer beating the drummer's march.

Unfortunately methods of recruitment were not always by such methods of kindly persuasion. It was about this time that a thousand men were press-ganged by the navy and, according to Trevelyan, transported to Flanders to serve in the army. They deserted in a body and joined the French. To aid the pressing need for soldiers, insolvent debtors were pressed into the army and, as the demand increased, convicted felons were released from prison on condition that they joined the colours. As soon as these sources started to fail, new Acts of Parliament were brought in to mobilise 'rogues, vagabonds and sturdy beggars' and finally 'to raise and levy all such able-bodied men as had not any lawful calling or employment or visible means for their maintenance and livelihood'.

It is not known on which method the officers of the 34th relied in their second recruiting drive, but the necessary men were raised remarkably quickly. By the spring of the following year they were already sufficiently up to strength to be sent post-haste to the North, to repel an expected invasion of Scotland by the French, in support of the Old Pretender. It could hardly be expected, however, that they were in any way a trained force, so it is perhaps just as well that the invasion fleet was dispersed by the British Navy when the 34th had got only as far as Leeds.

There followed a period when they formed part of a force which sailed menacingly up and down the French coast to keep the enemy guessing as to their intentions. Finally, they landed at Ostend and, after a short period, were sent to Antwerp for a year of garrison duty and much-needed training.

The war in Europe was now going Marlborough's way. His great victories at Blenheim, Ramillies and Malplaquet had disproved the myth of French invincibility and now, in the evening of that great soldier's career, he was ready to press home his advantage.

In view of the methods of recruitment, it is not surprising that the British Army was little better than a mob. There were occasions, when they were weakly led, that they got quite out of hand. The ill-fated expedition to Cadiz led by the Duke of Ormonde was an example of what could happen if the troops were not controlled with a strong hand. At Cadiz there were such scenes of violence and pillage that they remained for many years as a blot on the name of England. Marlborough, however, was a general of a different calibre. He subjected his men to the strictest discipline and trained them hard, giving them as little time as possible for their favourite pastimes of drinking, marauding and duelling. Duelling, incidentally, was by no means the prerogative of the officer class. In the ranks the slightest insult or most transient competition for the favour of a mere prostitute was settled by clash of arms, in spite of the most severe disciplinary measures if they were detected.

By 1710 the French, commanded by General Villars, had been almost driven out of Flanders. The advance to the frontier was held up by the strongly fortified town of Dousy, which had been held by the French since 1667. In April the 34th quitted their quarters and marched across country to join the Duke's advancing army. They were involved in a few skirmishes before finally arriving before the walls of Dousy. As comparatively fresh troops, they were selected to take part in the main assault and proved that, when it came to the point, they were of the stuff which has brought British arms victory all over the world. The young soldiers, well led by their veteran officers, carried the strongly-held fortifications and were amongst the first into the town. The cost was heavy. They lost one officer, six sergeants and seventy-five men killed and five officers, five sergeants and one hundred and twenty men wounded. In their weakened state they rejoined the main army, playing a minor part in further operations before going into winter quarters amongst the Walloon peasantry.

In April, 1711 the campaign was resumed. For the 34th the return to active service was marked by the honour of being reviewed by the Duke of Marlborough, who expressed himself as well satisfied with the standard they had attained. They soon afterwards took part in another successful siege, that of the fortress of Bouchain, which finally capitulated in early September. There followed another winter and more campaigning the following year but the war was at last drawing to an end. By the summer of 1712 Louis was desperately trying to negotiate peace terms. As a token of his sincerity, he handed the town of Dunkirk over to the British and the 34th were sent there as part of the occupying force, until the Peace of Utrecht was finally concluded in 1713.

The regiment returned to England, their heads held high, for

they had played a distinguished part in the campaign where the
enemy had been out-generalled and out-fought. The country was
briefly grateful, but it did not last long. Within weeks of their
arrival came the news that Parliament had decided to throw a
considerable portion of their victorious army on the scrap heap.
All the regiments from the 30th to the 39th were to be disbanded
and their officers placed on half pay. As Professor Trevelyan wrote:

Marlborough's victories helped to make England proud of her
soldiers, yet the treatment of Marlborough himself in the last years
of Anne shows how little, even then, the country cared for a redcoat
or was dazzled by the glory of war.

Soon a familiar sight in the streets was the discharged soldier,
begging for a crust of bread and, once more, an object of contempt.

'Good your worship, cast your eyes
Upon a soldier's miseries:
Let not my leane cheeks, I pray,
Your bounty from a soldier stay
But, like a noble friend,
Some silver lend,
And Jove will pay you in the end.'*

*From an anonymous old ballad 'The Maunding Soldier' or 'The Fruit of
War is Beggary'.

CHAPTER II

T HE GOVERNMENT heartily disliked standing armies but they were not long in a position to be without one. In 1714 Queen Anne died and was succeeded by George I. The Hanoverian was scarcely on the throne before trouble loomed again, this time in Scotland, where, in 1715, the supporters of James II raised his standard. At once the King ordered the strength of the army to be increased and the 34th, amongst other regiments, were restored with their former seniority.

In the event the Regiment was not used to quell the 1715 rebellion, which was suppressed by troops under the command of the Duke of Argyll. Instead, they remained in England until, in 1717, they were given orders to move to Ireland as garrison troops. Ireland was at that time, and for many years to come, a thorn in the flesh of the English. Impossibly poor and drained of capital by the absentee landlords, without any industry and dependent on the potato crop in order to exist, they had much to grumble about and there was always talk of rebellion against their oppressors. In a typically Irish way, on the other hand, they bore no personal grudge against the redcoats who were sent to keep them in order. On the contrary, they got on extremely well with the occupying troops and, providing there were no insurrections to quell – a task which the English soldiery found thoroughly distasteful – the army found Ireland a pleasant enough station.

The 34th remained there for two years before there came an interlude. Spain was once again under the French, and there were rumours that they were preparing to fit out an expedition in a further attempt to win the English throne for James II. Under these circumstances it was decided to strike first. An expedition, which included the 34th, was fitted out with the object of first capturing Corunna and then, to rub in the lesson, of taking Peru in South America. The Regiment sailed in the beginning of Sep-

tember 1719 and, the transportation of troops by sea in those days
being a lengthy and arduous business, eventually arrived off the
coast of Spain a month later. It was now decided to abandon the
plan to attack Corunna and to take the port of Vigo instead.

The harbour of Vigo was entered on the 29th September and
seven Spanish ships seized. On the following day the troops landed
and, in a short space of time, brought about the fall of the city
with small loss. Expeditions were then made into the hinterland.
The Spanish fled in panic from Rondondella and Pontevedra,
leaving behind massive quantities of military stores. Within three
weeks of the landing the King of Spain sued for peace. A treaty
was signed and the expedition to Peru abandoned. Shortly afterwards the 34th returned to continue their interrupted garrison duties
in Ireland.

It was not until 1727 that the Regiment was again called upon
for active service. This time the bone of contention was Gibraltar,
which the Spanish had been forced to give up under the terms
of the Treaty of Utrecht. It rankled sorely with them and in that
year they sent an army to besiege the fortress. The 34th were sent
for to reinforce the garrison and once more set sail for the south.
It was not an uneventful voyage. A violent storm blew up in the
Bay of Biscay. Part of the fleet was shipwrecked and six companies
of the regiment were lost. The expedition was so beset with bad
weather that they were almost two months on the voyage. When
they eventually arrived on the 26th March, they were at once
involved in a desperate defence action. The Spaniards had assembled
an immense force of artillery which carried on an incessant
bombardment of the Rock, often continuing far into the night.
Fortunately for the defenders their cannon were not as efficient
as they might have been. Many of them burst, killing numbers of
their own troops and those which were successfully fired caused
little damage. Nevertheless, the siege continued for three months
before the attempt was abandoned and peace with Spain signed
once again.

There followed a long period of quiet, passed by the regiment
partly in Ireland and partly in England. Indeed almost a complete
generation of soldiers passed through the ranks before the regiment
was again involved in hostilities. During this period there were
several changes in command. Colonel Chudleigh, who had reformed

the regiment in 1715, retired and the colonelcy was purchased by a Lieutenant-Colonel Robert Hayes of the First Foot Guards – the purchase of a command being a quite usual method whereby officers secured their advancement. Hayes died shortly afterwards and was succeeded by Colonel Cornwallis who, in turn, was succeeded by Lieutenant-Colonel Lord James Cavendish. Cavendish lived to command for only two years and was succeeded in 1742 by Colonel the Honourable James Cholmondeley and it was he who, in 1745, led the 34th once again into battle.

Although the names of these colonels of long ago are now mere entries in the records, each change was of the utmost importance to the men of the Regiment at the time. It has been said in modern times that there are no good or bad regiments – only good or bad commanding officers. If there is truth in it today, there was a great deal more truth in it two hundred years ago, for a commanding officer's power over the men of his regiment was complete and unquestioned. The system by which a commission and promotion in the service could be bought, created a situation whereby many senior officers had little military merit and even less interest in the troops they commanded. Often commissions were bought merely for social prestige and not for any desire to lead a soldier's life.

The life of the officer, except in battle, was in fact as far removed from that of the soldier as it is possible to imagine. He was a being apart, who could happily take five months leave out of twelve months every year, when not on active service, and confine his military activities in time of peace to the perfection of his turn-out and the niceties of social behaviour. It is surprising that when it came to a matter of bravery in the face of the enemy, the British officer class was second to none.

In matters of the welfare of the troops most officers showed themselves to be completely indifferent. When the 34th were in Gibraltar, they found themselves housed in the poorest of conditions. The reason was that, a few years earlier, the garrison had suffered a particularly cold winter and the soldiers, who had been provided with no means of heating, tore down their wooden huts and burnt them rather than freeze to death. It was twenty years before anyone thought about providing new ones.

It was, however, in matters of discipline that the calibre of officers in general and the commanding officer in particular most affected the daily lives of the men. Some officers were humane but too many treated their men like so many cattle. 'To see, as I have done,' wrote a retired officer in 1761 'a brave, honest soldier battered and banged at the caprice and whim of an arrogant officer, is really shocking to humanity.' An officer could order one of his men to be thrashed or to such minor punishments as 'the log', which required a man to go about his duties shackled to a heavy iron weight; but more serious crimes were dealt with by the commanding officer, who could award flogging with the rod or cat-o'-nine-tails.

The minimum number of lashes awarded would be twenty-five but anything up to a hundred would be regarded as 'getting off lightly'. Heavy penalties of 800 lashes and beyond were usually awarded by court-martial but these were drumhead affairs convened on the spot and merely instruments of the C.O.'s wishes. Some C.O.s had resort to flogging for the most trivial sins. Sergeant Teesdale of the 28th Foot records the state of affairs in his regiment whilst they were under orders to proceed for duty to the Continent in 1806:

> During the six weeks we had to parade morning and afternoon. The officers commanding companies had orders from Major B. to inspect their men closely and turn out such as they found dirty to the front; a square was then formed for punishment, and the men who had been found fault with were marched in, tried by drumhead court-martial and flogged to a man without reference to character. There was no remission of punishment – no, not a lash. I have known ten to fifteen and twenty-five fellows flogged at a parade under this frivolous pretext . . . until it was put a stop to by higher authority.

A dreadful example of the inhumanity of which some commanding officers were capable concerned a man of the Bengal European Infantry, who was sentenced to 1,500 lashes for some serious crime. When he was led out for punishment he suddenly siezed the drum-major's sword and made efforts to defend himself. He was duly overpowered and punishment administered to the last lash. He was then immediately tried again for mutiny, led out and shot.

On the other hand, the troops themselves did not always disagree with the punishments handed out. One member of the 34th is recorded as saying that he did not feel that 'he had become a man' until he had received a sentence of the cat. The really heavy punishments, however, disgusted the troops who were forced to

witness its administration. Napier records that, as the hundreds
of lashes mounted up 'the faces of the spectators assumed a look
of disgust, there was always a low whispering sound, scarcely
audible, issuing from the apparent stern and silent ranks – a sound
arising from the lips that spoke not; but a sound produced by
hearts that felt deeply . . . the punishment had become excessive . . .
the culprit had disappeared and the martyr had taken his place'.

Vicious though many of the sentences were, resulting as they
sometimes did in permanent injury to the victim and even on
occasions in his death, there were occasions which were not without
their humorous side. One such is related by Sergeant Lawrence of
the 34th in his memoirs. He describes how he was receiving his
one and only sentence of the lash. After a hundred and seventy-five
strokes, borne without flinching, he began to grow impatient. He
attempted to alter the position of his body on the triangle, whereupon the contraption, being insecurely fixed, moved also and began
to slip around the square, the drummers (whose duty it was to
inflict the punishment) having to run after it to apply their strokes.
This caused so much laughter in the ranks that the commanding
officer remitted the remainder of the sentence.

In 1743 the war of the Austrian Succession broke out in Europe
and a British army, 16,000 strong, was sent to Flanders to support
the claims of the late Emperor Charles VI of Germany's daughter,
the Archduchess Maria Theresa, whose claims were disputed by
the Prussians and the Bavarians, later to be joined by the French.
In June the following year the 34th joined the British forces on
the banks of the Scheldt. The British were under the command of the
King's younger brother, the brilliant but ruthless Duke of Cumberland. The following spring found the French under their most able
General, Marshal Saxe, laying siege to Tournay and the Duke
assembled his whole force, which included the Dutch and the
Hanoverians, to go to its relief.

The French took up a strong defensive position at the village of
Fontenoy and the Dutch were given the task of making the first
assault but, when they failed, the main brunt of the battle fell on the
British. They attacked with the greatest gallantry and actually succeeded in breaching the French line, whereupon they were exposed
to the most furious flanking fire. There were no forces available to
reinforce them and a retreat was ordered.

It was during the retreat, which the 34th had the task of covering, that the regiment played the conspicuous part which was to be forever remembered in its annals. Studded though the history of the British Army is with brilliant successes, some of their finest hours have been in defeat. So it was at Fontenoy. It is said that when the British and the French troops first came face to face at the start of the action, the officers of each side had raised their hats to one another and invited the other side to fire first. After battle was joined, however, there was no quarter. On the 34th, together with the Life Guards and the 42nd, fell the responsibility of seeing that the withdrawal of the British Army did not become a rout and that the force suffered as few casualties as possible. So well did they perform their task that the main body were brought safely out of the low ground to the comparative security of the town of Aeth. Their steadiness turned what might have been a military disaster into no more than a set-back.

A contemporary report describes the action in the following words:

With the French artillery ploughing through ranks and the triumphant squadrons of French horse riding around it, the regiment, with cool, soldier-like courage and discipline, covered the retreat of their comrades so effectually as to allow no trophies to the enemy.

In recognition of their fighting qualities the regiment were given the right to emblazon a laurel wreath on their colours, to which was added the further distinction of being allowed to wear the 'royal worm' in the lace of their drummers' coats. Oddly enough, at some later date, the wearing of the laurel wreath fell into abeyance. It is not mentioned in the Queen's Regulations governing honours in either 1844 or 1859. It was, however, later revived and the regiment is now the only one to bear the coveted insignia.

Following their hard-gained success at Fontenoy, the French continued to push forward and several fortified towns fell to them. For the British, however, a greater danger now threatened nearer home. Charles Edward Stuart, son of the Old Pretender, had landed on the west coast of Scotland and many of the Highland chieftains were rallying to his support. Almost daily the harassed Government received new reports of successes by the rebels. Something had to be done and the most urgent need was for more troops to stem the triumphant advance of the man who was now popularly known as Bonnie Prince Charlie.

It was in these circumstances that the 34th were disengaged from the European campaign and hurried back to England. They landed at Blackwall on the Thames on the 23rd September, 1745 and were brigaded with the 3rd, 13th and 48th Regiments. Then the whole force marched north as rapidly as possible to join the troops commanded by General Wade, which were stationed near Newcastle. The clans, meanwhile, had started their advance into England and were pressing south so rapidly as to menace London itself. Wade moved his force to cover Yorkshire, while Prince Charlie reached Derby. There he hesitated, halted and finally turned back on his tracks to head once more for what he hoped would be the safety of his native hills. The brigade, which included the 34th, were force-marched across country in an attempt to cut off the retreat, but the Scottish troops evaded them. The chase which ensued took the 34th for the first time back to their official headquarters at Carlisle Castle, which they had not seen for so many years. The wiry Scots moved too fast for the more encumbered Englishmen, who had to be content with the capture of stragglers from the main body. Those whom they managed to round up were incarcerated in Carlisle Castle, which had been recaptured after being taken by the Scots on their triumphant march south. The stone walls of the Castle dungeons dripped with water and the only light the unfortunate prisoners saw was when their gaolers opened the heavy wooden doors to throw in their food. It was from this grim prison that they were led out to be tried for treason and sentenced to death. In fact, the counsels of mercy prevailed and only eight were selected to be shot. The rest were transported, apart from a few who were allowed to go free. It is said that that infinitely sad song, 'The Bonnie Banks o' Loch Lomond' was composed by one of the condemned men on the eve of his execution:

> 'O ye'll tak' the high road
> And I'll tak' the low road,
> And I'll be in Scotland afore ye,
> But me and my true love will never meet again
> On the bonnie, bonnie banks o' Loch Lomond'.

Sung to one of his lucky compatriots, who was to go free, it refers to the Scottish belief that those who die away from their native land, return there after death by the secret 'low road' of the fairies.

The 34th, in a force now under the command of General Hawley, continued the pursuit of the main Scots force to Edinburgh and on towards the relief of Stirling, which was being invested by the Prince. Hawley, who was a rather spineless commander, encamped his army of thirteen regiments at Falkirk, about seven miles from the known position of the Scots. When dawn broke Hawley found that the Scots had advanced upon him during the night and were now ranged in battle order close to his own position. After some hesitation he led his men into attack. The Highlanders waited to fire only one salvo from their muskets before throwing them away and hurling themselves at the enemy with their claymores flashing. The ferocity of this traditional method of Scottish warfare was too much for Hawley's troops, who broke and fled leaving almost five hundred dead on the field of battle, including Lieutenant-Colonel Powell, who had commanded the 34th. This defeat, typical of several inflicted by the Scots, was due in part to bad English leadership, particularly in the higher echelons, and in part to the fact that the English troops, quite understandably, did not show the same spirit when fighting against their own countrymen as they did against the French.

The supreme commander of the English army, however, was now a man who was both able and without any such scruples as may have been felt by his subordinates. The Duke of Cumberland – 'Butcher' Cumberland, as he was to become known – had been brought back from the Continent to meet the new danger. Now he pressed hard on the heels of the Scots, driving them further and further north until mid-April, 1746 found the two forces encamped only a few miles apart – Cumberland's army outside Nairn and the Scots on the bare, inhospitable Culloden Moor.

The Scots made an abortive foray against their tormentors, hoping to surprise them with a dawn attack but their plans miscarried and they marched back to Culloden, tired and dispirited, having had no food for three days. Cumberland pursued them and, on the morning of the 16th April, the two armies faced each other in battle order. By midday those in the centre of the Scottish line, having been subjected to artillery fire, could stand still no longer and launched themselves forward. The suicidal attack lasted for scarcely an hour, by which time the pride of Scotland lay in serried ranks of dead. They had broken through the first two lines of the English at appalling cost but the survivors never reached the bayonets of the third line. They lay

5. The 34th (Cholmondeley's) Regiment covering the retreat from Fontenoy, 11 May, 1745.

6. The surprise night attack at Brandywine, 1777.

three deep, mown down by musket fire. A sad episode in the history of our islands was over. In the final battle, over a thousand High-landers perished, while Cumberland suffered losses of only three hundred. The 34th were in the front rank but on the extreme right of the line, where they were scarcely involved in the battle and lost only three men out of the twenty-four officers and four hundred and thirty-five other ranks.

Shortly afterwards the 34th returned to England and so played little part in the mopping-up operations in which Cumberland, by his ungoverned cruelty, earned his unenviable nickname.

There followed a period of retrenchment while the regiment was brought up to full strength and further instructed in the arts of war. They learned all the standard military manoeuvres such as forming defensive squares, firing volleys at the advancing enemy and, hardest yet simplest of all, how to attack by marching stolidly into the teeth of the enemy fire! Whatever action they were engaged in, it was always carried out in full dress. In those days the uniform of the 34th consisted of three-cornered cocked hats, bound with white lace and ornamented with a white loop and black cockade; scarlet coats, faced and lined with bright yellow and ornamented with white lace, scarlet waistcoats and breeches and white gaiters.

Culloden was the last battle fought on British soil and finally dashed the Stuart hopes of regaining the throne. The battle did not, however, resolve the struggle for power between the French and the English. That was to continue for many years and make it necessary for both countries to keep large standing armies. In 1752 the 34th were sent to Minorca as garrison troops, a station which one feels cannot have been too unpleasant. In 1755, however, war once more broke out with France, this time over the question of the British and French territorial boundaries in North America. At the same time, Frederick the Great was again at war with Maria Theresa and this time he enlisted England on his side, while the French supported Austria. One of France's first actions was to attempt to drive the English out of Minorca.

In April, 1756, they landed on the island and laid siege to Fort St. Philip, where the English commander had concentrated his forces. The defending troops consisted of the 4th, 23rd, 24th, 34th Foot and one regiment of artillery. The 34th mustered some 750 all ranks and the other regiments were about the same strength. The

French outnumbered them by about three to one. The long-fought action was a desperate affair. Little attention had been paid to the defences in the years of peace and they were in a shocking state of disrepair. Many of the officers were on leave of absence and the troops were not in peak condition. At the same time the French, under Marshal Richelieu, were thirsting for blood, highly trained and supported by a formidable weight of artillery.

As always in adversity, the English rose to the occasion. Their commander, General Blakeney, never changed his clothes during the whole of the siege and scarcely ever slept. The gunners dropped from fatigue beside their guns and the soldiers of the line fought with the ferocity of despair. There was only one chance of averting the inevitable and it lay in the hope of relief by the British Navy. Admiral Byng had orders to go to the aid of the beleaguered garrison and, on the 19th of May, when the defenders had been greatly reduced by casualties and had over 500 out of action through sickness or fatigue, the fleet hove in sight. For a time hope ran high; then, inexplicably, Byng turned tail and, scarcely firing a shot against the French Squadron, left the hard-pressed garrison to their fate.

For a further month Blakeney held out against appalling odds, while his numbers steadily diminished and supplies ran lower and lower. On the 27th June, with the defences almost obliterated by his artillery, Richelieu gave orders for a final assault against his crippled enemy. Every French gun opened up and the grenadiers stormed triumphantly forward, sure at last of final victory. The defenders, however, realising that a crisis had arrived, had every man in his place. Even the sick were carried from hospital to take their place in the firing line and the French could get no further than the earthworks. It was the final spurt of the flame of valour. The following day Blakeney, realising that no help from outside was to be forthcoming, made the decision to sacrifice no more brave men.

Of the defence of Fort St. Philip, Beatson observes in his *Naval and Military Memoirs*: 'Thus did four regiments and one company of artillery maintain the fort against such numbers of the enemy, by sea and land, for such a length of time as can scarcely be paralleled in history. The terms on which the fort was at last surrendered by a handful of men, so distressed, so shattered and so neglected, remains a lasting monument to their honour.'

Marshal Richelieu proved himself to be a chivalrous victor. He accorded the severely depleted force the full honours of war. They marched out 'with their firelocks on their shoulders, drums beating, colours flying, twenty cartouches to each man and also a lighted match, and all their private effects in addition . . .' Later they embarked on French vessels and were conveyed safely to Gibraltar. A fine gesture by one gallant commander to another.

News of the fall of Minorca was received with indignation by an England unused to military reverses. The Government came under harsh criticism for their lack of adequate preparation and safeguards. They decided on a scapegoat and Admiral Byng was court-martialled for his failure to save the situation. In spite of the fact that he had the able and eloquent Pitt to speak in his defence, he was found guilty and shot on his own quarterdeck. At the same time General Fowke, in command at Gibraltar, was dismissed the Service for not sending reinforcements. General Blakeney's courageous defence was recognised when he was made a K.B. and raised to the peerage, while many other officers received high honours.

As for the rankers of the 34th, and their comrades in arms, after a short stay in Gibraltar, they were shipped back to England, 'where their arrival was hailed with acclamations by the inhabitants of the towns through which they passed'. Once more they had proved their worth in the hardest circumstances which a soldier has to bear – defeat.

The action in Minorca was only a small part of the major conflict which was now raging in four quarters of the globe – Europe, Africa, America and India. In 1758 the 34th were again on active service against the French. This time they took part in a landing on the coast of Brittany to create a diversion in order to help the allied army in Germany. They marched on St. Malo, where they set fire to shipping and destroyed military stores before re-embarking. Later they took part in another raid, this time on Cherbourg, which was again successful. Amongst other stores they captured twenty-two fine brass cannon and two mortars which, on being brought back to England, were inspected by George II in Hyde Park and later taken in triumphant procession to the Tower of London. A further raid a month later met with less success. As they retired to re-embark after a fruitless foray, the French caught up with them and inflicted a considerable number of casualties.

There followed a period in England with the regiment living under

canvas outside Winchester. They were then under the command of
the Earl of Effingham and, on his being promoted to command the
first troop of Horse Grenadier Guards, by Lord Frederick Cavendish.
When he assumed the Colonelcy, Lord Cavendish presented the
officers' mess with the two fine silver vases which still ornament the
mess table.

With the accession to the throne of George III there was talk of
peace, but the negotiations fell through and, in 1762, Spain once more
joined in the war against England. At once a force, which included
the 34th, were sent to harass the Spanish in the West Indies. Their
first task was to take the strongly-held fortress of Moro, which was
the key to the taking of Havannah. It was an operation which
required both patience and courage. The siege was commenced on
the 6th of June but it was not until the 30th July that the fortress
was taken by storm. The final assault was short and bloody. The
Spaniards defended with determination and the Governor of the
island, Velasco, was slain, sword in hand, before final victory was
achieved.

To quote Beatson's *Naval and Military Memoirs* again:

> This conquest was, without doubt, in itself the most considerable,
> and in its consequences the most decisive, of any we had made since
> the beginning of the war; and in no operation were the courage,
> steadiness, and perseverance of the British troops and the conduct
> of their leaders more conspicuous. It was a military achievement of
> the highest class.

Apart from its military importance, Havannah proved a rich prize
to its captors who, according to the practice of the day, were entitled
to a portion of the spoils. In fact, the Commander-in-Chief reaped a
financial benefit to the extent of £122,697, Major-Generals received
£6,816, Brigadier-Generals £1,947 and so on down the scale until it
came to the Privates, who had done the fighting and who had to be
content with £4.1.8¼ each.

The following year, 1763, the Seven Years' War came to an end.
One of the terms of the peace treaty was that Havannah should be
restored to the Spanish in return for their ceding to Britain the
province of Florida in North America, and the 34th was amongst
the regiments sent to take possession of the new territory. In this
they were extremely lucky, for they might well have had to serve for

some years in the West Indies, which was a station dreaded by all the British Army. No troops were more neglected than those in the West Indies, where no troops more needed care and attention. Mortality from disease was generally higher than a regiment might expect to suffer in battle and constant reinforcements had to be sent out from home. There was little opportunity for recreation and many men had recourse to the rum bottle to relieve the boredom and the appalling conditions they had to endure. There was no such thing as home leave for rankers, so that they were trapped there for the whole period of the Regiment's service on the islands. One unfortunate regiment, the 38th Foot, was left for sixty years on the island without relief, so that for a recruit to be posted to them was tantamount to a sentence of transportation for life.

This was a fate which the 34th so luckily avoided. Instead, they were stationed for four years in the pleasant and fertile land of West Florida, before being returned to take up garrison duties in Ireland, where they were to stay for another seven years.

CHAPTER III

I⊤ IS NOW necessary to go back a few years in time in order to take up the history of the 55th Foot, who were, in the next century, to join with the 34th and take their place in the army as the second battalion of The Border Regiment.

In 1755, with the 34th Foot in Minorca, France and Britain were again on the brink of war and it was deemed necessary to increase once more the strength of the standing army to deal with the crisis which had arisen in North America. As has already been remarked, recruitment was becoming a more and more difficult matter in England, where they often had to resort to the sweepings of the gaols to fill the ranks. Scotland, however, was a different matter. After the unhappy events following the 1745 rising, the Scots had become a depressed race. The clan system, which had been the way of life in the Highlands, had been completely smashed. It was forbidden, on pain of death, to carry arms or even to wear the tartan. With the chiefs powerless to protect their people and the family communities abolished, many poor people became little better than beggars, wandering from place to place trying to scrape some sort of livelihood.

It was these circumstances which made Scotland a fertile recruiting ground for the army in the second half of the eighteenth century. The Scots were by nature fighting men and, if they felt any compunction for serving their erstwhile oppressor King George, their empty bellies soon overcame their scruples. Between the 1750s and the 1790s no less than twenty-five regiments were raised in the Highlands. One of the earliest was the 55th, raised at Stirling by Colonel George Perry, whose commission for the raising of the regiment was dated Christmas Day, 1755. Stirling was the centre of one of the best areas for recruitment in the country and the required recruits were obtained early in the following year.* For some odd reason the 55th were the only regiment raised north of the Edinburgh-Glasgow line which was not designated Highland.

So great was the need for troops by sore-pressed Britain that the 55th had scarcely been issued with their uniforms (which differed from the 34th only in that their scarlet coats were lined and faced with dark green) than they were sent to the west of Ireland in preparation for embarkation for North America. Perhaps fortunately, in that it enabled the young soldiers to have some sort of training, transports were not available until the 7th May, 1757, when, with six other regiments, they sailed in Admiral Holbourne's fleet for Nova Scotia. It was a long and tedious voyage and it was over two months before they disembarked at Halifax – months in which many of the troops had fallen ill through the insanitary conditions and the lack of fresh food. Almost immediately they were joined with a force of five battalions under the Earl of Loudon, which had arrived from New York and became part of an expedition sent against the French stronghold of Louisberg. As was to happen so often during the campaign, however, indecisive leadership caused a change of plan and operations were put off until the following year.

In the summer of 1758 a large British expedition set off up tne Hudson and the lakes leading to Montreal from the south, commanded in person by the Commander-in-Chief, General Abercromby. The French were under the brilliant generalship of the Marquis de Montcalm. The British advance was three-pronged – one column against Louisberg, another against Fort Ticonderoga and a third against Fort du Quesne. The 55th were part of the second force against Ticonderoga, which was composed of 6,300 regulars and 9,000 locally raised troops, together with heavy artillery support. On the 5th of July they crossed Lake George and advanced in four columns in heavily wooded country, which gave the enemy the advantage of being able to harass the British flanks from safe cover. The 55th were leading one of the columns and, in a sharp skirmish, their colonel, Lord Howe, was shot through the heart. Three days later they came upon the fortifications of Ticonderoga. They were an awesome sight. One of those present described the barricades as:

* In fact the Regiment was first numbered the 57th but, shortly after their being raised, the 50th and 51st were disbanded in America and the 57th promoted two places in the Army List.

Thousands of trees, the tops lopped off and the trunks piled one upon another. It was so high that nothing could be seen over it but the crowns of the soldiers' hats. Sods and bags of sand were piled along the top, with narrow spaces to fire through. All along the breastworks the ground was covered with heavy boughs, overlapping and interlaced, with sharpened points bristling into the face of the assailant like quills of a porcupine.

To a modern military tactician it would seem that General Abercromby had at least three possible courses of action. He could have made a flanking attack on the blind side of the fort. He could have brought his formidable artillery into play and smashed the fortifications to smithereens or he could simply have by-passed the fort and cut the French lines of communication. In fact, he did none of these things. Instead he ordered a frontal attack with the bayonet and broadsword.

The first line of attack was the picquets, followed by the grenadiers with the battalions in support. The 'reserve'* troops were the 55th and their fellow countrymen the 42nd (the Black Watch). The attack was launched under the blazing noonday sun with the leading troops struggling to force a way through the trees, whilst being subject to the punishing fire of the enemy. After an hour of bitter fighting a report was sent back to Abercromby, who was sitting in a sawmill two miles away, that the fort was impregnable. His only reply was 'Attack again'.

It was at this stage that the fighting men of the 55th and the 42nd took matters into their own hands. Infuriated by the agony endured by their comrades and, without waiting for orders, they threw themselves into the assault 'with a fury that would yield neither to discipline nor to death'. A few men managed to hack their way to the ten-foot high breastwork where, not having been provided with ladders, they climbed on each other's shoulders in an effort to breach the rampart. As fast as they climbed, so they were bayonetted. For four hours the desperate struggle continued 'until the inner abatis was hung with wisps of scarlet, like poppies that grow upon a hedge of thorns'. A ferocious fever had siezed the men, goaded on by the death of their comrades. Even when the order to retire was given, it

---

* The term 'reserve' did not have the same meaning then as it does today. The reserve meant a force of selected regiments, placed under a special commander and held available for any task which the Commander-in-Chief might see fit. Thus, on occasions, a reserve might even lead an attack.

was all the few remaining officers could do to persuade their men to obey.

The losses were tremendous – thirty-seven officers and five hundred and seventeen men killed, eighty-seven officers and one thousand, nine hundred and twenty-two men wounded. The reserve alone had thirty-five officers and over eight hundred men killed or wounded. An officer of the 42nd later wrote of Ticonderoga:

> The affair at Fontenoy was nothing to it – I saw both. So much determined bravery can scarcely be paralleled. Even those who lay mortally wounded cried aloud to their companions not to mind or waste a thought upon them, but to follow their officers and remember the honour of their country. Nay, their ardour was such that it was difficult to bring them off again. When shall we have so fine a Regiment again?

It is hard to imagine a more bitter baptism for the young soldiers of the 55th. They were not in any state to take a further part in the campaigning until the following year when reinforcements had been sent from England. In 1759 the 55th marched again. This time their grenadier company, under command of Brigadier-General Prideaux, was sent against Fort Niagara. Prideaux was killed at the very beginning of the siege by an exploding mortar but his second-in-command, Sir William Johnson, led his force with such energy that their objective was achieved in the short space of five days. In the meantime, the remaining companies of the 55th had again been sent, this time under General Amherst, to try and reduce Ticonderoga. Profiting by Abercromby's mistake, Amherst would not advance without his artillery, with the result that the French rapidly abandoned their fortifications, taking the precaution of blowing them up before they retired to Crown Point. The 55th were left to repair the damage until the season became too far advanced for further campaigning. Then they retired to New York for the winter.

In 1760 the war in Canada entered its final stage. The British troops were now, for the most part, battle-hardened and efficient and they were well led by General Amherst. In July a large force, including the 55th, set out on the long march to Montreal, which was the key to the possession of the country. By September, after capturing various forts on the way, Amherst landed on the island of Montreal, with six thousand men. At the same time, Colonel Murray arrived from Quebec with a further force of almost four thousand and, a day later, Colonel Haviland succeeded in capturing the Isle-aux-Noix. Surrounded on all sides without hope of relief, the French Governor-General, the Marquis de Vendreuil, sued for peace. Thus Montreal, without a shot being fired, fell and Britain found herself in control of the whole of Canada.

With the cessation of hostilities, the 55th took possession of the fort at Oswega on Lake Ontario, where they were to spend the winter before being returned to England. If they were looking forward to a peaceful time, however, they were to be considerably disappointed. The Indians, stirred up against the conquerors by the French settlers, soon started to give trouble. In the spring they broke out in open rebellion, simultaneously attacking all the frontier forts and capturing nine of them. The 55th had been concentrated preparatory to their being shipped home. Now the move was cancelled and instead the Regiment was sent to aid the hard-pressed frontiersmen. One party, consisting of ninety men of the 55th, under Lieutenant Culyer, left with provisions and ammunition for the beleaguered Fort Detroit but failed to get through, losing many men to the marauding Indians. A stronger force followed, under Captain Dalzell of the 55th, and succeeded in joining the garrison, which now considered themselves strong enough to attack their besiegers. On the 31st July, Captain Dalzell and his force crept out of the fort to surprise the Indians but some treacherous Canadians had revealed the plan to the Indian chiefs. They allowed the British to penetrate almost to their main camp before ambushing them. Fearful scenes of carnage followed as Dalzell tried to fight his way back to the fort. Wounded men left behind were immediately scalped by the Indians. Only half the force which set out managed to reach safety and Dalzell himself was killed fighting valiantly in the rearguard.

It was hoped that with the coming of winter the Indians would disappear again into the woods but it was not to be so. They kept up their siege until the following summer when a large force was sent to clear up the mess. Fort Detroit was relieved after a siege lasting fifteen months. The defenders were at once sent back to rest, while fresh troops took their place. Once again the 55th were scheduled for return to England and once again they were disappointed. At the last minute orders were given for all their men to be drafted to Florida to make the other regiments posted there (including probably the 34th) up to strength. It was a bitter disappointment for the men, who had more than earned a home posting. At the same time, the officers and N.C.O.s of the Regiment were sent back to Ireland with orders to recruit a new body. Thus it was that the 55th lost their Scotsmen, who had served them so well, to be replaced largely by the Irish. It was many years, however, before they forgot their Scottish origins and even as late as the turn of the century, it proved a popular choice of regiment for Scottish volunteers.

CHAPTER IV

BOTH THE 34th and the 55th remained in Ireland for the next ten years while peace reigned in Europe. It was, however, a period of growing discontent in North America, where the colonists were chafing under the yoke of heavy and often unfair taxation. Finally, in 1775, they broke into open rebellion against the British Crown, much to the surprise of Lord North, possibly the worst Prime Minister England has ever known.

Amongst the first troops to be sent to America to deal with the rebels was the 55th, who formed part of Sir William Howe's army. They were forced to evacuate Boston and sailed for Halifax where they waited for reinforcements. When these did not immediately materialise, General Howe lost patience and sailed his force to New York, where they made a virtually unopposed landing on Staten Island. The following day the American Congress took the step of publishing the famous Declaration of Independence, which put an end to any hope of a settlement without resort to arms.

Howe's expected reinforcements arrived about a fortnight after his landing, so that his army now numbered ten thousand men, supported by a strong fleet under command of his brother, Admiral Lord Howe. On the 22nd August the army crossed over Long Island and attacked the American forces strongly entrenched before Brooklyn, which in those days consisted, not of a sprawling concrete jungle, but of rolling wooded hills and valleys leading to the open plains beyond. The first assault was completely successful. The American lines were quickly broken and the retreating troops pursued with such energy that many perished in a deep morass in their efforts to escape. Just when it looked as if the victory would be overwhelming, however, General Howe called a halt and allowed the enemy to retrench.

The American losses were over a thousand men, while the British escaped comparatively unscathed. The losses of the 55th were only one man killed and three wounded. Howe did not follow up his advantage for almost three weeks. Then he took possession of New York and, in an attempt to attack Washington's forces from the rear, sent a strong detachment by ship to the mouth of the Hudson River. On the 28th September the battle of White Plains was fought, which resulted in the capture of Forts Washington and Lee and opened the way for General Cornwallis to advance into New Jersey. The virtually unopposed advance started with Washington's forces falling back in confusion when General Howe again took a hand. For some reason of his own, he ordered Cornwallis to halt his advance at the town of Brunswick. Thus Washington was able to get his army back over the Delaware River unmolested and wait safely on the other side for reinforcements.

This unexpected respite emboldened Washington to recross the Delaware when it had become frozen over and occupy a bridgehead on the other side. It was not a sound tactical move because soon afterwards the ice melted and he was left without a ready line of retreat. Whilst he was in this awkward situation, Cornwallis decided to attack and drew up his forces in battle order to launch an offensive the following day. Washington, however, left his camp fires burning brightly to deceive the enemy and slipped away during the night. The following day Colonel Mawood, at the head of the 17th and 55th Regiments and marching towards Maidenhead, was surprised to find the whole of the American Army advancing towards him. He immediately sent to Cornwallis for reinforcements and deployed his small force on some rising ground to await the American attack. As they approached, the British fire was so accurate that they fell back, closely pursued by the 17th, who drove them into a ravine at the point of the bayonet. If reinforcements had arrived at this time, the whole of the enemy force might have been destroyed. As it was, Washington himself arrived to rally his troops and managed by vigorous action to separate the 17th from the 55th and escape from his dangerous predicament. The 55th, encumbered by a considerable number of wounded, were then ordered to fall back to Brunswick to guard the military stores there, as well as the pay chest containing £70,000, the responsibility for which was a great anxiety to Cornwallis. The war now languished, due to lack of British supplies and, apart from some forays by Washington, no further action took place until the summer.

By July, 1777, Howe had been sufficiently reinforced and pro-
visioned to resume the campaign. General Burgoyne was known to
be advancing towards Albany and it would have seemed a natural
move for Howe to try to link up with him. However, for some reason
he decided to sail south and, much to Washington's relief, appeared
in August off the Delaware. Washington disposed his forces to protect
Philadelphia, an operation for which he was given plenty of time
due to the fact that so many horses had died during the sea voyage
that Howe was temporarily immobilised and could not start his
advance until the 3rd September.

Eventually, Washington was forced to make a stand and he chose
to entrench his troops behind the river of Brandywine. For once, in
this not too well conducted war, General Howe not only received
correct intelligence of the American plan but acted on it. Hearing
that Washington intended to send a force to harass the British troops
who, he had learned, were to ford the river Sehulkill, Howe anticipated him by sending the 42nd and 44th Regiments with the second
battalion of light infantry (which included the light company of the
55th) to surprise him. General Grey approached the enemy in
bivouac so secretly that he even ordered his men to take the flints
out of their muskets lest one of them be accidentally discharged; and
to rely solely on the bayonet. The plan was so well carried out that
the outposts were overpowered without the alarm being given and
they were able to fall on their enemy while they lay wrapped in their
blankets. Over three hundred died under the bayonet, a further
hundred were taken prisoner and the remainder only escaped with
difficulty, leaving all their baggage behind.

This bloodthirsty action had a curious sequel. The Americans
considered the attack to be not in the best of warlike tradition and
swore that in future they would give no quarter to any 'Light Bobs',*
who might fall into their hands. The 'Light Bobs' replied that 'They
were ready for them' and, so that they would be easily distinguished,
dyed the white feathers in their caps red. The red feather continued
to be worn in the thickest of the fighting for the rest of the war and
was later retained as a mark of distinction when the light companies
returned to their regiments. When, later, light (or flank) companies
came to be abolished, only the 46th Regiment of all those present at

---

* 'Light Bobs' as opposed to 'Heavy Bobs' was the name given to the light
infantry, who were mainly responsible for this night attack.

Brandywine chose to retain it and adopted it for the whole regiment. There is some doubt as to whether the red hackle, worn today by the 42nd, had the same origin but historians generally agree that it was not so. Undoubtedly, the 55th would have been entitled to the distinction if they had cared to adopt it.

While the distraction described was being executed, General Howe led his main force round to attack Washington on the flank. It proved a decisive defeat for the Americans and was one of the few occasions during this war when the British were able to force their opponents into engaging in a pitched battle. The battle of Brandywine opened the way to Philadelphia, where Howe wintered his troops.

The following spring, General Howe, who had been knighted for the dubious efficiency of his campaign, retired and Sir Henry Clinton was appointed in his place. By this time the French had joined the war and Britain found herself once more engaged on several fronts. Thus Clinton's first act was to obey the Government order to give up Philadelphia and retire to New York. This operation was carried out with the greatest difficulty, with Washington snapping at the heels of the retiring troops. At Freehold, Clinton turned to fight his tormentor, but the day proved so excessively hot that men on both sides were dropping dead from heat exhaustion and the battle was discontinued by mutual agreement. After arrival at New York, the 55th were used to take part in various forays to such places as the Acushnet River, Martha's Vineyard and Egg Harbour but, with the coming of winter, their part in the unsatisfactory campaign had come to an end.

During the autumn of 1778, the French fleet had been cruising up and down the American coast, closely watched by the British, and in November turned their attention to attacking British possessions in the West Indies. Before they could do so, however, a force, composed of the 15th, 28th, 46th and 55th Regiments, had been dispatched under Major-General Grant to defend them, and managed to turn the tables by attacking the French-held island of St. Lucia. The landing was successfully accomplished but shortly afterwards the French fleet, under Admiral d'Estaing, arrived with a vastly superior force. Some desperate fighting followed, during which the British naval squadron brilliantly out-manoeuvred the French. When d'Estaing decided to contest the matter on land, he fared no better. A small British force, consisting largely of all the light companies on the island, fought a spirited action in which there were more French killed and wounded than the entire numbers of the defenders. This signal defeat persuaded d'Estaing to give up further attempts to recapture the island.

The 55th then spent several years in the West Indies, mainly as the garrison for the island of St. Kitts. As has been remarked earlier in this book, the West Indies was far from being a popular station and the numbers of the Regiment who died from the various diseases to which they were prone, compared unfavourably with the number of their battle casualties so that it was with considerable rejoicing that they returned to England in 1785.

In the meantime, the 34th had not been left out of the American conflict, although the part they were destined to play was not to prove a happy one.

In the early spring of 1776, they embarked for Canada and arrived just in time to reinforce Quebec, which was being closely beleaguered by the Americans. With the comparatively small addition to his forces, the Quebec commander, Sir Guy Carleton, assumed the offensive and, sallying forth, routed the Americans and forced them to raise the siege.

The following year it was decided to carry the war against the enemy and to attempt to link up with Sir William Howe in New York. Accordingly, General Burgoyne set off with a force of approximately 8,000 men, including the 34th. It was to be an ill-fated expedition. A detachment sent under Colonel St. Leger to create a diversion on the shores of Lake Ontario, failed in its purpose, while the main army had much more to contend with than the enemy. The poisonous malaria from the swamps, through which they had to wade, seriously affected the men's health and the sick overfilled the field hospitals. When they were not wading through swamp, they encountered forest, which was so thick that trees had to be felled to enable the army to progress. All through the summer Burgoyne struggled to reach the plains of Saratoga. He did not achieve his objective until the middle of September when, at Stillwater, his weakened force came up against an American army under General Gates. A fierce battle ensued, which lasted the whole day, with no quarter given on either side. Towards evening the enemy abandoned the field but Burgoyne, with over 600 men dead and heavily encumbered with artillery and stores, was in no position to pursue his advantage and thus derived nothing from his victory.

All Burgoyne could now do was to dig in and give his battered army time to recover. In the meantime he sent off to Sir William Howe for assistance. Sir William, however, paid no regard to the trials of General Burgoyne and set sail with his force in the opposite direction. The Americans now attempted to attack Burgoyne from the rear and were only repelled at heavy loss to both sides. It now became apparent that the Americans were not to be tempted to another pitched battle but were concentrating on surrounding the British until they could be forced to surrender. Burgoyne, accordingly, by dint of abandoning his heavy equipment and surrendering his wounded, started to retreat back to Saratoga. From there he attempted to reach Fort George but found the road cut; he turned towards Fort Edward to find a similar situation. By now his army had dwindled to 3,500 men, of whom only a handful were fit to fight. The end was not far off.

On the 13th October the sorely pressed Burgoyne held a Council of War. By the most careful economies he was told he had food supplies for only a further seven or eight days. Any hope of help from Howe had long since vanished and his army was reduced to a state where it was no longer a fighting force. Under these circumstances, he had no alternative but to send emissaries to General Gates to ask for terms of surrender. Gates readily agreed that he would accept the capitulation of the British and that they would be allowed to march out of the fortified position with the honours of war. He further agreed that they should be marched to Massachusetts Bay for embarkation to England, under the condition that they were to take no further part in the campaign.

These were honourable terms but, when Burgoyne arrived at Massachusetts with his men, Congress disgracefully repudiated the agreement and the whole force were detained as prisoners of war. They were not to return to England until 1786, the year after the 55th returned from the West Indies.

The Battle of Saratoga, bringing about as it did, the capitulation of Burgoyne's army, has been described as one of the decisive battles of the world. It was followed by the recognition of American independence by France, Spain and Holland. When peace was finally declared in 1783, Britain had no option but to accept the loss of her American colony.

With all the events which had come about since both regiments left Ireland for America, their characteristics could no longer be said to spring from any part of the country. We have seen how the Scottish flavour was lost by the 55th and, with so many casualties from battle and disease, the Irish element of both regiments had become watered down by reinforcements raised in all quarters of Britain. On their return, both were well below strength as was the case with many other regiments of the line. Even the proud Highland regiments were no longer finding it possible to get the required number of recruits from their homeland. The 42nd, who had been so gallantly involved with the 55th at Ticonderoga, were reinforced before the end of the American war with men 'for the most part the sweepings of London and Dublin. They were of the most depraved character, and of habits so dissolute that one half of them were unfit for service'. The result was that the efficiency of this most Scottish of regiments was, for a time, impaired and there is no doubt that other regiments suffered in the same way.

The recruiting problem had become so acute that regiments resorted to the most extravagant bribes to fill their ranks, some offering as high as twenty pounds, as well as a handsome reward to anyone who might introduce a new recruit. Others resorted to flights of the most imaginative rhetoric to achieve their ends. An advertisement appearing in a northern paper offered five guineas to:

> You who, uncorrupted by the universal depravity of your southern countrymen, have withstood, unmoveable as a rock, all the assaults of Surrounding Luxury and Dissipation. You who, while others, effeminated by voluptuous refinements and irrecoverably lost to honour, lolling in the arms of Pleasure, can see the danger to their country with criminal indifference . . .

and so on for several paragraphs. Evidently the permissive society presented a problem, even in those days!

The Government, now more convinced of the need for maintaining a standing army, even in times of peace, was seriously worried about the situation and anxiously sought a solution. It was out of this anxiety that the scheme was devised of attaching regiments to certain territorial areas as recruitment areas, where it would be their duty to build up goodwill for themselves.

As a consequence of this plan, the following letter was sent to

Major-General Grant, commanding the 55th, whilst they were still in the West Indies, which demonstrates very clearly the thinking behind the new arrangement.

London   31 August 1782.

Sir,

His Majesty having been pleased to order that the regiment of foot which you command shall take the county name of the Fifty Fifth or Westmorland Regiment, and be looked upon as attached to that county. I am to acquaint you it is His Majesty's further pleasure that you shall, in all things, conform to that idea and endeavour by all means in your power to cultivate and improve that connection, so as to create a mutual attachement between the county and the regiment which may, at all times, be useful towards recruiting the regiment; but, as the completing of the several regiments, now so generally deficient, is, in the present crisis, of the most important national concern, you will on this occasion use the utmost exertion for that purpose by prescribing the greatest diligence to your officers and recruiting parties and by every suitable attention to the gentlemen and considerable inhabitants; and as nothing can so much tend to conciliate their affections as an orderly and polite behaviour towards them, and an observance of the strictest discipline in all your quarters, you will give the most positive orders on that head; and you will immediately make such a disposition of your recruiting parties as may best answer to that end.

I have the honour to be, etc.,

H. S. Conway.

To Major-General James Grant,
     Colonel of the Fifty Fifth or
     Westmorland Regiment of Foot.

At the same time Lord Frederick Cavendish, colonel commanding the 34th, received a similar letter designating his Regiment to the County of Cumberland. There seems to have been little reason for attaching the 55th to the County of Westmorland and only a slight one for attaching the 34th to Cumberland. In the latter case, apart from the Regiment's initial connection with Carlisle Castle, there was the circumstance that their commanding officer, Lord Cavendish, was the third son of the Duke of Devonshire, who had extensive estates in Cumberland and it might have been out of consideration for this family influence that the choice was made.

Whatever the reasons, the new territorial attachments of the 34th and the 55th were to have the effect of bringing them closer together, although their careers had already touched at several points. From now on they would both rely mainly on the hardy border men and the men from the fells to make up their ranks and it would be hard to imagine better material for the trials which lay ahead.

CHAPTER V

There is no record where either regiment was stationed on their return to England but it would be nice to think that they were sent to their counties of adoption to start the good work of influencing people and winning friends. By November, 1788, however, we know that the 55th had moved to Scotland and two years later was sent to Ireland and quartered in Londonderry. In the meantime the French Revolution had broken out and the peace was menaced once again. All the crowned heads of Europe watched with apprehension lest the revolutionary ideas should spread across their borders. When the ultimate step was taken and Louis XVI was executed it was felt that they could stand by no longer and England joined in a coalition with the other European powers against France.

Quite how the 55th reached France and under whose command is not now known. Perhaps they took part in the march from London to embark at Greenwich which was immortalised by an anonymous poet:

'Our march, interrupted by whisky and gigs,
Mad drivers, mad oxen, and obstinate pigs –
Men boxing, dogs barking, and women in tears,
Harsh concert that threatened the drums of our ears.
'Midst a bustle and uproar beyond all compare
At last we arrived at the Hospital Square.
Our Sovereign, God bless him! beloved and revered,
Benignantly smiling, amongst us appeared.
A Grenadier, drunk, from the centre rank reeled,
And, hiccuping, up to His Majesty wheeled,
"Never mind all those Jacobins, George, rest in quiet,
We'll quell them, my hearty! As quick as a riot!"
The King was delighted and laughed out aloud
While the soldier was hailed with three cheers by the crowd.'

It was not until May, 1794, that we come across definite news of
the 55th, when we find them fighting in the Hanoverian division
of the Austrian army in West Flanders. At the same time, the light
companies seem to have sailed for the West Indies with Sir Charles
Grey's expedition. What is most likely to have happened is that
the whole regiment were put under orders for the West Indies and
sailed with Sir Charles. They had hardly put out of port, however,
before news was received that the French, having beaten off the
Duke of York's attack on Dunkirk, were now menacing Ostend.
Sir Charles' force was therefore diverted to meet the new danger.
When the French withdrew, he must have continued his voyage,
leaving the 'heavies' behind with the Duke.

Whatever the circumstances of their involvement, the campaign
which ensued was as fiercely contested as it was obscure in detail.
The battalion companies of the 55th were brigaded, under Major-
General White, with the 12th and the 38th Regiments. The Allied
armies held a line approximately sixty miles long from Thielt on
the right to St. Amand on the left. At first there were minor
advances by the Allied armies, hotly contested by the French. Then,
at the beginning of the summer, the French (who were vastly
superior in number) started to drive the line back to the Netherlands.

It must be said here that although it was true that the French
held the advantage in numbers, they also held the advantage in
other directions. They were superbly led and, unlike the Allied
army, there were no disagreements and misunderstandings amongst
the high command. Above all, their soldiers, inspired by a burning
nationalism, rose above all their handicaps to form one of the most
formidable fighting forces Europe has ever known. Thomas Carlyle,
describing the French soldiers, wrote:

> The snows of winter, the flowers of summer, continue to be stained
> with warlike blood. The soldiers of the Republic are becoming the
> very sons of fire. Barefooted, barebacked: but with bread and iron
> you can get to China! It is one nation against the whole world; but
> the nation has that within her which the whole world will not conquer.

Gradually the inspired Frenchmen drove back their enemies.
Time and time again the Austrians broke and the Duke of York
had to withdraw the British troops to save them from becoming
isolated. In July the British and the Austrians finally separated,
the Dutch staying with the British. By November they had been

driven back to the line of the River Waal, where it was determined to make a stand. The Duke's army was in a sorry state. Since September it had been ravaged with disease. The troops were without winter clothing and many were without boots. The hospitals were grossly understaffed and without medical supplies, so that men were dying at a rate of fifty a day. £40,000 sent out to buy nourishment and wine for the sick, was never used for the purpose it was intended but found its way into the pockets of those whose duty it was to administer the fund. In an attempt to evacuate some of the wounded, five hundred of them were packed into a small river steamer, without water and with only one attendant. Its progress down the river was marked by the heaps of dead laid out on the river banks as it passed.

Now the French general, Pichegru, really had his tail up and was to give the Duke of York no peace. The British defensive position was centred around Nijmegen – a name to become immortal in another war – and was under heavy artillery fire. It was decided to attempt to silence these batteries and, accordingly, as strong a force as possible was gathered together to make a night attack on the French position. The main column consisted of the 27th, 28th, 63rd and 78th Regiments, led by the 55th. Unfortunately, there were traitors within the gates of Nijmegen and the French were alerted to the plan. As the sortie party crept forward, they suddenly came under heavy fire. General de Burgh, however, continued the advance without firing a shot in return and launched his attack at the point of the bayonet. The carnage which resulted was terrific, the French losing over 500 men and being completely driven from their position. Unfortunately, the demolition party which followed behind did not do their work properly, with the result that, when the victorious troops retired again to Nijmegen, the French were quick to resume their virtually undamaged positions and re-open fire on the town.

There was now nothing for it but further withdrawal. The winter was closing in and the conditions becoming worse, while the supply arrangements continued to be grossly mismanaged. General Pichegru, thinking it hopeless to try to follow up the British across country, saturated by the heavy rains and intersected by swollen rivers and canals, dug in and waited his chance with the coming of spring. It was at this stage that Fate took a hand. The winter proved to be the hardest of the century and so all the waterways were frozen solid. While the half-starved and half-clothed British suffered agonies from exposure, the French attacked again over the ice. So began one of the grimmest retreats in the history of warfare, rivalling in horror that of Sir John Moore's to Corunna and even Napoleon's retreat from Moscow.

The plan was to retire to Bremen, which was a hundred and fifty miles away, the communications with the Dutch coast being cut. The route lay over vast, trackless wastes with scarcely a human habitation and of such flatness as to offer little chance of finding suitable defensive positions for the rearguard. The sick and wounded were carried in 160 open wagons, in which they were exposed to the snow and rain, without a single blanket to cover them. Worse still, in accordance with the practice of these days, many of the soldiers were accompanied by their wives and even children. After one stage, when the night had been particularly severe, over three hundred bodies were left behind to mark the site of their pitiful camp. The 88th Regiment – the Connaught Rangers, who were often to be alongside the Border Regiment in the future – became so dispersed that no roll-call was possible. One of the 88th left behind this account of one incident during those terrible months:

> The whole of this day's march was marked by scenes of the most calamitous nature. We could not proceed a hundred yards without perceiving the dead bodies of men, women and children and horses in every direction. One scene made an impression on my memory, which time will never be able to efface. Near a cart we perceived a stout looking man and a beautiful young woman with an infant about seven months old at the breast; all three frozen dead. The mother had most certainly expired in the act of suckling her child as, with one breast exposed, she lay upon the drifted snow, the milk to all appearance in a stream, drawn from the nipple by the babe and instantly congealed. The infant seemed as if its lips had just then been disengaged and it reposed its little head upon the mother's bosom with an overflow of milk frozen as it trickled from its mouth; their countenances were perfectly composed and fresh, resembling those of persons in a sound and tranquil slumber. About fifty yards advanced was another dead man, with a bundle of linen clothes and a few biscuits, evidently belonging to the poor woman and child; and a little further was a horse, lying down but not quite dead, with a couple of panniers on his back, one of which contained, as we discovered, the body of another child about two years of age, wrapped in flannel and straw. This, we afterwards heard, was the whole of one

family, a sergeant's wife of the 55th, her brother and children. The man found with the horse and bundle had remained behind his regiment to assist them during the march thus memorable for its miseries. He had just gained sight of a distant hamlet, where they might have obtained shelter from the inclemency of the weather, when his strength failed him. The commanding officer of the 55th rode by at that criticial moment, but too late to render them any service ; and, as the battalions passed the spot, the troops were witnesses in their turns of this melancholy scene.

Even the Dutch villages, through which the tragic procession passed, proved hostile, little caring that the campaign had been launched to assert their independence. In the middle of this desperate situation, the Duke of York was recalled and the command devolved on the Dutch General Walmoden. The Prince of Orange distinguished himself by deserting and soon all resistance from the Dutch ceased. It is surprising that, in this calamitous situation, any order was maintained, but maintained it was. With a force of 50,000 Frenchmen worrying at their heels, the British painfully dragged themselves back to safety. The final stages were almost the worst for a thaw set in and they had to wade many miles through water up to their middles before finally arriving at Bremen. Of the original army of 13,000 there were only 6,500 to embark for England on April 10th, 1795.

In the meantime, the flank companies of the 55th were in the distant West Indies, where they were also to suffer severely, although from totally different causes. Arriving early in 1794, they had an early success in the capture of Martinique, after which they attacked St. Lucia, which had once more fallen into the hands of the French. This they also accomplished without much difficulty and, leaving a small garrison behind, continued their victorious way to Guadaloupe.

It was at this stage that yellow fever broke out amongst the troops with such severity that they were rendered more or less noncombatant. As the plague swept through the ranks, the French appeared off the island and landed a strong force of 1,500 men. Lieutenant-Colonel Gomm of the 55th and his few remaining fit soldiers were almost over-run and retreated to a fortified position. Sir Charles Gray made strenuous efforts for their relief. Every available man on the other islands was sent to Guadaloupe. Fierce fighting ensued, without much impression being made by either side until, once again, disease took a hand. On the 1st September, out of a total force of 1,760 men, only 389 were fit to stand. A month later the effective force had been reduced to 125. The French did not seem to suffer to the same extent and, when they received fresh reinforcements, the British force had no alternative but to surrender. The French agreed that they should be allowed to march out with the honours of war and be shipped back to England but, as had happened earlier in America, the pact was later repudiated and they were all made prisoners of war. Colonel Gomm and many of his officers died during captivity. Of the handful of survivors few, if any, were to rejoin their Regiment. Most of them were drafted to the 45th Regiment to make up their strength.

Matters were going so badly for the British in the West Indies that it was decided to send a major expedition from England to deal finally with the French. Accordingly, a force of over 3,000 cavalry and 22,000 infantry was assembled under Sir Ralph Abercromby, which set sail at the end of 1795. The force included the reconstituted 55th, newly returned to full strength after the drubbing they had received on the continent. The whole huge force was transported in a fleet of 300 ships, which must have been an impressive sight as they sailed down the English Channel. The intention was to sail the Atlantic in convoy and make such a show in the Caribbean as would strike terror into the hearts of the enemy. Unfortunately, heavy storms forced the expedition to return after only a few days out. Many ships were lost and others so badly damaged that the first part of the fleet had to sail without them early the following year. Much of the impact it was hoped to make was thus lost.

The task allotted to the force which included the 55th was the recapture of St. Lucia for the third time. It was accomplished after some severe fighting in which the local population of Caribs proved most troublesome. They retreated to the centre of the island, together with a number of runaway slaves and French deserters, from which point of vantage they continued to rob and plunder long after the main hostilities had ceased. In consequence, the 31st, 44th, 48th and 55th Regiments were left behind to deal with them, while the main force sailed on to further victories.

Whilst garrisoning the island, the dreaded yellow fever again made its appearance and all the regiments suffered severely. Of the total force stationed in various islands during that year, deaths from disease reached the horrifying total of 264 officers and 12,387 men.

The 34th also found themselves in the West Indies at this time and were involved in suppressing the Caribs on the island of St. Vincent. On this occasion, however, the native population became so uncontrollable that orders were given for the whole tribe, numbering about 5,000, to be rounded up and shipped off to South America, where they were allowed to settle. Having accomplished this task, the 34th sailed for home to be followed the next year by the 55th, who had had their numbers partly made up by the remnants of the 44th and 48th Regiments.

The terrible losses suffered by the army during the last years of the century rendered the ever-pressing problem of recruiting more acute than ever. When they got back to England, the 34th were ordered to bring their Regiment up to strength by enlisting boys between the ages of 12 and 16 from the orphanages and the poorhouses. By this means the Government sought not only to gain recruits but to relieve itself of the expense of maintaining the unhappy youths. The enlistment was hardly completed before the regiment was sent off to the Cape of Good Hope and afterwards on to India. It is remarkable that such unlikely material was later to be turned into a first-class regiment. Perhaps, after all, life in the army for a boy, however young, was preferable to the rigours of the poorhouse.

The battered 55th were not left long to lick their wounds. Although its total strength was scarcely more than 400 men, they set sail for Holland that year following their return from the West Indies, as part of an expedition led by General John Moore. Its object was again the liberation of the apathetic Dutch from the French. The 55th took an important part in the capture of Helder Fort and campaigned with varying success during the summer of 1799. With the approach of winter, however, and memories still green of their last experience in the Dutch marshes, the Duke of York signed a hurried treaty and sailed his force (already with a formidably high sick list) back to England.

In the year 1800 the 34th embarked for service at the Cape of Good Hope and two years later, the Cape having been returned to the Dutch, under the terms of the Treaty of Amiens, they sailed on to India, where they became garrison troops in the Madras Presidency.

In 1802 the 55th again sailed for the West Indies, this time Jamaica. Thus both Regiments missed the military excitements which were to be produced by the Peninsular War.

PART II

The Nineteenth Century

CHAPTER VI

ALTHOUGH BOTH Regiments, whose careers we have been following, were stationed far from home at the beginning of the nineteenth century, the 34th was still to have an important part to play in the argument with Napoleon in Europe. This was because the Government, with its troops scattered all over the world, was anxious about the defence of the country against a possible French invasion. It therefore ordered that many regiments were to raise second battalions and the 34th was one of those selected to do so.

It would have been thought that, with the identifying of the 34th with Cumberland only twenty years before, that county would be the recruiting area for the new battalion; but the inscrutable ways of the War Office did not permit such a logical course. The area of Cumberland and Westmorland had been allotted to the 2nd Battalion of the 25th or 'Sussex' Regiment, while the 34th were ordered to be formed at Ashton in Kent. They were placed on the establishment on the 25th April, 1804, and for several years were pawns in a frantic game of military manoeuvring. They were sent first to Hanover but were returned to England without being required to strike a blow. Then they were ordered to Ceylon but sent to Cork instead, where they formed part of a secret expedition being organised under General Beresford. Nothing came of this but they were sent to Madeira and put under orders for India. When this fell through, they returned tamely to Jersey. Finally, in the summer of 1809, having been made up to a thousand men strong, they embarked for the Peninsula to join the army of Sir Arthur Wellesley, shortly to be created Lord Wellington.

The campaign on which they were now embarked was to be one of the most glorious in British military history. The vast French army, which had poured over the Pyrenees and advanced irresistibly through Spain, now threatened to drive Wellington's army out of Portugal and into the sea. The Spaniards had proved to be ineffective

soldiers, largely because they were so badly led. The Portuguese
were equally ineffective allies so all that stood between Napoleon
and his ambitions was the battered red-coat army, poorly equipped,
on short rations and frequently with their pay months in arrears.
They had been enlisted from the poorhouses and the jails, some
of them were boys and most of them with little experience of war –
yet they fought like tigers, showing a bravery in battle which has
never been surpassed, and a sense of discipline in their dealing
with the civilian population which won them the gratitude and
admiration of those they strove to liberate.

By the time the 34th joined the Peninsular Army, Wellington
had pushed the French out of Portugal and was on the point of
marching into Spain. The formidable massing of the French army
under Marshal Massena, however, was of such proportions that
he delayed his advance and concentrated instead on the defence of
Portugal. It was under these conditions that the battle of Busaco
was fought, in which the 34th received their baptism of fire.

Marshal Massena was the most successful of the French generals,
Napoleon's favourite, with the reputation of never having been
defeated in battle. A man of less self-confidence might never have
attempted to drive the British out of their position, high in the hills,
with their guns perched amongst the rocks, looking down on every
movement of the enemy. The attempt, however, was made and
carried through with fanatical spirit. Five columns of the French
advanced against the British massed on the high ground. Again and
again they threw themselves forward to be met by a withering fire.
Then, when the attacks started to weaken, the British rose with that
terrible cheer, which was to be known to every fighting Frenchman
in the months to come, and swept down the mountains, their bayonets
sparkling in the sunshine until they became reddened with French
blood. It was an overwhelming victory and one which gave much
heart to the Portuguese, who were beginning to think of the French
as unbeatable.

For a time Wellington lay in his impregnable lines of Torres
Vedras. The 34th were brigaded with the 28th and 29th Regiments
under Colonel the Hon. Alexander Abercromby, which moved out
of their defensive position to lay siege to the town of Badajoz.
Marshal Soult, who now commanded the French, moved to relieve
the town and Abercromby's brigade was amongst the troops under

7. The uniform of a private of the 34th Regiment in 1811.

8. Drummer of the 34e Regiment of French infantry in 1811, great rivals of the English 34th Regiment by whom they were routed at the Battle of Arroyo dos Molinos.

9. Display of French colours captured by British Troops in 1811.

10. A Crimean scene, with men of the 34th Regiment playing skittles with French Colonial Troops. The group on the right are playing 'Housey-Housey'.

11. The 55th (2nd Battalion Border Regiment) taking Russian rifle pits at the Battle of Inkerman, 5 November, 1854, from a painting by Orlando Norrie.

supreme command of General Beresford, who were placed in position to meet them. At first sight it looked like an unequal contest. Beresford's force was probably equal in number to the 30,000 French but only 6,000 of them were British and the French were all seasoned troops.

At first the battle took the course which might have been expected. The French attacked at nine in the morning and, almost at once, the Spanish and the Portuguese were routed. At one stage there was such confusion that the Spanish and the British were firing on each other and it looked as if the day was lost. Suddenly a line of Fusiliers, together with Abercromby's brigade, emerged in perfect order from the smoke which covered the battlefield and threw themselves against the heavy masses of the enemy. Napier describes the conflict which followed in these words . . .

the Fusilier battalions struck by the iron tempest, reeled and staggered like sinking ships. Suddenly and sternly recovering, they closed on their terrible enemies, and then was seen with what a strength and majesty the British soldier fights. In vain did Soult, by voice and gesture, animate his Frenchmen ; in vain did the hardiest veterans, extricating themselves from the crowded columns, sacrifice their lives to gain time for the mass to open out on such a fair field ; in vain did the mass itself bear up, and fiercely striving, fire indiscriminately upon friends and foes, while the horsemen, hovering on the flank, threatened to charge the advancing line. Nothing could stop that astonishing infantry. No sudden burst of undisciplined valour, no nervous enthusiasm, weakened the stability of their order ; their flashing eyes were bent on the dark columns to their front ; their measured tread shook the ground ; their dreadful volleys swept away the head of every formation ; their deafening shouts overpowered the dissonant cries that broke from all parts of the tumultous crowd, as, foot by foot, and with horrid carnage, it was driven from the incessant vigour of the attack to the farthest edge of the hill. In vain did the French reserves, joining with the struggling multitude, endeavour to sustain the fight ; their efforts only increased the irremediable con- fusion, and the mighty mass, giving way like a loosened cliff, went headlong down the ascent. The rain flowed after in streams, dis- coloured with blood, and one thousand five hundred unwounded men, the remnants of six thousand unconquerable British soldiers, stood triumphantly on the fatal hill.

This battle was one of the turning points in the campaign and the 34th were given the honour of inscribing 'Albuhera' on their colours for the gallant part they played in it.

One of the most remarkable officers to serve in the 34th joined the Regiment shortly after Albuhera and remained with them throughout the rest of the campaign. His name was George Bell, at that time a lieutenant but later to rise to the rank of general and to be knighted. Throughout his military life he kept a diary of events, which was later published as *Rough Notes of an Old Soldier*. This record was put into a shortened form in 1956 and published* under the title of *Soldier's Glory*. It is one of the best accounts of life in the army of those times ever printed.

There is an amusing story concerning the circumstances of George Bell's joining the regiment he was to serve so well. On receiving his commission he was ordered to join the 34th on a troopship at Portsmouth. His mother took him by coach from Appleby but, to their dismay, they arrived at Portsmouth to find that the fleet had already sailed. They learned, however, that the wind had dropped and the Fleet had become becalmed just west of the Isle of Wight. Undaunted, they set off in pursuit and duly caught up with it. No sooner had they boarded the troopship, however, than the wind sprang up and there was no way of getting George Bell's mother ashore again. Bell must have been one of few soldiers to arrive on the Peninsula with his mother in tow! History does not relate how the lady got back home again.

One of the elements which added spice to the 34th's part in the campaign was the special rivalry which existed between them and their opposite number, the 34th French. The 34th English, nick-named 'The Cumberland Gentlemen', called their counterparts the *Parley Vous* and it was their greatest ambition to meet them and overcome them in battle. Their opportunity came on the 28th October, 1811.

At that time they were serving in the brigade commanded by that able General, Sir Rowland Hill. The French were causing a great deal of trouble in the area of Estremadura and he decided that they must be driven out. On the night before the battle it was learned that they had been quartered in the village of Arroyo dos Molinos and, accordingly, Hill moved his force to a position where they could attack at first light.

Let George Bell, whose first action this was, here take up the tale:

'All was still, and cold, and cheerless, until about two o'clock in the morning of the 28th, when the word was gently passed through

* Coincidentally by George Bell & Sons Ltd.

all the regiments: "Stand to your arms!" The whole division was now in silent motion, and moved on to the plain some few miles, pretty close to the enemy, who were quartered and encamped in and about the little town of 'Arroyo-Molino'. The division was now divided into three brigades, cavalry on the flanks and centre. It was just before the dawn of day, with a drizzling rain. We could just see our men to call the roll.

'Our gallant and worthy General, riding along our front, said, "Are you all ready?" "Yes, Sir". "Uncase your colours, and prime the load." All this looked very serious, and I began to have a queer fear of mortal danger stirring my nerves. As I took the King's colour in charge, being senior ensign, the Major said, "Now my lads, hold those standards fast, and let them fly out when you see the enemy."

'Away we went across the plain to be baptised in blood. Our skirmishers in advance had come across the French outlying pickets, and had begun operations. A cannon-shot came rattling past, making a hissing noise, such as I had never heard before. Four sergeants supported the colours in battle; my old friend Bolland from Beverley was one of them. I said, "What's that, Bolland?" "Only the morning gun, sir; they're just coming on them now." A little onwards, and I saw two men cut across by that last shot, the first I had ever seen killed. I was horrified but said nothing.

'The French were getting ready to be off again when our advance got up to their pickets and began the quarrel. Their horses were saddled and tied to olive trees, infantry gathering from different points for their alarm-post – artillery taking up position – all getting on the defensive, when they were skilfully hemmed in on three sides; behind the little town the 71st and 92nd Regiments brought up their left shoulders, and came pouring into the streets with a destructive fire; the French were now falling by fifties, but fighting and struggling hard to maintain their ground. We had lined the garden walls, and kept pitching into their ranks while our cavalry gave them no time to reform; a thick mist rolled down the craggy steep mountain behind the town; there was a terrifying cheer, such as is not known except amongst British troops on the battleground; it drowned the clatter of musketry, while the driving storm carried with it the enemy up this sierra, the 28th and the 34th Regiments at their heels. We pressed them so closely that they threw off their knapsacks, turned round, and fired into us; still our men pushed on until this body of Girard's brave army dropped their firelocks, dispersed, and as many as could got clear away over the mountains. . . .'

In his tactical plan, General Hill had ordered that the 28th and the 34th be sent round the village to cut off the retreat and it was to

them that the spoils of war fell. Fifteen hundred prisoners were taken
at a cost of only seven British killed and sixty wounded. The 34th
were virtually unscathed but they had played a vital part in a great
victory. Of them General Hill wrote in his dispatches:

> 'No praise of mine can do full justice to their admirable conduct;
> the patience and goodwill shown by all ranks during the forced
> marches, in the worst of weather; their strict attention to the orders
> they received; the precision with which they moved to the attack;
> their obedience to command during the action; in short, the manner
> every one of them has performed his duty, from the commencement
> of the operation, merits my warmest thanks.'

Arroyo ever since has had a special place in the annals of the
Regiment. They had met their opposite number of the French Army
and had made them their prisoners, including the band with their
drums and the drum major with his long cane. These trophies are
a proud possession of the Regiment to this day, in spite of periodical
requests from the French to have them returned, and Arroyo Day
has been kept every year in remembrance of an unique occasion.

Now Wellington intensified his siege of Badajoz and the 34th were
once more involved, although in a minor capacity. George Bell was
again a witness of the whole action and his account of it is given here
at some length, both as an example of the heroism of which the
British soldier is capable and as a demonstration of Bell's quality
as a descriptive writer:

   ... the men dashed forward under a terrible fire, spread and raised
their ladders against the castle walls, and with unexampled courage,
ran up under a shower of shot and shell, stones and small arms, while
the fearful fire was kept up on the red-coats from flanks and centre.
The leading men on the ladders were met by pikes, bayonets and
musketry, their ladders pushed from the walls. Now the deafening
shouts, crashing of broken ladders, and shrieking of the crushed and
wounded men became loud amongst the din of war. Excited to madness, the comrades of the undaunted brave below, who swarmed
again round the ladders, swiftly ran up, and were tossed over from
the enemy above, who cried, 'Victory!' and 'Why don't you come into
Badajoz?'.
   The brave Colonel Ridge, with a voice like thunder, called to his
men to follow, raised a ladder to the wall a little further off, and
met with but little opposition until he got in. Another ladder was

raised and our men went pouring in, took the enemy in the flanks, and delivered a volley which very much astonished and staggered them. Here another fight commenced, and here poor Ridge fell – no man died a more glorious death in battle, although multitudes of brave men fell who deserved great military glory.

The frightful tumult at the main breach all this time, the incessant roar of the cannon, musketry, bursting of shells, yells of the wounded, and the cheering of those who had so short a time to live, rent the air in a fiery lava of exploding shells and barrels of powder.

Every flash showed the French ready and prepared on the ramparts ; showed their glittering arms, dark figures, heaps of live shells, and an astonishing amount of artillery, every man having three loaded muskets beside him. Yet our men leaped into the ditch, of whom 500 volunteers, being foremost, were dashed to pieces with shot, shell and powder barrels. The Light Division stood for a moment in horror at the terrific sight ; then, with a wild shout, dashed with one accord into the fiery gulf and, with the light of a blaze of fire-arms from above, the 4th Division followed in an excited fury. One hundred men were drowned in the inundation (for, at this time, the sluices were opened and the water let into the ditch from the river). They now turned off to the left, seeking the main breach, and got crowded and mixed together. The only light was that of the flashing guns, pouring death and destruction among them. The confusion was great, but all cheered like thunder ; the French cheers were also loud and terrible. The bursting of grenades, shells and powder barrels, the whizzing flight of blazing splinters of barrels, the loud voices of the officers, the heavy groans of the dying, were sufficient to create terror indescribable. Now they found the way and went at the breach like a whirlwind. Sword-blades, sharp and pointed, fixed in ponderous beams, were in their front as they ascended ; planks, too, filled with iron spikes ; while every Frenchman had three or four loaded muskets at his feet, with leaden slugs over the usual bullets. Hundreds of our men had fallen, dropping at every discharge, which only maddened the living. The cheer was for ever on, on, with screams of vengeance and a fury determined to win a town. The rear pushed the foremost into the sword-blades to make a bridge of their bodies, rather than be frustrated in their success. Slaughter, tumult and disorder continued. No command could be heard ; the wounded, struggling to free themselves from under the bleeding bodies of their dead comrades ; the enemy guns within a few yards, at every fire opening a bloody lane amongst our people, who closed up and, with shouts of terror as the lava burned them, pressed on to destruction. Officers, starting forward with a heroic impulse, carried on their men to the yawning breach and glittering steel, which still continued to belch out flames of scorching death.

About midnight, when 2,000 men had fallen, Wellington, who was looking on, sent an order for the troops to retire and re-form for another attack. In the retreat from the ditch there was great confusion and terrible carnage under the continual fire of the French. The groans and lamentations of the wounded, trampled on and expecting to be left to the mercy of an exasperated and ferocious enemy, were awful. Who could explain their feelings? The bitterness of death to them was past. The 3rd Division had gained the Castle. The 5th Division was also engaged at another point. The town was girdled with fire ; General Walker's brigade were escalading – the Portuguese were unnerved and threw down the ladders. Our men snatched them up and raised them against the walls, nearly thirty feet high. The ladders were short, yet the men clambered up them. The fire of the French was deadly ; a mine was sprung under the soldiers' feet, live shells and beams of wood were rolled over them with showers of grape ; man after man dropped dead from the ladders. Other points were attacked and won. The French fought like demons. A death struggle of fiery antagonists took place at every corner, while our men most thoroughly maddened with rage and excitement, dashed to the breach with wild resolution: for is it not recorded 'who shall describe the martial fury of that desperate soldier of the 95th, who, in his resolution to win, thrust himself beneath the chained sword blades, and there suffered the enemy to dash out his brains with the ends of their muskets.'

Here was now a crushing and most desperate struggle for the prize ; the bright beams of the moon were obscured with powder-smoke. The springing of the mines, powder-barrels, flashing of guns and small arms, rendered our men marks for destruction. Death's grasp was just on the remnant of the brave, a total annihilation of humanity on our side, when the troops who had escaladed the Castle made a dash at the breach and, with one loud cheer for England, and a sweeping volley and another mad shrieking yell, rushed on with the bayonet and cleared the bloody gap for those below, who now rushed in, driving the French from every point – and Badajoz was won!

This sort of action, so vividly described by George Bell, was to be fought again and again during the long campaign. The losses on both sides were appalling. Badajoz alone cost Wellington 5,000 brave men and the call for more and more reinforcements from England became ever more urgent. They came straight from their homes – or more probably from prison – and were thrown into battle with only the most cursory of training. Yet they proved superb fighting men. The secret lay in the outstanding leadership they were given. Wellington himself was hero-worshipped and his frequent appearances at the battle front greeted with scenes of the greatest enthusiasm. 'There he comes with his long nose – give him a cheer' would be the cry when he was spotted, quietly riding into the lines of some outlying battalion. His constant battles with authority at home for better supplies and weapons for his men were well known, so that none of the discontent at the shortcomings of the commissariat was laid at his door. He was truly a soldiers' general.

Where Wellington set an example, the other officers followed. Those in the fighting regiments lived as roughly as their men, sharing the same meagre rations and bivouacking in the open as they did. In the battle they were in the thick of things, leading every charge with drawn sword and exhorting their men to follow them. When an officer was killed in front of his men, their rage knew no bounds and they redoubled their efforts to get at the enemy.

By the same token the French were honoured and brave opponents and there were many examples of chivalry between the two sides. Bell records an occasion when a French cavalry officer was leading a charge of his men and was about to decapitate a British officer when he noticed that his opponent only had one arm. At once he brought his upraised sword down in a smart salute and passed on. The French soldier's great dread was that he should be captured by the Spanish or Portuguese, from whom he might expect the cruellest treatment, even if he escaped death. In the hands of the British he was assured of being accorded the full honours of war. There was no more awesome figure in the battlefield than the British soldier in full lust of battle but once his enemy was at his mercy, he was the first to tend his wounds and share with him the last of his rations.

After Badajoz the 34th were, for a time, left behind while Wellington advanced to the northern frontiers of Portugal in preparation for his entry into Spain. Confronting Wellington were two great French armies, one under Marmont, north of the Tagus, and the other, under Soult, to the south of the river. Anxious to cut communications between the two, Wellington now sent Sir Rowland Hill, whose force included the 34th, to destroy the bridge, which Marmont had constructed for the purpose. It was protected at each end by a fort and a powerfully fortified castle on the only approach road denied access by artillery. Boldly, Hill decided to leave his guns behind, by-pass the castle and attack the bridge with his infantry. Marching at night, the British force struggled through the mountain passes and at daybreak fell on the enemy and stormed the bridge. Such was the element of surprise that the ladders were erected and the breach achieved before the French were aware of the attack. The British then turned the French guns on the fort at the other end of the bridge and, in a short time, were in possession of that also. Sir Rowland was created Lord Hill of Almarez for this daring exploit in which the 34th played a prominent part.

With Napoleon's forces divided, Wellington now pushed north against Marshal Marmont, while General Hill's force remained in the south to contain Marshal Soult. In June 1812, Wellington won a brilliant victory at Salamanca and entered Madrid, but shortly afterwards considered it expedient to retire again to the frontiers of Portugal, where he spent the winter.

In the spring of 1813, Wellington again advanced at the head of a refreshed and reinforced army – probably one of the finest British armies ever put in the field – and this time the advance included General Hill's division. They played a prominent part in the great victory at Vittoria, where they attacked on the left flank. As the battle reached a climax and the final fortunes were still undecided, the 34th forced a defile and led an attack, which turned the tide in favour of the British. The mighty French army broke and fled, leaving behind them, in addition to all their supplies, five million dollars in gold and silver. A few of the fighting troops filled their pockets with the spoils as they passed in pursuit of the defeated army, but by far the greater part was left to be picked up by the non-combatants and the camp followers, who dogged the footsteps of both armies at a safe distance. None of this great sum of money came to the Treasury as prize money but finished up in the hands of the human jackals who never hesitated to plunder even the bodies of the dead, if richer prizes were not available. At the time of the Battle of Vittoria, the British army was in a very poor state. In the retreat of the previous year, Wellington's army had been so badly supplied that for nineteen days they had no other food than the acorns, chestnuts and berries they could pick up. During the advance to Vittoria, they had been little better served. Most of the soldiers were barefoot and even generals had little more than the clothes they stood up in.

The Marquis of Wellington, as he now was, was almost as much concerned with the plight of his men as he was with the business of beating the French and, indeed, the two were inextricably bound together. There was an occasion when Sir Thomas Picton, one of his commanders, told his Commissary that if he did not find rations for his men, he would hang him on a tree. The indignant Commissary at once went to Wellington to complain of how he had been insulted. The great general listened quietly to the man's tale and then said quietly, 'Did Sir Thomas really say so?' 'Yes, my Lord, these were his very words.' 'Very well, you had better get the rations, or you may be sure he will keep his word. Good Morning!' Miraculously the rations were produced.

With the French now in full retreat, Wellington chased them to the Pyrenees, where they made a last stand to avoid being driven out of the Peninsular altogether. They held on tenaciously to the mountain passes but the blood of the British was up and they would brook no opposition. The towns of San Sebastian and Pampelona were besieged and the army pressed on until they were looking down on the sea and the encamped French troops, which were spread out below them.

It was during a week when it was the turn of the 34th to be the advance body that they ran into serious trouble. The outposts were attacked at dawn on Sunday the 25th July, and the 34th were alerted to go to their rescue. On the sounding of the signal gun the men at once paraded in full marching order – it was a rule that the men never went on parade except with their full kit, just as if they were never to return to the same spot. They raced uphill as fast as they could manage, with Lieutenant-Colonel Fenwick conspicuous at their head. They were badly blown by the time they came up with the enemy, who held the narrow pass with ten thousand men. Almost at once, Fenwick was knocked over, followed at once by Captain Wyatt of the Grenadiers, who was shot through the head. Several other officers fell, including the Adjutant, but still the advance continued. The odds, however, were to prove too much. The outposts were already dead or taken prisoner and three hundred men of the 34th were to become casualties before reinforcements arrived. For a small action it had been an extremely costly one. Colonel Fenwick, who had gained clasps at both Albuhera and Vittoria, had his leg amputated at the knee and command of the battalion devolved on Major Henry Worsley.

Step by step the French were pushed back until, by the end of October, they had been driven right out of Spain and the two armies faced each other across the river Nive on French soil, the 34th having

played a prominent part in the crossing of the Nivelle, which gained
for them another battle honour. When the Spanish had entered
France, they had at once set about wreaking vengeance against their
oppressors. They pillaged the countryside, murdering the civilian
population and looting everything which was moveable. Wellington
took instant action. Many of the looters were summarily shot and
the majority of the Spanish forces sent back to Spain. It was, therefore, almost an entirely British army which faced the French in their
own country.

Now there followed a period of inactivity with the Commanders
and General Staff on each side taking careful stock of the situation.
In the ranks there was less anxiety. They were camped in full view
of each other on either side of the river and passed the time in
cautious fraternisation. French brandy was exchanged for English
tea and some of the French, who had formed attachments when in
England as prisoners of war, sent notes across the river for onward
transmission to their loves.

It was at times like these that the army benefited from the great
number of soldiers' wives who followed the Colours through thick
and thin and were ever ready to give comfort to their menfolk. They
were not, however, always popular with higher command. They were
not amenable to any form of discipline, getting in the way and
generally impeding progress, particularly in time of retreat, when
they often blocked the line of march with their donkeys and
paraphernalia. They were, however, the most indefatigible band of
women, enduring fearful hardships, foraging like terriers for some
delicacy to give to their husbands at the end of a long day's march
and earning small sums of money by doing washing for the officers
– when the officers had any money with which to pay them! Of all
the followers of the 34th Mrs. Skiddy was the acknowledged leader
and was a familiar figure around the battlefields with her two chief
lieutenants, two more Irish ladies, called Biddy Flyn and Betty
Wheel. George Bell gives a graphic account of the day that, after
repeated orders that they were to follow in the rear of their respective
corps, the women were told that if they did not obey, their donkeys
would be shot:

'I'd like to see the man that wud shoot my donkey' says Mrs. Biddy
Flyn. 'Faith, I'll be too early away for any of 'em to catch me. Will

you come wid me, girls?' 'Aye, indeed, every one of us', and away
they all started at early dawn, cracking their jokes about division
orders, Wellington, commanding officers, and their next bivouac.
Mrs. Skiddy led the way on her celebrated donkey, called the 'Queen
of Spain'. She was a squat little Irishwoman and as broad as a turtle.
'Dhrive on, girls, and we'll bate them to the end of this day, at any
rate' says Mother Skiddy. 'And the morrow too,' says Mrs. Flyn. 'An'
the days after that', cried Betty Wheel, and then a chorus of laughter
by the whole brigade. Alas! the Provost-Marshal was in advance – a
man of authority and a terror to all evil-doers. In his department the
Habeas Corpus Act was suspended throughout the war and he was
waiting there in the narrow turn of the road for the ladies, with an
advance guard, all loaded. He gave orders to fire at once on the
donkeys, killing and wounding two or three, *pour example*. There
was a wild, fierce and furious yell struck up at once, with more weep-
ing and lamentations than one generally hears at an Irish funeral,
with sundry prayers for the vagabond that murdered the lives of these
poor, darling, innocent crathers! As we came up, the cries of distress
echoed in the hollow trunks of the old cork trees. It was 'Oh, bad
luck to his ugly face – the spy of our camp – may he nivver see home
till the vultures pick his eyes out, the born varmint,' and so on. They
gathered up what they could carry and marched along with the
troops, crying and lamenting their bitter fate, with not a dry rag on
their backs: It was wonderful what they endured; but, in spite of all
this warning, Mother Skiddy was foremost on the line of march next
morning, as she said. 'We must risk something to be in before the
men, to have the fire and a dhrop of tay ready for the poor crathers
after their load and their labour. An' sure if I went in the rear, the
French, bad luck to them, wud pick me up, me an' my donkey, and
then Dan would be lost entirely.' She was a devoted soldier's wife,
and a right good one, an excellent forager and never failed to have
something for Dan when we were all starving . . .

The peaceful interlude was broken on the 9th December when,
just before daylight, the British advance troops, which included the
34th, plunged into five feet of freezing, fast-running water and made
the other shore in spite of continuous rifle fire from the opposite
bank. Referring once more to the women folk, George Bell records
that they had been given the strictest orders that, under no circumstances were they to cross the river.

Indignantly, Mother Skiddy, the Brigadier-General of the Amazons,
called a midnight meeting and addressed her ragged army: 'I have
the wee-est donkey of you all, an' I'll take the wather, if I'm to swim
for it and let me see who's to stop me, Bridget Skiddy, who thravelled

from Lisbon here into France. If Dan falls, who's to bury him? God save us! Divil a vulture will ever dig a claw into him while there's life in Biddy, his lawful wife. Now, girls, you may go or stay ;' and so she began to saddle her ass.

Once over the Nive, the British found every yard of ground strongly contested. For a time Lord Hill's division was cut off from Wellington in the angle between the Nive and the Ardour and it required the utmost courage and perseverance to extricate itself. On the 10th December Soult mounted a counter attack with 55,000 men but was thrown back with great loss. The battle raged for five days, culminating in Lord Hill's force finally destroying the enemy. Napier records 'that five thousand men were killed or wounded in three hours, upon a space of one mile square'. On the morning of the 14th Wellington rode up to his gallant commander and, shaking him by the hand, declared, 'Hill, the day is your own.' So the 34th added one more battle honour to their colours.

Now Napoleon's days were numbered. Wellington pursued Soult across France, leaving him little time to form a defensive line. A stand was made at Orthes but nothing could stem the victorious British advance. Wellington pressed on across the Garonne and again caught up with Soult, who tried to establish a defensive position at Toulouse. This was to be the last battle of the campaign and the French showed themselves to be stubborn to the last. Wellington carried their position but twice they rallied and twice they were thrown back with great loss. Then came the news that the Allies had entered Paris and that Napoleon had abdicated. The Bourbons were restored to the throne in the person of Louis XVIII and all hostilities ceased on the 21st April, 1814. At that time, after a long and terrible campaign, the British were faced by an enemy who had once been all-victorious, but who now were completely broken.

The 'Cumberland Gentlemen' could claim an honourable share in the great victory which had left the bones of nearly 100,000 men to be picked over by the vultures. To commemorate its distinguished service in the Peninsula and the south of France, the Regiment bears on its colours the names of Albuhera, Vittoria, Pyrenees, Nivelle, Nive, Orthes and Peninsula.

After the declaration of peace, the Regiment remained for a short time in France, where they were made much of by the inhabitants, many of whom (particularly the women), seemed to prefer the company of the British to their own heroes. Within a few months, however, they were sent back to Ireland, where they were instrumental in quelling an insurrection in Tipperary. Then they lay idle for four years, in spite of the eagerness of all ranks to rejoin the conflict against Napoleon, which culminated at Waterloo. In 1817 the British Government again felt secure and ordered a reduction of the armed forces. The 2nd Battalion was amongst the first to go.

To the eternal shame of the authorities, let it be recorded that a great number of the veterans, who had fully earned the pension of a shilling a day for life, which had been promised, were often fobbed off with sixpence, and that only granted for a limited time, like twelve or twenty-four months. After that many gallant soldiers, bearing honourable scars, were reduced to paupers.

After the disbandment, the colours of the 2nd Battalion were handed over to the 1st, who retained them for many years. As they became frailer, it was decided to preserve them in a glass case and they were sent to London for the purpose in 1857. Unfortunately, the tradesman's premises were burned down and only the charred remains were recovered. These were placed in a silver urn, which was used as a centre-piece for the officers' mess table.

Although the 1st Battalion had not nearly such a colourful story to tell as their comrades in the Peninsula, their stay in India was far from devoid of incident and hardship. In the early days of the nineteenth century, India was not such a pleasant station as it was later to become. Apart from the constant outbreaks of cholera, the natives were far from reconciled to being governed by the British Raj and were constantly in a state of insurrection. Moreover, the conditions under which the troops had to serve were thoroughly unsatisfactory. Quarters were poor and often insanitary and the climate greatly added to the discomfort of all ranks, who were inadequately equipped to endure either the heat or the monsoons.

Soon after they arrived in India the 34th lost their commanding officer, Lieutenant-Colonel Fancourt, killed in a Sepoy mutiny; but it was not until June 1814 that it undertook offensive action against the Mahrattas, who were the chief trouble-makers in the country. In that year the 34th marched to Seringapatam to relieve the 69th but, finding the living conditions there so affected the soldiers' health, they soon moved on to Vellore, which became their base of operations.

The campaign reached its peak in 1817, by which time the Mahrattas and Pindarees had assembled a force of 130,000 cavalry, 87,300 infantry and 589 guns. Against this the British commander, Lord Moira, had only 116,400 of all services and 295 guns. The native troops were, however, no match for the British, who, early in 1818, inflicted a crushing defeat from which the insurrectionists never recovered. As was usual, the flank companies and the heavy companies of the 34th were employed on different operations. The flank companies joined Brigadier Munro's force at Adoni and penetrated the South Mahratta country. They captured the fortresses of Dummul, Kooshgul and Darwar, where they halted for the rainy season. Then, early in 1818, they overtook the rear of the Mahratta army at the Salpee Pass, who fled before them in confusion. In the meantime, the battalion companies proceeded to Bangalore to join Major-General Long's division, but they suffered so severely from dysentery that they were rendered non-combatant for some time. They were eventually joined by their flank companies at the end of 1820 in preparation for embarkation for England. The Regiment had been detached on active service from headquarters for over three and a half years and lost one officer and eighty-one rank and file in operations. Their most severe hardship, however, had been disease and uncomfortable campaigning conditions.

They were not to return home immediately. Instead, they moved to Wallajabad, where they were stationed until January 1823. Then volunteers were called for to serve in other corps, who were staying in India. Five hundred and thirty-seven opted to stay on in India, with the result that the regiment embarked on the 8th March only one hundred and sixteen strong and sailed for England in the East India Company's ship 'Coldstream'.

We must now return to the 55th Regiment, whom we left, in 1802, en route for Jamaica. As was to be expected, their stay on the island was characterised by enormous fatalities from disease. They remained on the island for ten years, moving their station only twice. They were first in barracks in Maroon Town, then moved to Up Park Camp, and finally finished their service at Spanish Town. The monotony of their service was relieved only by being called upon to form part of an expedition to St. Domingo, where a small French force was being contained by the Spanish. The Spanish were, however, not strong enough to dislodge them from the capital and they called on their English allies for help.

San Domingo had had a troubled history. In 1798 the negroes had risen against their French masters, who had reduced them to slavery. The revolution succeeded and for a time there was anarchy. The freed slaves committed every sort of outrage against the whites and all restraint was thrown to the winds. It was in this situation that a great native leader emerged, in the person of Toussaint L'Ouverture. He brought all the revolutionaries into line, restored law and order and declared himself the First Consul of a new Independent Republic. A strong man, he was also moderate in his views and had a great capacity for statesmanship. Napoleon, however, considered him an upstart and a critic of his own omnipotence. He therefore sent a strong force to retake the island. Toussaint managed to negotiate a peace without much bloodshed but the French treacherously took him prisoner and shipped him back to France, where he was imprisoned and cruelly tortured. Finally Napoleon had him starved to death *pour encourager les autres.*

When the 55th landed with the British force on the island, the French were hemmed in by the Spanish with no hope of reinforcement and, in 1809, they surrendered without a blow being struck.

In 1810 the Government started another drive to reduce their forces in the West Indies and four companies of the 55th were ordered home to Carlisle. The following year two more companies were shipped home, leaving behind four companies consisting of sixteen officers and rather more than two hundred men. It was almost as if the authorities, by delaying the return of other ranks, hoped that disease would take its toll and save them the expense. In fact, after two years, there were only enough survivors to form one company, which was put under command of the Military Secretary of the station and left to languish on the island, while the remaining officers, sergeants and drummers, were brought home. As so often happened, service in the West Indies had turned for many privates into a sentence of transportation for life.

The remnants of the 55th were now gathered at Carlisle Castle and occupied with recruiting again to full strength in order to supply reinforcements for Wellington, who had just begun his victorious march into Spain, which has already been recorded in this history. At the last minute, however, the plan was changed. The regiment was not left to bring itself up to full strength but hurried off, only four hundred strong, to join a force under General Sir Thomas Graham, to drive the French out of Holland.

The first task given to the force was to join with the Prussian General Bulow and lay siege to Antwerp. All went well until General Bulow and his troops were ordered to join the Grand Army and Graham was left with too weak a force to continue the blockade. Under these circumstances he withdrew to the area of Bergen-op-Zoom, where he lay inactive for over a month. Finally, on his own initiative, he decided to try to capture the extremely strong fortress.

Bergen-op-Zoom was at the time considered to be almost impregnable, the fortifications having been constructed by the great Dutch engineer, Coehorn. The only factor in General Graham's favour was that the garrison consisted of less than three thousand men, where it was considered that at least twelve thousand were required to man the elaborate defences properly.

On 8th March, 1814, the four thousand British troops were formed into four columns, the 55th forming part of the second column with the 33rd and the 69th Regiments.

The attack had an early success when the fourth column, marching up the bed of the river Zoom at low water, reached the ramparts without loss. When their presence was discovered, however, they were so hard pressed that they had to consider retiring. Then they discovered to their dismay that the tide had risen behind them and that their line of retreat was cut off. The French general, realising their plight, was able to leave them isolated and turn his attention to repulsing the attacks being made by the other columns. Fighting was bitter but, on the whole, the British had the best of it, the third column gaining a foothold at great loss. The first and second columns were on the left and now made their attack across the ice which allowed them to come close to the walls. In spite of terrific defensive fire, they descended into the ditch and set their ladders against the defences. To their great chagrin they discovered, as British troops had discovered so often in their campaigns, that their ladders were too short and they had to withdraw with the loss of two hundred men. Later the first column gained access at a point which was undefended and, having left their ladders in place, the remnants of the 55th and their brigade were also able to scramble into the fortress.

12. Private Thomas Beach of the 55th Regiment fighting off Russian troops over the wounded body of Colonel Carter of the 41st Regiment, for which he was awarded the VC. (*Illustrated London News*).

13. The storming of the Redan, 6 October, 1855. (*Illustrated London News*).

A GRUESOME RELIC OF THE MUTINY 18 8
THIS BABY'S CAP WAS PICKED UP ON THE
EDGE OF THE WELL AT CAWNPORE AFTER THE
ENTRY OF BRITISH TROOPS. IT HAS A FEW BLOOD
STAINS.

14. A grim reminder of the Indian Mutiny, 1858.

There now occurred a great misfortune for the attackers. The French were on the point of conceding defeat and had retired to the centre of the town with the idea of giving themselves up in the morning. Unfortunately, the British forces were unable to establish contact between the various columns. Those outside thought the town had fallen and not only did not advance but turned away a German Brigade who, hearing the firing, had come to their aid. Worse – Colonel Henry, commanding the third column, also thought the job done and withdrew his troops to their quarters. As dawn broke the startled French realised that they had only three isolated parties of British to deal with and, with their superior knowledge of the streets and fortifications, were able to deal with them individually. The Guards of the first column had to retire in the face of a sustained counter-attack and were only saved by the 55th and the 69th Regiments, who coolly covered their withdrawal. The 55th itself fought bravely to maintain its position after most of the ladders had been shot away, cutting their line of retreat. But it soon became apparent that their position was hopeless. General Bizanet, the French commander, called for their surrender and the British commander had no option but to agree.

When the decision was made known to the 55th, the first concern was to save the colours from falling into the hands of the enemy. Ensign Goodall was carrying the King's colour and Ensign Ring the regimental colour. They tore these from their staves and wrapped them round their bodies under tunics, where they remained undetected. Under the terms of the surrender agreement, the regiment was released the following morning on condition that they took no further part in the campaign against the French. Thus the colours were saved and later deposited in Carlisle Cathedral.

Oddly enough, although all the other regiments who took part in the assault upon Bergen-op-Zoom were sent home, the remnants of the 55th were not. They continued with the army, whilst taking no part in operations, until Napoleon abdicated. Then they formed part of the victorious force which marched into Antwerp. It was not until June 1814 that they sailed for England. Once more they had been involved in an operation which had not been crowned with success but in which they had acquitted themselves well. Of the Bergen-op-Zoom assault it was written by a contemporary historian, 'it was the very quintessence of pluck and deserved the success it very nearly obtained'.

In March 1815 the sensational news reached England that Napoleon had escaped from Elba and was marching on Paris at the head of a great army. Shortly afterwards he reoccupied the throne, which was hastily vacated by Louis XVIII. In a trice all the toil of years was undone and the whole of Europe was again called to arms. The great Duke of Wellington was put at the head of the allied armies and on June 18th annihilated Napoleon's army once and for all at Waterloo.

It was a pity that neither the 34th nor the 55th were called upon to take part in this final victory, to which they had contributed so much in the years which preceded it. It was not to be. Instead the 55th were marched up and down England in a haphazard manner, as if the authorities could not make up their minds what to do with them. From Harwich they marched to London, where they were quartered in the Tower until it was decided to move them to Chelmsford. Thence they went to Colchester and then back to London. August saw them in Brighton and the following February they were in Bristol. A short period in Ireland followed until, at the end of 1821 they set sail from Gravesend for Cape Town, where they were to remain until September, 1827.

CHAPTER VII

W ITH THE awesome figure of Napoleon finally removed from the European scene, there was entered upon a period sometimes known as 'The Long Peace'. To an extent it is a misnomer because, with the expansion of the British Empire and the Government's increasing responsibility for the maintenance of law and order in places far from home, the army was continuously involved in minor actions in many parts of the world.

At home, after twenty years of almost continuous bloodshed, the country now experienced a natural revulsion against war which, unfortunately, manifested itself by the profession of soldiering becoming again degraded in the eyes of the public and, more significant for the army, in the eyes of officialdom. As has already been remarked, the country were quick to applaud their soldiers when they stood between them and their enemies but, when the crisis was passed, they were even quicker to complain at the expense of maintaining in idleness men who had suddenly become reduced in their eyes to the status of a drunken mob.

The nineteenth century was a time when legislation generally was becoming much more benign, as evidenced by the abolition of slavery, the improvement of prison conditions, the general cleansing of the public services and the passing of such measures as the Reform Bill. That the army did not benefit to the same extent from these stirrings of public conscience was largely due to the army itself. The whole officer class, from the summit downwards, were dyed-in-the-wool traditionalists. To change any of the army traditions or to relax its out-dated code of discipline was to endanger the whole structure which had stood so well the test of battle. The only things they did change related to matters of dress. While the troops continued to be disgracefully housed, grossly overcrowded and abominably fed, their uniforms became more and more gorgeous. The mounted troops in particular were adorned with fantastic head dresses and elaborate trappings of all kinds. The infantryman was fitted out with a huge shako, shaped like a large inverted bell, which had the effect of making him something of a laughing stock in the eyes of the public. When it came to the officers' own turnout, the styles adopted were even more comical. Fashions were exaggerated to an absurd degree and trousers cut so tight that the wearer had difficulty in sitting down. Even 'working' uniforms were heavily embroidered with gold lace and the whole effect was one of Ruritanian splendour. The expense of the cavalry officer's outfit in particular was so great that the cavalry became a sort of means test – only the very rich could afford it. Regiments of the line, like the 34th and the 55th, were not so unrestrained. The result was that a gap was created between the expensive and the inexpensive regiments, which was to develop down the years.

Even the great Duke of Wellington, although politically all-powerful, did nothing to improve the lot of the soldiers who had served him so well. He opposed any increase of pay, not on the grounds which were generally supported in Parliament – that it would lead to an increased drunkenness, but in the belief that, if the army became more expensive, the country would insist that the numbers were reduced. The Duke went in constant fear that the country would refuse to support an army and sought by every means to prevent such a catastrophe. Thus, instead of trying to show that the army was an honourable and exciting profession, he tended to hide them away and make them as inconspicuous as possible. The result was that the recruiting officer's job (showing the flag being discouraged) became doubly difficult and numbers declined anyway.

Although the British soldier was not nearly such a rogue as he was painted, his liking for strong liquor was far from being a fiction and created one of the main problems in time of peace. It became the practice never to pay neighbouring units on the same day for fear of creating a conflict. Soldiers habitually got drunk on pay nights and rival regiments took great delight in pitching into one another when they had taken a glass or two too many. It is related of the 42nd Highlanders, when they returned from Waterloo, that their back pay and prize money was doled out to them bit by bit as they marched north. A little at Cambridge, a little at Nottingham, a little at Durham and so on, for fear that they would render themselves unfit to continue the march the following day if the paymaster was too open handed. They received the balance when they got to Edinburgh and the celebrations which followed lasted almost a week.

Such efforts as were made to improve the soldiers' lot by individual officers or outside philanthropists were often defeated by the soldiers themselves. For example, shortly after Waterloo, an attempt was made to give them greater comfort by the issue of additional blankets. The soldiers promptly got together in groups of three, each of whom contributed a blanket. Two were sewn together and then cut into three, while the third was sold for beer money.

There was, however, one development in the early part of the nineteenth century, which was very much welcomed by the army. In 1826 Sir Robert Peel brought into existence the Metropolitan Police Force which, as it expanded, gradually relieved the army of some of its more unpleasant duties in relation to the civil population. The growth of the Industrial Revolution brought with it a great deal of social unrest, which often led to popular demonstrations and disturbances. Until the formation of the police force, it was the army which was called upon to maintain order, if necessary by force. The unfortunate events which gave rise to the incident known as 'the Peterloo Massacre' is an example of the sort of situation in which the army were likely to find themselves. In that instance the authorities lost their heads and ordered the Cheshire Yeomanry to charge a massive demonstration at St. Peter's Fields, Manchester, with fatal results which have long been remembered. Although the troops were only obeying orders, such actions did not increase their popularity.

If anything, to be stationed in Ireland in the 1820s was worse than being stationed in England where, with its rigorous discipline and endless parades, the soldier's life was a trying one. When the 34th went to Ireland in May, 1824, they were plunged almost at once into the job of policing a country which was in a ferment of unrest. It was a most unpleasant job. Officers of the rank of major and captain were given magisterial powers over the civilian population and sergeants were given warrants authorising them to enter private houses by day or night in search of weapons. Any civilian found out of doors after sunset was immediately imprisoned and anyone carrying a weapon, even if it were only a billhook, ran the risk of being summarily shot. In retaliation the 'Rockites', who were the chief troublemakers, raided army barracks, often setting fire to them (they frequently consisted of little more than wooden huts) and

generally conducted a guerilla warfare against the oppressors. It was
not a situation which the British soldier enjoyed, and the men of the
34th must have been considerably relieved when, in August, 1829,
they were sent to perform duties in North America. Later they were
sent to various stations in Novia Scotia and Canada – in January
1838, they assisted in quelling the Canadian rebellion.

It was while the Regiment was in Canada that a part of regimental
tradition was established. After the Battle of Arroyo dos Molinos,
the second battalion of the 34th were accorded the right to wear the
red and white tuft or pompom of the 34th French on their shakos.
For some reason the privilege had fallen into disuse and it was found
necessary to re-apply for the right: as a result of some correspon-
dence, a letter was received giving permission for the tuft to be
resumed. It was some years later, in 1845, that Queen Victoria
ordered that the tuft be abolished and a battle honour awarded
in lieu. In fact, when adding Arroyo to their list of battle honours,
the 34th did not lose their distinctive 'Ball Tuft'. A year after the
battle honour was granted, the dress regulations show that they were
allowed to wear a pom-pom which was half red and half white, and
later when the cap badge of The Border Regiment was passed in
the 1880s, the pom-pom continued to appear in the centre. Thus
they seem to have managed to achieve the best of both worlds!

Towards the end of their stay in Canada the Regiment was
stationed in Amherstberg, one of the most remote townships of the
West, under command of Lieutenant-Colonel Airey (later Sir
Richard Airey, G.C.B.). He proved to be one of the most advanced-
thinking commanders of his time and made a contribution to the
welfare of the army in general which was to be far-reaching. At the
time when Airey commanded the 34th, the soldier was provided
with no food from his dinner at mid-day until breakfast at eight the
following morning – a fast of twenty hours if the soldier had not
the means to forage for himself. Feeling that this must be injurious
to his health and strength, Colonel Airey introduced an evening meal
for all ranks. It caused the greatest opposition from all the authorities, who tried everything in their power to block the idea. Airey
appealed to Lord Hill, then Commander-in-Chief, and that excellent
soldier gave him his whole-hearted support. In a short time the
innovation became accepted by the whole army. That it should have
been a commanding officer of the 34th who brought about such a

great benefit, is a matter of considerable regimental pride. Airey
did not stop there. Because his station was so remote and provided
so few facilities for his troops, he started the idea of a regimental
canteen. This idea, too, spread rapidly and was soon adopted by all
the regiments in the service.

With Colonel Airey in command, conditions cannot have been
too bad for the 34th. When, in May, 1841, orders were received to
return to England, four sergeants, nine corporals and two drummers
and two hundred and one privates volunteered to serve permanently
in Canada. Their request was granted and local recruits enlisted in
their place. It was, therefore, a rather mixed bunch which arrived
back in England in August, 1842. Soon after their arrival at
Portsmouth, there was an urgent call for them to proceed to
Birmingham to aid the police in their efforts to control disturbances
in the manufacturing districts. Not many years previously this would
have entailed a rigorous period of forced marches. Now they were
embarked on the South Western Railway to London at eight a.m.,
marched across London to the Birmingham Railway Station and
arrived at their destination before midnight on the same day. At last
some conditions were changing, in spite of the diehards.

In the meantime, the 55th, whom we left in Cape Town, were
having an adventurous time. The year after their arrival at the Cape,
the Kaffirs became very troublesome on the frontiers of the colony.
A punitive expedition was mounted consisting of a detachment of
the Royal Artillery, the 55th, a detachment of Cape Mounted Rifle-
men, some Dutch Boers and a party of Hottentots. This mixed force
advanced far into Kaffir territory before they eventually caught up
with the enemy. A stand was made by the Kaffirs on the banks of
the Umtata River but they were no match for the superior arms
of the British force and were defeated with great slaughter.

Shortly after this incident the Regiment was ordered to prepare
for service in India, and in August 1830 embarked for Madras. The
voyage took two months and they arrived to find three fresh companies from the depot waiting to join them. The whole force then
marched to Bellary, where they were to remain for five years as
garrison troops. It was towards the end of this tour of duty that the
55th, at the beginning of 1834, were called upon to take part in an
expedition against the rebellious Rajah of Coorg. This Indian
potentate was giving a great deal of trouble to the British authorities,

so that it was decided to depose him as Rajah and take possession of his territory. For this purpose a force of over seven thousand was assembled, of which the 55th formed the advance guard. They entered Coorg territory on the first of April and immediately came up against great difficulties. Not only was the country extremely mountainous and heavily wooded, but the advancing troops were faced by formidable artificial defences. These consisted of deep ditches in front of ramparts up to twenty-five feet high, which must have been created to stem some ages-old invasion long before the occupation of India by the British for, in many cases, great trees grew on top of the ramparts. To make the passage of troops still more difficult, the defenders had cut down more trees and piled them across their line of advance. As the 55th struggled through the jungle at the head of the column, they also had to contend with enemy snipers and occasional vigorous attempts to cut the head of the advancing force from the tail.

On the third day the vanguard came up against a strongly fortified position at Soamwar Pettah. Here a particularly high rampart was loopholed for musketry and protected by stone blockhouses and a tough bamboo fence. The only approach was by a narrow defile, which was obstructed with felled trees. An attempt was made to get parties round the flank of the obstacle by cutting a way through the dense jungle on either side but, through some miscalculation, or more probably through being misled by treacherous guides, the flanking parties came together again just in front of the defences. Major Bird, who was in command, decided that the only course now was a frontal attack, which was promptly launched but was repelled with heavy musket fire. Colonel Mill, who commanded the regiment, now arrived on the scene with reinforcements and ordered a further attack, which he led himself with the greatest bravery. The defences, however, proved to be too formidable and they were again repulsed. The Colonel fell mortally wounded and the casualties in the regiment were heavy. Two officers and thirty-six men were killed and six officers and a hundred and twenty-six men were wounded, some of whom later died – a formidable total out of the three hundred and twenty all ranks engaged.

The whole advance had been six-pronged. Two other columns failed to get through but three succeeded and the Rajah's capital of Mercara was taken. Later the Rajah himself was captured. The remainder of the 55th, having caught up with the main advance, were put in charge of the important prisoner, whom they escorted to Bangalore. The following year the Regiment left their base at Bellary and were stationed at Secunderabad, where they remained for a further three years. Then, in October, 1836, with their ranks much depleted by sickness, they marched back to Madras. They had done eighteen years' continuous foreign service and were due to be posted home.

The long periods that regiments spent abroad, without any hope of home leave, were not perhaps as onerous as they would seem to modern eyes. Many serving soldiers had few connections left at home and, as we have seen, it was customary for wives to accompany their husbands even on active service. Most important of all, in the soldier's eyes, was the fact that home service was much more trying than service overseas. Discipline was extra strict, drill parades were endless and pay was less, without any hope of prize money. Time and time again we have instances of soldiers preferring the rigours of campaigning to life at a home station.

If there were some members of the 55th, however, who were now looking forward to a spell at home, they were to be disappointed. On the very month that they arrived in Madras, the Emperor of China issued a decree ordering the massacre of all Europeans within his realm. This order came on top of a long series of insults and violence offered to British merchants in China and it was obvious that the Government could no longer ignore the situation. It was determined to send a strong punitive force to Hong Kong and the 55th were selected to join it. Before they sailed, the 55th were issued with the new percussion musket, which replaced their old flint-locks. They were the only regiment in the whole force to have the new rifles and were therefore considered as something of an élite corps.

The expedition sailed on the 23rd May, under Sir Hugh Gough. His command, in addition to the 55th, included the 18th, the 26th and a wing of the 49th, the 37th Madras Rifles and supporting sappers and artillery. They were carried in a fleet of nine sailing vessels and four steamers, with the formidable total of three hundred and twelve guns. They arrived at Hong Kong in July, where they remained for almost a month before proceeding to Amoy, a heavily fortified port. All day the fleet pounded the shore batteries, but the Tartars stood to their guns remarkably well, so that it was not until late afternoon that the return fire was silenced. It was then attempted to land the troops but it was blowing a near gale and it proved to be a very slow and difficult operation. In the end, with only one company of the 55th on shore, the attempt was given up until the following morning. When they finally moved into the attack, the British troops found that the enemy were not nearly so keen on hand to hand fighting and the town was soon taken. Spoils of war included over five hundred cannon and twenty thousand dollars worth of silver.

Within a week Sir Hubert Gough was on the move again. This time he sailed for the island of Chusan, which had been captured by the Chinese the previous year. The town was strongly defended with dug-in positions above the town, manned by over two thousand Tartars and Chinese. In the plan of attack the 55th, with two other regiments, was given the task of assaulting the prepared defensive positions. Because of exceptionally strong currents, the landing proved far more difficult than had been anticipated and they were swept off course. This meant that they were forced to land on an extremely exposed position, right below the defences. Even before the whole force had landed, the advance was sounded and the 55th led the charge up the hill. The enemy poured out of their trenches down the hill to meet them, so that, for a time, the hill appeared from a distance to be 'blazing with the fire of their gingalls and matchlocks'. Nothing, however, could stem the impetus of the attack and the summit was gained. It was just as they reached the crest that Ensign Duel, who carried the regimental colour, was shot dead. As he fell the colour was caught by Colour-Sergeant Davidson. As he handed it over to another ensign, the spearhead was shot away but it was still carried forward to wave triumphantly over the hill top. There they paused to wait for the reinforcements to arrive from the beach; then scaling ladders were procured and the advance continued to the city walls, which were soon taken and forces joined with those which had attacked the city from the right flank.

It was during the assault on the hill that Lieutenant Butler, who was acting Adjutant, distinguished himself by engaging a Chinese single handed and capturing the only imperial standard to be taken during the whole war. This standard was afterwards given by Lieutenant Butler to Captain, later Major-General Sir H. C. B.

Daubeney, G.C.B., who, on the 18th July, 1874, deposited it in Kendal Church over the regimental memorial.

The story of Ensign Richard Duel, who was killed while carrying the regimental colour, is a less happy one. On the morning of the landing he had heard that he had been promoted from the rank of Sergeant-Major. Although his name had not yet appeared on general orders, he asked if he could have the honour of carrying the colour into battle and this was granted him. He landed in the forefront of the attack and was killed almost as he reached the objective. Thus he did not live to enjoy the promotion to commissioned rank, which he had earned after thirty-two years of service.

The next target, after the fall of Chusan, was the large city of Ningpo, which was even more strongly defended than Chusan. Indeed so formidable were the defences that the Chinese were confident that the British would not venture to attack. The expedition arrived off Chinhae on the 9th October and an assault was immediately planned. The force was divided into three columns – on the right 641 men under Captain Herbert R.N., in the centre 440 men under Lieutenant-Colonel Morris and on the left 1,000 men under Lieutenant-Colonel Craigie of the 55th. The attack was made simultaneously by all three columns, the 55th being ordered to capture the bridge on their front and to advance as rapidly as possible so as to get behind the Chinese, should they try to retreat. Once again the defenders proved no match for the determined British and were driven back at all points. When the 55th appeared to the rear, as planned, many surrendered but many others fled to the river in the hope of escaping and were mown down in their hundreds. The road now lay open to Ningpo – and a day later the Royal Irish marched through the open gates, headed by their band playing 'Garry Owen'.

These victories, gained in quick succession, had the effect of teaching the Chinese a salutary lesson and were followed by three or four months of quiet, which gave the troops the opportunity of a well-earned rest and brought the time nearer when they could be reinforced from England. By the end of 1841 a strong draft had arrived for the 55th, under the command of Major Warren.

At the beginning of 1842 trouble flared up again with the Chinese recovering their courage sufficiently to attack Ningpo and Chinhae. These attacks were easily repulsed but shortly afterwards it was considered politic to evacuate both places and to show the flag in

other parts of the country. The first objective was Chapoo, which
was defended by at least eight thousand troops. Again the 55th
distinguished themselves in a well conducted attack against resolute
defenders and again the British forces carried the day.

At the beginning of June, 1842, further considerable reinforcements were received, including the 98th Regiment, fresh from
England, and three native corps and a regiment of volunteers from
Bengal. Sir Hugh Gough now had quite a considerable army under
his command and decided to pursue a more adventurous course of
action. It appeared that none of the defeated Mandarins was prepared to tell the Emperor of China the obvious truth – that the
British forces were superior in every way to his own and that his
empire was seriously threatened. It was decided, therefore, to launch
an attack on the imperial city of Nanking to impress the Emperor
with the hopelessness of his cause. Sir Hugh Gough now divided his
command into four brigades, promoting Colonel Schoedde of the
55th and Colonel Bartlett of the 49th to be Major-Generals in
command of the centre and left brigades respectively. Then,
supported by sappers, miners and engineers, he set sail up the
Yangtze-Kiang in a fleet of ships seventy strong.

On the 20th of July the fleet anchored off Golden Island, where
they could intercept traffic on the Grand Canal to Pekin and cut
communications between Nankin and Tching-Kiang-Foo. On the
following day the troops were ordered to land and commence the
offensive. General Schoedde's Brigade was ordered to occupy the
two hills commanding the north and east faces of the walls of Nankin.
The first to land were four companies of the 55th and they quickly
attained their objective. The purpose of their manoeuvre was to
distract the attention of the enemy from an attack on the city itself,
to be made by General Bartlett's Brigade; but General Schoedde had
the discretion to mount his own attack on the city if he felt that the
tactical situation warranted it. After a careful reconnaissance, he
decided to scale the north-east wall and to use the grenadier company
of the 55th for the task, supported by the 6th Madras Infantry.

The action which followed was one of which the regiment ever
afterwards was to feel justly proud. In spite of tall ramparts,
looped-holed on both storeys and resolutely defended by Tartars, the
walls were successfully scaled with Lieutenant Cuddy of the 55th
calmly sitting on top of the wall in a hail of fire, helping his men

over. Major Warren of the 55th commanded another assault and both parties were involved in desperate hand-to-hand struggles to force their way into the many guarded houses within the city walls, from which the enemy kept up an incessant fire. Lieutenant Cuddy fell, badly wounded, leading his men into an attack. Major Warren killed two Tartars and was about to be felled by a third when one of his men bayonetted his attacker in the nick of time. One doorway, through which it was necessary to pass, was so narrow that only one man at a time could get through. Private Kelly rushed forward but fell at once and was nearly hacked to pieces. Sergeant Maitland, followed by Corporal Clements, immediately dived forward – both were killed instantly. There is no knowing how many more brave men would have sacrificed themselves, had there not been an explosion on the other side of the doorway, which knocked out the defenders and allowed the grenadiers of the 55th to pour through.

Such determination was shown by the 55th and their supporting Madras Infantry that they soon had the portion of the town surrounding the north gate under control. Shortly afterwards the Royal Artillery blew down the gate and, entering the town, were astonished to see their own side in occupation. They brought with them their rockets with which they did considerable damage and helped to complete the taking of the city. The whole of this battle was fought under the glare of a pitiless sun, which was so fierce that two officers and sixteen men fell dead from sunstroke.

The taking of Nankin so terrified the Mandarins and so impressed the Emperor that China now sued for peace. Terms were agreed upon, which included the payment by the Emperor of an indemnity of twenty-one million dollars, the throwing open to British merchants of five of his principal ports and the ceding of Hong Kong to the British Empire. That such a small force should have been able to wrest such a considerable concession from a large and powerful nation is an extraordinary example of the power of British arms in the nineteenth century. In May, 1843, the House of Lords and the House of Commons recorded their thanks to Sir Hugh Gough and his men for their remarkable achievement. The 55th were singled out for a special honour. In consideration of their distinguished services, they were given authority to bear the word 'China' on their colours as well as the device of a dragon.

This brilliant campaign, however, ended sadly for the regiment.

They were sent to Hong Kong to await a passage home but, during their stay there, suffered from an epidemic of fever, which was so severe that they lost two hundred and sixty-seven men out of a total strength of just over five hundred. On the voyage home a further forty-four died. When they arrived at Portsmouth, after twenty-three years of continuous service abroad, they had on their strength only nine members of the original force which had sailed for South Africa in December, 1821.

During most of the Chinese campaign the 34th had remained in Ireland. They were in Athlone in August, 1845, when they received new colours, the old ones being laid up in Carlisle Cathedral. Almost immediately afterwards they sailed for the Mediterranean and remained on Corfu for three years. Then, after a short stay at Gibraltar, they sailed for Barbados and Trinidad in the West Indies.

There they suffered as usual from the ill health which was part and parcel of serving in those stations, but there was one tangible result of their stay which is pleasant to record. The naval vessel H.M.S. *Dauntless* was also in the Barbados and her crew suffered very badly. The 34th must have been of considerable assistance to them, as two years later they were presented with a fine silver pedestal inscribed:

Presented by the Officers of the Royal Navy and Royal Marines to the Officers of Her Majesty's 34th Regiment, in grateful remembrance of the unbounded kindness and generous aid afforded by them to

The Officers and Crew of
Her Majesty's Ship Dauntless
When suffering and disabled by Yellow Fever at
Barbadoes 1852.

This fine tribute became the centrepiece of the Officers' Mess table.

The 55th did not stay long in England after their return. In the autumn of 1846 they moved to Ireland, where they became engaged in the suppression of the Smith O'Brien rebellion and witnessed some of the fearful hardships endured by the Irish people following the failure of the potato crop. It must have been a happy day when, in February, 1851, the order came for them to divide into service and depot companies. The depot companies went to Carlisle and the service companies sailed for Gibraltar.

These shuntings were, however, insignificant when compared with the great events afoot which, before long, were to engage the attention of both regiments to an extent that they could hardly have foreseen.

CHAPTER VIII

I T WOULD NOT, at first, seem likely that a dispute between the Greek and Roman Churches in the Holy Land would be a matter of much concern to Britain. This, however, was the excuse which the Czar of Russia needed to invade Turkish territory in 1854. It immediately became obvious to the Western Powers that the presence of the Russians, whose territorial ambitions they much suspected, in the Turkish capital could have a serious effect on the delicate political balance in Europe. Thus the extraordinary situation came about that the traditional enemies, France and Britain, joined together for the first time in their history to go to the aid of the Turks. It was the beginning of the Crimean War, one of the most rigorous wars ever fought by British troops.

When war was declared the 55th were still in Gibraltar, but were under orders to proceed to the West Indies the following spring. For two months the regiment remained on tenterhooks, hoping that their destination would be changed and that they would be given the opportunity of having a shot at the Russians. In April the orders arrived. They were to be brigaded with the 30th and 95th and sail for the Crimea. As they were rather under strength, their companies were made up from other regiments stationed on the Rock. Notably 250 men from the 92nd Highlanders were transferred, giving the 55th a distinctly Scottish flavour. It was a long time before the 92nd recovered from the loss of so many of their best men but it was the 55th's gain and they proved themselves to be brave and loyal soldiers in the stern test that was to come.

The regiment sailed on the 10th May, 1854. There then followed some months of acclimatisation. The 55th brought with them their band under Senor De la Vega which played for them most nights, while there were also swimming expeditions and cricket matches, the latter causing considerable amazement amongst the Turkish population. Dr. 'Billy' Russell, the distinguished correspondent of *The*

Times recorded seeing them embarking for Varna:

> On Thursday last the 2nd Division embarked in excellent order. Sir De Lacy Evans, his brigadiers, Pennefather and Adams, were aboard before nine o'clock. The 1st Brigade – 30th, 55th, and 95th Regiments – and the 2nd Brigade – the 41st, 47th and 49th – constituted a very fine division, which has suffered less from sickness than any other division of our army. They moved with great regularity down the rude piers, and embarking, regiment after regiment, on board the steamers, were soon aboard their respective transports.

Major-General John Hume,* who later wrote a book about the Crimean campaign, put the freedom from disease amongst the men of the 2nd division down to the fact that they had already served for some time in the Mediterranean. Whatever the reason, they were extremely lucky; the regiments newly out from England were being decimated by the dreaded cholera.

It was not until the end of the summer that the regiment saw its first action. Then, on 20th September, they were plunged into the battle of the Alma. For the Russians, perched on the Alma heights, it must have been a formidable sight as sixty thousand men moved steadily towards their position. The Turks were on the extreme right next to the sea, then the French in the middle and the British occupied the left and most exposed flank. The march up to the Alma was a long and tiring one under a very hot sun, but the British remained undismayed. Hume even records:

> During the advance a number of hares were started. We had some difficulty in preventing our men from chasing them. One man, in his excitement, threw his rifle after a hare, quite forgetting that in a short time he would want to use it against the Russians.

At one of the periodical halts the generals commanding, both French and British, rode down the ranks, surrounded by their respective staffs. It is recorded that as Marshal St. Arnaud passed the 55th he exclaimed to them 'English, today you will see the Russians. I hope you will fight well!' 'Hope!' exclaimed an Irish voice from the ranks. 'Shure, ye *know* we will!'

It was not, in fact, until 11 o'clock the following morning that the British came in sight of the Heights of Alma. Even from a distance

---

* One of four distinguished brothers, he served with the 55th during the whole of the Crimean campaign, as did his elder brother, later General Sir Robert Hume, K.C.B. Both later commanded the regiment, holding it between them for twenty-one years. Another brother became Colonel Sir Gustavus Hume who with the fourth brother Captain Walter Hume served in the 38th Regiment. All four were at the siege of Sebastopol. Probably a unique record.

of two miles the immense strength of the position was obvious. The plan for the assault was simplicity itself – to march forward in battle order until the Heights were taken. Before this took place, however, a halt was called for ninety minutes. This proved a severe test for the soldiers. During this time they were under heavy shell fire – many for the first time. All they could do was to lie down in an effort to reduce casualties. Then, when the long-awaited order was given, they rose to their feet and strode forward in all their magnificence. The Turks and the French had the task of crossing the estuary of the Alma and turning the Russian left flank. The British had to advance across the river and make a direct frontal attack on the main Russian position. The first brigade of the 2nd Division, which included the 55th, were the link between the French and British forces.

It may be appropriate here to remark on the changing tactics – if such a word can be used to describe such a simple manoeuvre – which were adopted in the Crimean campaign. There had in the past been a marked difference between the fighting methods of English and Scottish troops. The Scots, when ordered to advance, would do so in a rush, throwing themselves down from time to time to avoid the enemies' volleys. The English, on the other hand, simply proceeded at walking pace and considered it beneath their dignity to take any evasive action. The advance up the heights of the Alma incorporated the best of both systems. The troops moved forward steadily but every now and again were ordered by their officers to lie down for a breather.

The 55th adopted this system and advanced in the centre of the line through a perfect storm of round shot, grape, shell, canister, case shot and musketry fire. Colonel Warren rode ahead of his men on his charger signalling to them to lie down whenever he felt that the fire was becoming too intense to be bearable. He himself, however, never deigned to alight from his horse. W. B. Pemberton in his *Battles of the Crimean War* records of him that he 'sat bolt upright on his horse like a statue with a single glass to his eye, never moving when shot or shell passed close to him.'

Eventually the Regiment, after suffering heavy loss, reached the banks of the river from which position they were at last able to return the fire, using the new Minié rifles with which they had been issued before the start of the campaign. The 47th were the first to cross the river, followed by the 30th and 55th. Once across, General Pennefather ordered Colonel Warren to form a line. This was attempted but the fire of the Russian guns was so intense that any group which formed was immediately struck down. The advance then became a matter of the 55th following their Colonel as best they could.

In the final assault on the Heights great deeds of valour were performed by the British regiments in the van of the attack which have now become a glorious part of British military history. By half past three in the afternoon the Russians were retreating at all points and another famous victory had been won. Colonel Warren, who had conducted himself with such bravery, remained miraculously unscathed through most of the action whilst his officers and men fell about him. Toward the end of the battle a Russian bullet shot away his epaulette and bruised his shoulder.

After the battle there followed the melancholy duty of burying the dead. Then, on the 23rd September, the advance of the allied army continued. The line of march was strewn with Russian knapsacks and equipment of various descriptions which had been jettisoned in the withdrawal. There were several lessons learned at the Alma, not least of them being that the ridiculous shako was completely impractical in battle. General Hume recorded:

My brother thought that we would look more uniform in forage caps so we hung our full-dress headgear on one of the shrubs. No doubt they now figure as trophies in some Tartar cottage.

It was an example which was widely followed; the British army were now beginning to go to war in earnest. True, whenever there was a halt for any length of time the cricket bats came out and inter-unit matches took place on any flat piece of ground available, while the band played in the officers' mess tent, but, with the passing of summer, conditions became steadily grimmer.

On 29th of September the 2nd division moved up to the plateau overlooking Sebastopol, which gave them a magnificent view of the Russian fleet and the formidable batteries which protected the town. Morale was at a high point and there could be few who would have thought that over a year would elapse before the final assault and capture would take place. In the meantime, the weather was getting colder and cholera was again starting to rage through the ranks. In a short space of time the 55th lost three officers and a dozen men.

Almost a month later the Russians launched a counter-attack to recover Balaclava, which had been occupied by the British. They brought up 4,500 infantry and two squadrons of Cossacks who hurled themselves against the defences. It resulted in terrible losses to the Russians whilst the British were left virtually unscathed. The 55th, who played a prominent part in the action, which became known as 'Little Inkerman', only lost one man. It was, however, the prelude to the battle of Inkerman which began on 4th November. This time the Russians showed their real strength. General Dannenberg was in charge of the main attack with 40,000 infantry and 135 guns, whilst Prince Gortschakoff was to lead 22,000 men in a feint against the French division covering Balaclava.

The main British camp, which included the 55th, were in the process of scraping together a miserable breakfast of green coffee and salt beef when the alarm was raised. The 55th, in fact, were providing some of the forward pickets, and these now retreated, fighting desperately. Knowing the whole safety of the army depended on them they managed to delay the Russian advance until they were almost surrounded. Indeed, but for a timely relief by the 41st regiment not a man would have survived.

It was a result of these effective delays, and partly because the Russian attackers took a wrong turning, that the British defences were not cut. Even so the battle soon developed into a desperate affair. The Russians hurled themselves forward against a narrow front between a gun battery on the right and a ravine three-quarters of a mile distant on the left. Inkerman has been well termed the 'soldier's battle', for in the broken country crowded with opposing troops it was every man for himself. William Russell described it thus:

> It was a series of dreadful deeds of daring, of sanguinary hand-to-hand fights, of despairing rallies, of desperate assaults – in glens and valleys, in brush-wood glades and remote dells hidden from all human eyes, and from which the conquerors, Russian or British, issued only to engage fresh foes.

For over four hours eight thousand British troops, out numbered four to one, held off the furious assault. Then the French appeared on the right flank and gave new courage to the exhausted battalions. Almost immediately, however, the Russians, too, brought up fresh troops and the contest was renewed with even greater vigour. A strong column of Russians advanced straight onto the position held by the 55th. Both sides were fighting in greatcoats and, in the confusion, the 55th mistook the Russians for British reinforcements and allowed them to approach to within a few yards of their position before discovering their mistake. Then they rose as one man and charged the Russians, driving them back in disorder.

The battle continued until 2 o'clock in the afternoon, although any hope of a Russian victory had long since disappeared. When it was all over it was found that the British alone had lost nine generals and well over two thousand killed or wounded. The 1st Brigade of the 2nd Division (the 30th, 55th and 95th) suffered so severely that they could only muster 700 men between them on the day after the battle, while the whole division had only 18 officers above the rank of captain who had not been killed or wounded. Russell reported:

> If it is considered that the soldiers who met the furious columns of the Czar were the remnants of three divisions which scarcely numbered 8,500 men; that they were hungry and wet and half famished; that they were men belonging to a force which is generally 'out of bed' four nights out of seven; which had been enfeebled by sickness, by severe toil, sometimes for twenty-four hours at a time without relief of any kind; that among them were men who had within a short time previously lain out for 48 hours in the trenches at a stretch, it will be readily admitted that never was a more extraordinary contest maintained by our army since it acquired a reputation in the world's history.

It would be almost invidious to single out individual instances of valour, but it should here be recorded that Private Beach of the 55th gained the coveted award of the Victoria Cross for rescuing Colonel Carpenter of the 41st. The colonel was lying desperately wounded and surrounded by several Russians who were stabbing at him with their bayonets when Private Beach rushed forward and drove them off single-handed.

Of the events which followed the gallant defence of Inkerman it must forever be remembered with shame that British soldiers should have been allowed to suffer such privation as they did that winter. Through appalling administrative incompetence and not least through scandalous profiteering by the contractors who were responsible for supplying the army, they faced conditions which far exceeded anything which had been known during the Peninsular War.

Much has been written about the dreadful conditions under which officers and men had to live during the winter of 1854-55. The cold was of such arctic intensity that even the horses died from exposure. Each morning regiments found some of their own numbers frozen to death, unprotected by the warm garments which should have been sent from home. Others, in a desperate attempt to find some warmth, were suffocated in their tents by the fumes of charcoal fires and, peering over everybody's shoulder, was the ever present spectre of disease. By mid-winter deaths in the British Army alone averaged 100 a day. At the same time there were onerous fatigues to perform. Deprived in large measure of their horse transport, the rank and file had to portage cannon balls and other supplies from the ships to their lines in preparation for the spring campaign. Men, drenched in perspiration from their efforts and seriously under-nourished, fell ready victims to disease. The hideous total of deaths mounted week by week. At the same time arrangements for the nursing of the sick were so inadequate as hardly to be considered. At the base camp at Scutari, Florence Nightingale earned undying fame by her outspoken criticism of the inadequacies of the medical services, but in the front line conditions were even worse. There was no bedding for the sick and no medical supplies. Devoted surgeons and their assistants slaved night and day but, without proper facilities, much of their effort was in vain. The 55th were particularly fortunate in having Surgeon Ethelbert Blake and Assistant Surgeons Cowan and Rendell, but in spite of their devotion to their tasks nothing could overcome the pitiful lack of adequate medical facilities and supplies. By the beginning of December there was only one officer in the regiment fit for duty. A draft, consisting of one officer and 130 men, on the 10th of December made a welcome addition to their numbers but the new recruits, unaccustomed to the rigours of life in the Crimea, were soon found to be even more vulnerable than the veterans.

Almost daily there were sales of the effects of officers who had died and the simplest luxuries fetched enormous prices from those who had no other way of spending their pay. A bottle of French Cointreau brought the sum of £30 and several pounds for a pair of socks or boots with good soles was not unusual. Most officers and men were reduced to a single set of clothing, so that in the event of their getting wet – a common occurrence – they had no dry clothes to change into. Some were completely without footwear and others had no greatcoats to protect them against the severe climate.

These almost impossible conditions gradually became known at home and a wave of indignation swept the country. As the British army shivered in front of the defences of Sebastapol the women of Britain, led by Queen Victoria herself, set about rectifying the short-comings of those whose job it was to see that the army was properly clad. In every home socks, jerseys and the famous Balaclava helmets were knitted by loyal and willing fingers. Alas, they only started to reach the Crimea by the time the worst of the winter was over.

The heavy casualties from sickness and disease meant that new drafts had to be continuously sent from home and amongst those that arrived at Balaclava on 19th December was the 34th. The Regiment was by now hardly recognisable as the one which had so recently left the West Indies. Earlier in the year they had been forced to give up a number of their best men to make up the strength of other regiments bound for the Crimea. In 1854 they were moved, for the summer, to Corfu but many of their serving soldiers were still in their teens and were not considered old enough for the rigours of a Russian winter. Two hundred of the youngest were left behind so that when the Regiment finally sailed it was scarcely 500 strong.

No sooner had the 34th arrived than they were plunged into the most onerous duties, picketing the front line trenches outside Sebastopol and carrying out all the fatigues required of front line troops. Throughout the winter both sides bombarded each other incessantly which contributed to the general cheerlessness of the situation.

The 34th had their baptism of fire on the 22nd March, 1855 when the Russians, taking advantage of the improving weather conditions, launched a ferocious attack on the British position. The battle took place at night and casualties on both sides were severe. When dawn came the enemy retired, leaving over a thousand dead behind them.

With the coming of spring the dreadful conditions of the winter were largely forgotten. Fresh supplies were arriving from home and spirits were high. Everyone was anxious to get at the Russians, but it was not until June that the first determined attack was made – an attempt to capture the fortifications in front of the Russians' main

defensive position which was known as the Redan. Both the 34th
and 55th were engaged in what was to be one of the most bloody
conflicts of the war. Fortunes swayed to and fro – the British rapidly
obtained their first objective, the Quarries, and as quickly were
driven off again. The position changed hands no less than five times
before, in the small hours of the morning, the Russians finally retired
leaving a very much depleted British force in triumphant possession.
It was as a result of this and similar actions up and down the line
that the allies gradually moved closer to the main Russian position.
A major attack could not now be postponed for much longer. It
came on the 18th June, after the heaviest bombardment of the war
aimed at breaching the defences and preventing the enemy from
concentrating their forces. The assault was made in three columns,
four hundred men of the 2nd on the left, the 4th in the centre, and
400 men of the 34th on the right. Beyond the 34th were the French,
whose main object was to divert the enemy's attention. The advance
started at 3 a.m. instead of the more usual 6 a.m. and was at once
successful. The 34th and the 4th rapidly reached the Redan itself,
leaping over the parapet on the flank in the hope of surprising the
Russians. The latter, however, were fully prepared for this move and
at once opened a murderous fire of grape and musketry. It was
during this attack that the French were seen to be retiring, and as a
result it was impossible, even if the Redan was taken, for the British
to hold it on their own, and so they too were recalled. Three-quarters
of the 34th were put out of action.

The second phase of the attack was conducted by the gun batteries
with which the British managed to all but silence their opponents.
Lord Raglan then proposed to the French General Pélissier that
another attack be made with fresh troops, but the French had
suffered more heavily than the British and were unable to take the
field. The 34th had acquitted themselves with conspicuous bravery
and several of their members were awarded gallantry decorations,
Private Simms winning the Victoria Cross for saving many of his
wounded comrades whilst under enemy fire.

Both armies were now almost continuously involved in hostilities
and on the 16th August the Russians made a last desperate attempt
on the Allied positions. They were met by the French and the
Sardinians on the banks of the Tchernaya and were hurled back
with great loss. By this time the British were losing about 250 men

a week in the trenches, but in the period from 17th to 31st August the Russians admitted losses of 11,000 men. It was obvious that the end could not now be far off. The final assault by the French against the Malakoff and the British against the Redan came on the 5th September, when an artillery bombardment opened and continued for three days before the troops advanced. The conflict was now even more furious than before, with the 55th playing a particularly prominent role. Their commander, Brevet Lieutenant-Colonel Cuddy, whose bravery in China has already been mentioned in this history, was killed at the head of his men, the two Hume brothers were both wounded and many others besides. The ramparts of the Redan were gained by the 55th, where Drummer Doyle distinguished himself by standing on the highest point and sounding the advance. Private Seabright rushed forward waving a red, white and blue handkerchief and plunged into the enemy ranks. In spite of all the British could do, however, the Russian defences proved too strong, and once more they were forced to retreat.

It had been decided to make a further assault the following morning, but when dawn broke it was discovered that the Redan had been deserted by the enemy. After cautious reconnaissance it was found that they had withdrawn entirely from Sebastopol, having sunk their fleet in the harbour and set fire to many of the buildings. At long last the flags of the French and the British flew proudly over the stronghold which their enemies had defended so tenaciously, and at such terrible loss to both sides.

During the armistice, before peace was finally signed, there was a great deal of fraternisation between the allied armies and the Russians. They visited old battlefields together and played games against each other. Later, when the peace treaty was ratified, the generals had their fun reviewing each other's troops and analysing past campaigns.

The 34th were the first to reach home. They embarked on the 14th June and finally arrived in England on the 11th August. They camped at Aldershot and then moved to Glasgow and, later, Edinburgh. The 55th left the Crimea on the 21st May but were posted to their old station of Gibraltar, where they remained for fifteen months. They then returned to Ireland.

*   *   *

In many ways the Crimean campaign may be regarded as a land-mark in the development of the British army. It was about time, for no army could have been worse equipped for the rigours they were expected to endure than the army the British government sent to fight against the Russians. The upper echelons of the service were hopelessly blocked by senile senior officers who ought to have been retired many years before. On the eve of the Crimea there were thirteen generals with over 70 years' service each, and two hundred with over fifty years. Only seven generals had less than forty years behind them.

Few officers had any idea about the welfare of their troops and still believed firmly in the use of the lash to maintain discipline. Amongst the records of the Border Regiment to be seen at Carlisle Castle today is the following extract from General Orders:

Horse Guards
August 15th 1810.

At a General Court-martial, held at Maidstone on the 25th June, 1810, and continued by Adjournments to the 25th July following, Private Robt. Chilman, of the Bearsted and Malling Regiment of Local Militia was arraigned upon the following charges, viz ;

1st. For Disobedience of Orders, Having on the 1st June, 1810, Refused to obey the Orders of Lieut Col The Honble T. W. Stratford, and having resisted in the Streets of Maidstone going to the Barracks, when he was ordered to be confined for gross irregularity of conduct.

2nd. For having on the same day made use of Mutinous, threatening and Disrespectful Language to the said Lt Col The Hon T. W. Stratford.

3rd. For Mutinous and Improper Behaviour having on the same day having kicked James Chittendon, then a Sergeant in the Bearsted and Malling Regiment of Local Militia while in the execution of his Duty, (Escorting him a prisoner to the Barracks), and having struck other persons, who assisted in securing him, such conduct being contrary to the Rules and Articles of War.

The Court found the Prisoner guilty of the Crimes laid to his charge and sentenced him to receive Eight Hundred lashes upon his bare back with the Cat o' Nine Tails.

Such condign punishment for what amounted to a drunken escapade was not by any means unusual. About the same time, for example, there was the record of a British regiment stationed at Fort Charles in Jamaica. It was an appalling site, surrounded on three sides by the sea and on the fourth by a fever swamp. There were no recreation facilities and no military action to divert the soldiers' attention from drinking and other idle pursuits. In the course of two years the 300 men of the Regiment received 54,000 lashes between them in the interests of maintaining discipline.

The French Army, by contrast, did not use the lash mainly because their army was constituted in quite a different way. Officers and men alike were drawn from roughly the same middle class so that there was much more fraternization between them. The Duke of Wellington records dining with a high ranking French officer who told him that he had spent the morning playing billiards with some of his men. Such a situation would have been quite impossible in the British Army of those days. The officers were drawn from some of the most aristocratic families in the land and the men from the lowest classes. The more fashionable the regiment, the less the officers had to do with their men. Many of them did not know the simplest drills and spent practically no time on duty in time of peace. The worst offenders were perhaps the cavalry who, because of the influence of their officers, seldom served abroad in peace time. They were familiar figures at the fashionable assemblies in London, lisping affectedly and so elegantly dressed that they were suspected by less dandified officers of wearing corsets. Promotion was almost entirely by purchase. It is recorded that Lord Lucan paid £25,000 for the colonelcy of the 17th Lancers and Lord Cardigan almost twice that sum for the 15th Hussars. It is only fair to record of these foppish officers that in battle they were 'brave unto madness' – men like Lord George Paget who lit his cigar at the beginning of the Charge of the Light Brigade and noted that it lasted him right up to the Russian guns.

The first annual camp, held for training purposes, was ordered in 1853 and, about the same time, there were the first proposals for examinations of applicants for commissions and for officers seeking promotion. The old brigade considered the matter of examinations to be outrageous but gradually wiser counsels prevailed so that by 1871 promotion by purchase came to an end. The question of the education of the rank and file was also taken up. Sixty per cent of the army which fought in the Crimea were illiterate but, after their return to England, army school-masters were appointed for the first time to teach reading and writing. At the same time the number of lashes which could be awarded was reduced to a mere 200.

Many of these reforms which foreshadowed the shape of the modern army, were brought about, not by the army itself, but by the improvement of communications which enabled correspondents like 'Billy' Russell of *The Times* to let the man in the street know something of the privations which the army suffered, and personalities like Florence Nightingale to capture the popular imagination. Public indignation at a corrupt and inefficient administration caused questions to be asked in the House of Commons and power to be given to the hands of the reformers. From the time of the Crimea onwards there dawned a milder regime for the serving soldier.

While the struggle was going on in the Crimea there was another danger looming inside the Empire itself. For some time there had been considerable discontent amongst the natives of India, which burst into open rebellion on the 10th May, 1857, at Meerut. Soon the mutiny spread through the north-western provinces and Bengal and news was received daily in England of new outrages. Station after station was fired, British officers shot down and women and children put to death with appalling cruelty.

Within four days of the first news being received reinforcements were on their way to India to support the small force of four or five thousand men which was all that could be mustered by Lord Canning, the Governor-General.

The 34th embarked at Portsmouth on the 24th August – part of a steady stream of troops being hurried out to India. They disembarked at Calcutta and were immediately sent up the Hoogly River to Chinsurah as the first stage of an arduous journey – the last part in covered carts – on their way to Cawnpore. There they came under command of General Wyndham, who had been given the task of protecting the city as well as keeping open communications from Lucknow to Allahabad. Soon after the arrival of the 34th it became known that the rebels had advanced to within fifteen miles of the city and were poised to attack. It was also known that the native force numbered in the region of twenty-five thousand men, while General Wyndham had only about two thousand under his command. Nevertheless, he at once moved to meet the enemy – the 34th under their commander, Colonel Kelly, taking the left flank.

When battle was joined the British were at once successful, driving the enemy back several miles. It was not considered practical to continue the pursuit and Wyndham withdrew his troops to a defensive position to the north of Cawnpore. The following morning there was a counter-attack mounted in great strength which was successfully held, until it was discovered that a further enemy force had out-flanked the British and were menacing the city behind them. Wyndham was thus forced to make a precipitate withdrawal leaving behind him much of his baggage. The 34th lost all their kit, together with their tents and bedding.

A position was now taken up behind Cawnpore, allowing the enemy entrance to the city but taking advantage of a strongly fortified position from which a counter-attack could be launched. During the retreat through the narrow city streets one of the guns was accidently overturned and had to be abandoned. Later, however, it was decided to try and recapture it. A party of the Naval Brigade were charged with the task of righting the gun, protected by E Company of the 34th. This exceedingly perilous operation was carried out at night, the raiding party creeping into the city occupied by twenty thousand of the enemy. It proved entirely successful and the gun was recovered without a shot being fired, for which the men engaged received a special message of thanks from the Commander and a welcome extra issue of rum.

There followed several days of fierce fighting for possession of the city, but Wyndham was so greatly outnumbered that he could make no progress. After the third day news came of the approach of that gallant soldier, Sir Colin Campbell, who was retiring from Lucknow with a large body of sick and wounded as well as women and children whom he had brought out of the beleaguered garrison. Sir Colin's train was five miles long and it was obvious that they could neither stay in the dangerous vicinity of Cawnpore nor get to safety without a strong guard. Accordingly 500 men of the 34th, under Colonel Kelly, were given the dangerous task of escorting them one hundred and forty miles to Allahabad, through a district infested with mutinous Sepoys. By dint of forced marches, however, the task was accomplished in five days without any loss.

When the 34th returned to Cawnpore, it was to find that Sir Colin had cleared out the enemy and was now preparing to march back to the relief of Lucknow. The 34th were brigaded with the 38th and 53rd and, on the 10th February, took up their position about nine miles from the city. To this brigade fell the lion's share of the fighting as the British force marched remorselessly on Lucknow. It was hard going, because every palace or large house (of which there were a great number) was heavily fortified. It took eight days of tough fighting before the King's Palace, the last stronghold in the heart of Lucknow, fell.

Sir Colin Campbell, as Commander-in-Chief, was now faced with the difficulty of having to dispose his very limited forces over a vast territory, in such a way as best to keep the rebels in order. Thus the concentration of troops in Lucknow was dispersed, the 34th being sent two hundred and fifty miles as part of a force commanded by Sir Edward Lugard, to the relief of the important town of Azimghur. Unfortunately although the Oude could now be reported free from rebels, there were many who had escaped into Nepal. The Indian ruler would have none of them and asked for British help in having them expelled. There followed a game of hide-and-seek, with small packets of British troops engaging rebel concentrations wherever they could be found. After completing their task at Azimghur the 34th joined in the chase. At Bhootwul they attacked a strong native force and routed them completely, capturing three guns, six elephants, thirty camels, more than three hundred horses and a great quantity of baggage. They killed four hundred of the enemy without a single casualty to themselves. It was actions such as these which finally convinced the mutineers that their cause had no hope of success. By the spring of 1861 the rebellion was, to all intents and purposes, over. The 34th remained in India until the beginning of 1867 when they were ordered home, arriving at Portsmouth on the 10th July of that year.

In the meantime the 55th had spent several years in Ireland and, in 1863, they too were sent to India. The practice of allowing wives to accompany their husbands on active service had ceased after the Crimean campaign, but by 1863 India was again considered a peacetime station. Thus it is interesting to note that the Regiment sailed thirty-five officers and nine hundred and eleven men strong, accompained by one hundred and ten women and one hundred and seventy-three children. Their first station was Hazareebaugh, then considered a fine and healthy cantonment. It was later condemned as unfit for European habitation, but the Regiment found their stay there most enjoyable. They were not, however, to be there long.

In November 1864 they found themselves in Lucknow and the following month, there being trouble with the hill tribes on the frontier, they joined a field force acting against Bhootan, leaving their women and children behind.

It was two months before the 55th, under Colonel R. Hume (whom we have already met as a captain in the Crimea) arrived at the scene of the operations at Koomreekhatta and almost at once plans were made for the attack, it being rather late in the year for European troops to be in such a malaria-infected area. The enemy position consisted of eight block-houses and several large boulders behind which they could take cover, positioned along the crest of a ridge of hills with a very steep ascent, which offered no cover to the attackers. In spite of this a successful assault was made. There followed some brisk skirmishing extending over several days, but the Indian irregulars were no match for the trained British troops armed with Enfield rifles. By the time the rainy season arrived in earnest, they had been taught their lesson and the British retired again down the Brahamapootra.

Unfortunately, the withdrawal did not take place before the first signs of Bhootan fever had shown itself amongst the 55th. By the time they reached Dum Dum there were one hundred and eight men in hospital. Within a month there were four hundred admissions, scarcely a man escaping from at least slight infection. Mortality amongst the 55th was the highest of any regiment in India that year, and the state of health so poor that they had to be taken off their operational role with the field force. By the time they were made up to strength again, peace had been concluded and they returned to Lucknow almost exactly a year after they had left it.

In March 1869 they moved to a new hill station called Chukratta—so new, in fact, that the 55th were largely employed in constructing its defences, building its huts and making new roads. They remained there for three years before moving to Peshawar—the 'graveyard of India'. Inevitably, they suffered again from disease, so it was with relief that they received orders to move to Delhi in December 1873. Shortly afterwards they were posted to Aden.

CHAPTER IX

It WILL BE remembered that, in August 1782, the 34th and the 55th were attached to the counties of Cumberland and Westmorland respectively with the intention that they should cultivate their county connections in order to create a fertile recruiting ground for the future. In fact, as we have seen, neither regiment was given much opportunity of furthering the ties with their adopted counties. Even during the rare times when they were stationed at home, the War Office seemed to take a perverse delight in quartering them as far from their counties as possible.

From the point of view of the Regiments, efforts were made from time to time to observe the spirit of the original instruction. A regimental memorial tablet was placed in Carlisle Cathedral on behalf of the 34th and, in 1873, two sets of colours were also placed there. The 55th established a regimental memorial in Kendal church and placed their old colours there in 1851, to which was later added the Chinese standard in 1874. On the whole, however, the links were rather tenuous and it was not until almost a hundred years after they had first received their county descriptions that official steps were taken to strengthen the bonds.

In 1871 a committee sat under General McDougall for the purpose of preparing a new scheme for the localizing of the army. As a result, the 34th and the 55th were linked together in the 2nd Sub-District, known as the Cumberland and Westmorland Brigade. This arrangement was given practical expression when, in November 1872, two companies of the 55th were sent to Carlisle Castle to lay the foundations of the headquarters for the new formation. In April the following year Colonel Newdigate took command at the Castle and the 34th also sent two companies to take up their quarters there. Thus a relationship which may be said to have started when the 34th first were quartered in Carlisle shortly after their formation in 1702, became for the first time of a permanent nature. From now on both

15. Men of the Regiment in the firing line at Spion Kop, January, 1900.

16. Unpacking the Royal Gift, Orange Free State, 1900.

17. On a trawler just before landing at X Beach, Gallipoli, 25 April, 1915.

18. Men of the Regiment dug in at Cape Helles, Gallipoli.

Regiments, who for so many years had drawn their recruits from all parts of the kingdom, were to become localised, filling their ranks with the hardy fell men from their own counties.

The time was also not far distant when it would be possible to talk of the two Regiments, which had already become so closely linked, as one. In 1866 the Eversley Royal Commission on Recruiting had strongly urged the linking of two existing battalions into a single regiment but it was not until two years later, when Mr. Cardwell became the Minister for War in the new Gladstone administration, that a series of much needed army reforms were put into effect.

Cardwell was faced with a difficult task and one which was, to some extent, contradictory. He was charged first of all with placing the army on a new and efficient basis whilst, at the same time, he was required to effect all those economies in expenditure which had been a familiar cry down the years. His first step, carried through against considerable opposition, was the introduction of the Short Service Act. This was passed in 1870 and achieved three desirable purposes. Firstly, it did away with the long-service soldier and brought into existence instead the Army Reserve. Secondly it did away with the enlistment bounty and the evils inherent in the bounty system. Thirdly it enabled regiments to discharge 'incorrigible' or 'worthless' men. From the time of the passing of this Act, the army started to lose its image as a refuge for jail-birds and ne'er-do-wells.

Cardwell's next step, which has already been mentioned, was the abolition of the inquitious system of the buying and selling of commissions and promotions, thus altering the whole position and status of the professional soldier. Examinations for officers by this time had become established so that it was no longer easy for the dim-witted to find themselves amongst the higher ranks.

None of these improvements, however, would have helped recruitment very much had they not been accompanied by some increase in pay and this, too, Cardwell managed to achieve, By 1873 a free daily ration of food was introduced which had the effect of raising the man's daily pay to a clear one shilling and, a few years later, an amount of twopence a day deferred pay was granted to be kept for the man in order to give him a start in civilian life when the time came for his discharge. The shilling a day was, of course, subject to the usual stoppages for such items

as groceries, supper, washing and other extras and it was not until
1890 that the infantry soldier was guaranteed a daily payment of
twopence in cash, clear of all stoppages. Nevertheless, the improvements introduced to the pay scale by Cardwell were a step in the
right direction.

Oddly enough the most important of all the reforms attributed
to Cardwell did not come into effect until 1881, some years after
he had given up his office, although it is generally known as the
'Cardwell system'. The system was in fact Cardwell's brain child,
but it met with such fierce opposition from the Duke of Cambridge,
then Commander-in-Chief, that it was not until some years after
its original conception that it could be put into effect. It was based
on the principle of linking two battalions into one 'corps', of which
one would serve at home and the other abroad. The home battalion
was to consist of a cadre of officers, non-commissioned officers and
experienced soldiers who would train young soldiers up to a required
standard before they were sent abroad to serve with the sister
battalion.

It was, of course, natural, when the Cardwell system came into
effect, that the 34th and the 55th should be paired off together.
Thus was born The Border Regiment, the 34th being the first
battalion and the 55th the 2nd.

Almost inevitably, it was not an arrangement that was at once
warmly accepted by the two Regiments, however great their
admiration for each other. In the last pages of his book, about the
part played by the 55th in the Crimea, John Hume, by now a
veteran Major-General, voices what must have been the most
generally held objections to the new scheme of things:

> Many changes have taken place in the army since the old Crimean
> days ; old officers and men of the 55th and other regiments have great
> difficulty in recognising their dear old regiments under their new
> names. The 55th has been turned into the 2nd Battalion of the Border
> Regiment ; the 34th is the 1st Battalion. If the authorities had not
> taken the old numbers entirely away but had, for instance, called
> regiments by their new titles, retaining the old numbers, e.g. 34th, 1st
> Battalion Border Regiment, 55th, 2nd Battalion Border Regiment, we
> would have been satisfied, and the individuality of the old regiments
> would not have been destroyed ; there would have been no necessity
> to put the numbers on the ornaments or accoutrements ; they need
> only be used for parade purposes and to let people know what regi-

ments were called in the old wars. Soon after I left the regiment in 1879, the 55th was ordered to discontinue their old regimental march-past tune, 'The Lass o' Gowrie,' to which they had marched past for over one hundred years, and to replace it with 'John Peel.' The old green facings were taken away. The regiment was given, as compensation, the names of battles it never took part in, to wear on the colours and the cap ornaments. In fact the old 55th ceased to exist in 1880, when it was made the 2nd Battalion of the 34th Regiment, both making a new regiment called 'The Border Regiment'. I trust that some day the old numbers may be given back, and that the 55th in the future may have as good a record to show as the old corps that fought in China and the Crimea, as well as in America and the Low Countries.

One can feel for the grand old soldier as he saw so much of what he cared for swept away. At least his last wish was to be fulfilled. The old numbers were never to be restored but the two Regiments under their new name were to go forward to even greater glory.

At the same time that the 34th and the 55th became the 1st and 2nd Battalions, the County Militia were made the 3rd Battalion and the Westmorland and Cumberland Volunteers became respectively the 4th and 5th Volunteer Battalions.

Following the linking of the two Regiments both became involved at one time or another in various operations in India. In 1886 Lord Dufferin had almost casually added Upper Burma to Lower Burma (which had been annexed by Lord Dalhousie in 1852), and the whole now became the 11th Province of British India. Trouble broke out in 1889 and the 1st Battalion were amongst the troops sent to restore order. The expedition was directed against the troublesome Dacoits, who were continually raiding the more peaceful tribes. It was altogether successful and had the effect of bringing peace to a country which, before British intervention, had been torn by centuries of strife. From that time on Burma was to grow in prosperity and in loyalty to the Crown – a shining example of a country which benefitted greatly by being conquered by the British.

The 2nd Battalion was involved in operations in Waziristan in 1894 before finally returning home in 1897, when the 1st Battalion was sent to Malta. There they provided two Companies to quell disturbances in Crete. They were still in Malta in 1899 when the South African War broke out and they were at once sent to Cape

Town to join the force commanded by Sir Redvers Buller in Natal.

The war in South Africa was entered into by the British Government with, if possible, even less preparation and foresight than they had devoted to the Crimean campaign. Accustomed to easy victories against native troops armed with ancient rifles and even bows and arrows, little thought had been given to improving tactics or even to providing the troops with suitable dress for the type of campaign in which they were now to be involved. There was a general feeling that it was only necessary to show the flag in order to demoralise the Boers, and that the whole affair would be over in a matter of weeks.

In fact, the Boers soon showed themselves to be a most tenacious and resourceful enemy. They were well-armed and excellent marksmen who knew the country over which they were fighting intimately. Moreover, they were not encumbered with the strict rules of battle which were imposed on the British soldier. They were guerilla fighters who could attack suddenly and silently before disappearing again into the veldt. Before many months had passed it was obvious to the British command that they had a stern affair on their hands, and one for which they were singularly ill-equipped.

As soon as the 1st Battalion joined Sir Redvers Buller's force they were placed under orders to go to the relief of Ladysmith. Shortly after the expedition had set out they had the first taste of what they were up against. An armoured train was ambushed and the small force which accompanied it lost no less than 75 men killed and wounded. The Border Regiment were not on guard-duty at the time of the incident, but took part in the burying of their comrades—killed by an enemy they had never seen.

Shortly afterwards, on the 15th December, 1899, they were involved in the bitter battle of the Tugela River. Here the Boers were strongly entrenched on a hillside to the north of the river, with advance defences on the south side protecting the town of Colenso. The British decided on a set-piece attack, the Border Regiment being brigaded with the Dublin and Inniskilling Fusiliers and the Connaught Rangers under General Hart, on the left of the line. They rushed the forward trenches but, when they came to the river they found that not only had the bed been covered with barbed wire entanglements but that it had been cunningly dammed so that it reached a depth of ten feet. An attempt was made to cross it under heavy fire from the opposite bank, but it proved quite impossible. A few men managed to struggle over, only to be taken prisoner, while many were swept away and drowned. In the meantime, the attack on the right of the line had failed and in the centre the Boers had advanced and captured two gun batteries consisting of eleven guns. At 4 p.m. a retreat was ordered, nothing having been achieved and heavy casualties suffered in eleven hours of fighting.

Early in January of the following year, the Boers launched yet another attack on Ladysmith, but were again repelled. Meanwhile, they had given up their position on the Tugela River and Buller was able to cross it unopposed and continue his advance towards the beleaguered city. It was one of the weaknesses as well as one of the strengths of the Boers that they were an irregular force. They were ideally equipped to harass the British but at the same time they could not maintain prepared positions for long. Their fighting men were also farmers and they were quite likely to return to their farms whenever they were not actively engaged in a fight.

After the Tugela River the next defensive position between the advancing forces and their objective was a 4,800 foot high mountain, Spion Kop, which was regarded as the key to the whole of the enemy's defences. This was attacked by Buller on the 10th of January and it was taken after five days of heavy fighting. Once in possession, however, the British found it untenable and again withdrew, their total loss in the operation being over 1,500 men. After a short rest Buller again advanced, this time seizing the heights of Vaal Krantz and again having to abandon them when it was discovered that the position was under heavy fire from concealed Boer artillery on the opposite hill.

The part played in this prolonged action by The Border Regiment is perhaps best described in a letter written by a Border soldier, Pte Thomas Heyliss of Workington, to his friend Mr. Joe McCourt of Strand Street, Whitehaven:

We had seven days' fighting right off at a stroke, and our regiment lost very heavily. The first day we lost 121 men and we had hardly been twenty minutes in action, and the worst of it is that we cannot see where the Boers are firing from, because they are so deeply entrenched. We took their position that day and we stopped there for seven days. The reason of it was to draw the enemy to our position while General Warren's troops got through at another place, but all to no avail. We had to retire after losing many a valuable life. We went up there with twenty-five officers and came back with eleven officers. The night we retired the Boers knew it as well as us, and they attacked us just as we were leaving. My company and the 'L' Company of our Regiment were told to hold them in check, which we did. Our good old Colonel* fell three times that I saw, and I heard him say: 'God bless you my lads ; come on all.' Our regiment are sorry for him, as he was very well liked. We feel the want of him now. I do not know how many rank and file we lost but I know we lost over 200 men. The men told off to go for water got shelled, and many lost his life while doing good for another. We got into camp, and we were thankful, because we had not had any cover fighting night and day for those seven days. We were not to remain long at rest. We got thirty-six hours' rest, and then we got dispatched to a place called Vaal Krantz. We stopped there for three days, fighting day and night. We lost very few men there. Other regiments fared worse than ours. We had to retire all through a big gun of the Boers. They fired weights of 100 lbs., and the shell buried itself eight feet in the earth. It's a good job that the shells don't burst, or else there would not have been any of our regiment left. Anyway we retired and the troops were cursing, I can tell you and saying we will never relieve Ladysmith. We came back to our old fighting ground called Colenso, where our regiments fought and behaved so gallantly. We were in General Hart's Brigade, better known as the Irish Brigade. General Buller is pushing the advance slowly but steadily with very little loss, and, from the time of writing this, he thinks we will relieve Ladysmith in about four days. I am sending you one of the Queen's chocolate boxes. The civilians out here would give any amount of money for them. I am sending you this piece of poetry made up on the battle of Colenso by a friend, Private Williams, and myself. You can insert it, if you wish, in the *West Cumberland Times,* as I would consider it a great favour to see it in the columns of the paper which everybody reads.

The poem, some forty heroic lines, was duly published, notable perhaps for its expressions of patriotism rather than for its lyric qualities.

The forecast that Ladysmith would be relieved in four days proved a sanguine one. Buller realised that he was attempting the impossible by trying to conduct the campaign in Natal and at the same time supervising the operations from Cape Colony. He therefore appointed General the Lord Roberts to take personal command of the relief force, and it was he who finally effected the relief on the 28th February. The siege had lasted four months during which the most ter-

---

* Colonel Hinde who was later invalided home.

rible privations had been endured by the inhabitants. When the news was made public all England went mad with delight and the names of the regiments which had taken part in the operations were on everybody's lips.

Yet the war in South Africa was still not going well. True, the British army had thrown away their red coats and been equipped, for the first time, with the more practical khaki dress, but they still went into battle in traditional style, marching steadily forward into the enemy's fire until the objective was reached. Against the sharp-shooting Boers it proved immensely expensive in lives and was by no means always successful. Often they would arrive at the enemy position only to find that he had slipped away and the whole business had to be gone through again. Often enough they never even reached the first objective. General Colville records one such occasion when he watched with awe as the thin British line marched across the open plain into a hail of lead.

> Thinner and thinner it grew and thicker and thicker the brown patches on the grass behind it. What men were able to do, they did ; but there seems a law which fixes the exact amount of thinning which a body of civilized men can stand. It has nothing to do with fear ; a battalion will advance without a waver, under a storm of bullets, up to a certain point ; on reaching that point it is possible that the enemy' fire may have slackened, but if the gaps are too big it will halt.

After the relief of Ladysmith, Hart's Brigade, containing the 1st Battalion, came under Lord Roberts's command and the scene of operations was switched to the west. By this time the pattern of war was beginning to change. Most of the big set-piece battles had been fought and it now became a matter of hard marching in pursuit of the Boer forces. First of all Hart's Brigade marched to the relief of Wepener, a little border town in the Orange Free State where a detached British force was being besieged. A fierce battle took place at Bushman's Kop where the Border Regiment were part of the frontal assault, supported by the Cumberland Volunteers, who had by now sent companies out from home. This time the weight of the attack was too much for the Boers who melted away, and some days later the Border Regiment marched into Wepener to the strains of 'John Peel', loudly cheered by the inhabitants, many of whom were emigrant Cumberland miners.

There followed more rigorous marching over difficult ground. Sometimes they had to wade waist-deep through swamp land, at others cover long dusty miles across the veldt while their equipment became steadily more and more inadequate. To quote another soldier, Private Starkie of Cockermouth, in a letter home:

> We had a doctor's inspection, but he said that he would not allow the men to do more than 16 miles a day. They wanted us to do 24 miles a day, but there is not a man in the Regiment who could have done it – we are all so weak and no shoes on our feet, knees and the seat out of our trousers – such a sight as you never saw, and nothing but skin and bones.

In spite of this depressing picture the Regiment acquitted itself well and was singled out, with the Dublin Fusiliers, for special praise by General Hart, in a message dated 17th May, 1900;

> Major-General Fitzroy Hart congratulates the 1st Battalion of the Border Regiment and the 2nd Battalion Dublin Fusiliers upon the recent instance of their marching. For military reasons it was needful after the march forward yesterday to march back to Fourteen Streams. As far as he can arrive at a tolerably correct estimate of the ground covered, these two battalions in the course of yesterday and last night marched twenty-six miles in the space of nineteen hours including all stops and rests, and the strong point of it is that they did it in such good style that they arrived at the end of it in compact formation while going at a good pace and with no straggling and falling out.
> The Major-General accordingly puts this march on record.

The Regiment were not left long in one place. After leaving Fourteen Streams, they marched 200 miles to Lichtenburg, forty-five miles south-east of the still-beleaguered Mafeking; then to Johannesburg where they expected to be able to take a rest. Instead they set out again the following morning for Pretoria, leaving behind, to their great regret, their old friends the Dublin Fusiliers. The Border Regiment now became part of Colonel Mahon's command. They entered Pretoria on the 13th July, where they had an opportunity of seeing Lord Roberts, cheering him as they passed by, the band striking up 'John Peel'.

This stage of the South African War was proving singularly unglamorous for the British soldier; no heroic actions, only a monotonous foot-slogging which must often have seemed, to those taking part, to be quite pointless. Here is another extract from a letter home, this time from Corporal Carter of Maryport:

You'll be wondering when you are going to hear from me again, but opportunities for writing seldom occur when on the march. We are camped here about ten miles from Pretoria, waiting for orders. We are in, I think, the most degenerate state of unpicturesque vagrancy – worn-out boots and clothing, men unkempt, dirty and rarely washed, subsisting on a bare ration that never satisfies the appetite, in a part of the world that appears to have never evolved beyond the first stage of creation, a bare, desolate, cheerless place, where you can never buy, beg, nor steal anything eatable. I've devoured my day's allowance of biscuits for my breakfast, and must trust to anticipation to allay the appetite. I'm now smoking a raking up of pockets – tobacco dust, biscuit dust, and shreds of khaki, not a very fragrant mixture but better than nothing. Closing as I am at the end of my paper, with love to all and hoping to be home soon, for 'Hope springs eternal in the human breast,' and hunger infernal reigns in the human stomach. Yours affectionately, William the Famishing.

Since writing the foregoing, I've managed to beg a little more paper, so will continue the motion. I received the socks and tobacco, a mercy to be thankful for, now when postal delivery is so uncertain. We've been tramping through the Transvaal under General Hunter. It's bitterly cold at night with a cruel keen wind that pierces through one like the point of a dagger. How much longer is this confounded war going to last? We have no news beyond rumours, and what appears in brigade orders from time to time. It is putting ages on us all. I'm not 30, I look 40, and I feel 46. I assure you that often with many others I've prayed to be knocked over. If it's fatal, you're finished. If it's simply a wound, you enjoy all the comforts of hospital. I'm as thin as a cigarette paper and about as vigorous as a centenarian. . . .

After the fall of Mafeking rumours that the peace was about to be signed became more and more frequent, but no sooner was the Regiment settled into one camp than it was rushed off to another. Eventually the rigours to which they were constantly exposed told on their health and sickness began to run through the ranks. The letters home of the men themselves provide the best description of what they had to endure so no apology is offered for quoting yet another – this time by a private in the Volunteer Company:

Convalescent Camp, Bloemfontein,
Sunday 23rd September 1900.

When I arrived at this camp from the Green Hill Convent Hospital ten days ago I found about half a dozen of my Company here and also a very large number of the Border Regiment, and the number is increasing daily. Never a day passes but what three or four of the regiment arrive here from the hospitals round about Bloemfontein. The day I came here the Border Regiment contingent numbered eight. I reckon there are over a hundred belonging to the regiment now in this camp, besides a good number in the rest camp, and between 30 and 40 at the Garrison Duty Camp.

The regiment has been completely knocked up with the hardships and privations it has gone through in this country. If there was any heavy marching to be done it was 'Where is the Border? They can do it.' And consequently whenever it arrived in any place where there was any likelihood of the regiment having a bit of a rest, it was no sooner there than it was packed off again on the tramp elsewhere and some other regiment left behind. The regiment has proved itself 'second to none' out here as regards its marching powers and endurance. This is not mere bravado, for when General Ian Hamilton formed his brigade about the middle of July he had the pick of a large number of regiments round about Pretoria. The Border was sent for from Uitport nearly thirty miles away from Pretoria to join the Brigade, which also consisted of the Berkshires, Argylls and K.O.S.B.'s. The regiment had then been almost continually on the march line since April 15th, when it started off from Aliwal North for the relief of Wepener. There is however, a limit to all things excessive, and the limit to the endurance of the men belonging to the 1st Border Regiment was reached on the return of the regiment from Rustenburg towards Pretoria when large numbers of the men went sick and were sent to the hospital. The remainder of the Battalion were then given a rest, and they were sent to guard Commando Nek about the 11th or 12th August. The regiment was still there on September 10th, and for aught I know to the contrary is there at the present time.

When copies of the *Bloemfontein Post* arrived here containing the news of President Kruger's flight to Delagoa Bay there was great jubilation amongst us 'Tommies' and loud cheering was freely indulged in by all. There is a persistent rumour floating about today that peace has been proclaimed. Even if it is only a rumour, the end cannot be very far off. Soon the last blow will be struck and the last shot fired, and tired feet will follow the heart's longing homewards, whether it be to Great Britain, Australia, Canada or any other part of Her Majesty's dominions which has furnished troops for this war which has now lasted so long and so fiercely in this country.

In fact the war was to be prolonged for over another year, although the Border Regiment were only to take part in one more battle. Under General Clements and with their old comrades the Inniskillings, they took part in the action fought at Megaliesburg in December 1900, where they acquitted themselves with distinction. When peace was finally declared early in 1902 they returned to England. Then, after a short rest, they were sent abroad again, first to Gibraltar, then briefly to Wellington in India before moving to Burma, where they were to remain for a number of years.

The 2nd Battalion went out to do garrison duty in South Africa in 1905, but returned to England before the outbreak of the Great War, at which time they were stationed at Pembroke Dock. The 4th and 5th Volunteer Battalions, both of whom had sent Companies on active service to South Africa, lost their description of Volunteer Battalions in 1908 and became part of the newly formed Territorial Army.

PART III

The Twentieth Century

CHAPTER X

IT HAS BEEN said that the army was totally unprepared for war in 1914. In fact this was very far from the case. The South African War had almost as great an effect on the authorities as had the Crimean War some fifty years earlier, and the ordinary citizen had been deeply stirred by the obvious inadequacies of higher command which had made that war such a tedious and costly affair.

The reforms instituted by Cardwell after the Crimean War had greatly improved the soldier's lot and raised his status in the eyes of the public. Now, after the Boer War, there came another great reformer, who was to put into effect an improvement in the organisation of the army more far-reaching than anything Cardwell would have dared to attempt. This was R. B. Haldane, a lawyer by profession, who had a clarity of vision which was to prove of the greatest long-term value to the army as a whole. Haldane's greatest work was altering the historic status of the militia so that they now became the feeders of reserves to the Regular Army in time of war, an arrangement which was soon to prove of inestimable value. Next, he collected together all the volunteer organisations throughout the country and formed them into larger bodies, thus giving them an importance which they had never hitherto possessed. Haldane even had the courage to set about the reorganisation of the high command, creating the Army Council and a new general staff. He must have been a man of immense tact and persuasive powers, for he managed to put through all his reforms with the minimum of opposition from the die-hards.

In the first years of the twentieth century a new doctrine swept through the British Army. A hundred years earlier a sergeant had written:

> . . . but let soldiers be taught that they have a character to uphold ; give them to understand that they are made of the same materials as those who command them ; capable of feeling sentiments of generosity

and honour – let officers evince by their conduct that they believe that
the men they command have feelings as well as themselves (although
it would be a hard task to make some of them think so); let them
be encouraged to improve their minds – and there will soon be a
change in the army – one honourable to all concerned.

It was only with the coming of the twentieth century that any
attempt was made to carry out what the sergeant of long ago had seen
so clearly. Ferocious punishments had now become a thing of the past
and the soldier was at last being treated as a civilized human being.
In 1909, at Aldershot, Sir Horace Smith-Dorrien – a few years later
to gain undying fame at Le Cateau – laid it down that soldiers must
be 'placed on their honour'. Public houses were no longer to be out
of bounds, the seven-hundred-strong picket which patrolled the
streets nightly was to be abolished and discipline generally was greatly
relaxed. The results showed that there was no increase in crime
but rather that the soldier took a greater pride in himself.

At the same time, great efforts were made to improve the soldier's
general standard of living. Bit by bit the old cold-water ablutions
were swept away. Reading rooms, writing rooms and libraries became
commonplace, and the standard of cooking improved to an extent
that the soldiers were eating better than their civilian counterparts.
At the same time he was given plenty to do. He became an expert at
handling the more sophisticated weapons with which he was steadily
being equipped, and took part in manoeuvres designed to teach him
the principles of war – even if those principles were soon to prove
outmoded.

The result of all this was that the British Army in 1914 was a com-
pact, highly-trained body of men. It was at about this time that H. G.
Wells wrote that to enter a barracks was to be transported into
another world in which men did not strive after personal gain, but
after an intangible ideal which influenced all their actions. It was,
perhaps, an idealistic view, but there is no doubt that the peace-time
soldier, under the improved conditions, was a very different man from
his predecessors.

In Britain, the people who were unprepared for war were the
civilian population but, when it came, they embraced it with an
enthusiasm that knew no bounds. It says much for the new image
which the army had created for itself that the whole country tumbled
over themselves to join the Forces. There was no conscription, but

19. Sergeant Riley (2nd Border) driving back the enemy by machine-gun fire at Gheluvelt, 29 October, 1914, for which he was awarded the DCM.

20. Resting in a front-line trench, Thiepval Wood, August, 1916.

21. Regimental recruiting poster, 1922.

when Lord Kitchener issued his famous appeal for volunteers, the response was tremendous. At first it was only the regular battalions which were to be sent overseas, and it was these that the civilian volunteer was anxious to join. He wanted to become a real soldier, for there was no more admired figure in the land than the Regular.

At the end of July the 2nd Battalion were engaged in military exercises at Rosebush Camp, about thirty miles from Pembroke Dock, their headquarters. Already the authorities knew that war was inevitable. Along with other battalions all over the country, they had their training interrupted and they were ordered to return to their headquarters for a 'precautionary period prior to mobilisation'. General mobilisation was ordered on the 4th August and parties of reservists started to arrive from the depot at Carlisle. By the 29th August the 2nd Battalion was 27 officers and 1,068 other ranks strong, and ready for action. They formed part of the 7th Division, being in the 20th Infantry Brigade consisting of the 1st Grenadier Guards, 2nd Scots Guards, 2nd Border Regiment and 2nd Gordon Highlanders.

In the meantime, all over the country, men were rushing to join the colours. In Cumberland and Westmorland they flocked in from the hills and the mining villages, all anxious to do their bit for King and Country. It was not long before the supply of men far outstripped the availability of equipment with which to train them or uniform for them to wear. As the Expeditionary Force were having their first taste of the bloody conflict which lay ahead, men in civilian clothes were frantically trying to master arms-drill with broom-sticks in place of rifles, and wooden dummies in place of artillery. Perhaps one of the most remarkable regiments to be raised at this time was what was to become the 11th Battalion The Border Regiment.

One of the greatest nobles in the country was the Earl of Lonsdale whose vast estates were centred round Penrith and extended over most of the Lake District as well as including the whole of the mining town of Whitehaven. The Earl himself was nothing if not colourful, and he now set about raising a regiment of his own to go to war against his erstwhile friend the Kaiser. There were already nine battalions of The Border Regiment in process of formation; the authorities were embarrassed by the rush of volunteers but it did not deter Lonsdale from issuing his own call to arms. He had a poster printed in his racing colours – red, yellow and white – with which he flooded the two counties. It was altogether a remarkable document:

ARE YOU A MAN

or

ARE YOU A MOUSE?

Are you a man who will for ever be handed down to posterity as a Gallant Patriot

or

Are you to be handed down to posterity as a
rotter and a coward?

If you are a Man

NOW

is your opportunity of proving it, and ENLIST at once and go to the nearest Recruiting Officer.

REMEMBER

if you can get 15, 30 or 60 of your Comrades to join you, you can all ENLIST together, remain, train, and fight together.

THE COUNTIES – CUMBERLAND AND WESTMORLAND – HAVE ALWAYS BEEN CELEBRATED FOR THE FINEST MEN, THE GREATEST SPORTSMEN AND THE BEST SOLDIERS.

NOW IS YOUR OPPORTUNITY OF PROVING IT

HURRY UP!

Please take my humble advice before it is too late.

THE COUNTRY HAS NEVER BEEN IN GREATER PERIL.

LONSDALE.

Lowther Castle.

The poster raised a storm of protest. The Mayor of Whitehaven, feeling that it was a slight against the patriotism of his borough, drove furiously to Lowther Castle to protest. Lord Lonsdale was too busy designing uniforms, appointing officers and ordering ammunition and weapons at his own cost to spare time to see him. Because the wiry dalesmen who crowded into the recruiting office were very often under the required height of five foot eight inches, Lonsdale telegraphed the War Office for permission to waive the regulation. Back came an agonising wire 'Stop repeat stop collecting recruits.' Blandly he announced that anyone over five foot six could now join. The War Office gave up in despair and allowed him to christen his private army 'The Lonsdales', with the official title of the 11th Battalion The Border Regiment. To his great disappointment he was not allowed to send them to war in the hodden grey uniform he had designed for them. They had to wear khaki like everybody else.

Part of the reason for all the frantic activity was that everybody believed that the war would be over by Christmas, and they were determined to have a hand in the final defeat of the Hun. It was some relief, therefore, to the 2nd Battalion when, on the 3rd October they were ordered to embark for the Continent, and it was evident that they were going to see active service.

The main object of the expedition was the relief of Antwerp. Accordingly the force of 53,000 men, of which the 2nd Battalion formed a part, landed at Zeebrugge and then proceeded by train to the suburb of St. André. It was touch and go whether they arrived in time; in fact, they only reached their position on the day the evacuation of Antwerp began. There followed some confused manoeuvring while the Germans poured in troops against the small British force. It soon became apparent that the battle was not to be an offensive one to save Antwerp but a defensive one to protect the Channel ports. So began the Battle of Ypres, in which the 2nd Battalion played a vital role. With their comrades in the 7th Division they hung on grimly to their positions, whilst suffering the most appalling casualties. This was war such as it had never been known before.

> 'Day after day', wrote one war historian, 'the same British battalions, jaded, depleted of officers, and gradually dwindling into mere skeletons, were called to withstand the attacks of fresh and fresh troops. It was not merely that the Germans had superiority in numbers on each occasion when they attacked . . . but they also had the unspeakable advantage of being able at any time to direct a stream of fresh troops against any given part of our thin, weary, battered line . . .'

During those anxious days when the British stood firm, the 7th Division was reduced from 400 officers and 12,000 men to 44 officers and 2,336 men. Two members of the Border Regiment were awarded the Victoria Cross, Privates Abraham Acton and James Smith,

For conspicuous bravery on 21st December, at Rouges Bancs, in

voluntarily going from their trench and rescuing a wounded man who
had been lying exposed against the enemy trenches for 75 hours, and,
on the same day again leaving their trench voluntarily, under heavy
fire, to bring into cover another wounded man.

They were under fire for 60 minutes while conveying the wounded
men into safety.

As the first year of the war ended the Commander of the British
Expeditionary Force issued the following message to all troops:

> In offering to the Army in France my earnest and most heartfelt
> good wishes for Christmas and the New Year, I am anxious once more
> to express the admiration I feel for the valour and endurance they
> have displayed throughout the campaign, and to assure them that to
> have commanded such magnificent troops in the field will be the
> proudest remembrance of my life.

It might be appropriate here to say a word about the other battalions which were raised immediately following the outbreak of war.
They were:

The 3rd (Special Reserve) Battalion, which had originally been the
Militia Battalion, the cadre of which, before the war, had served the
Regimental Depot. They were a draft-finding unit during the whole
of the war, training and sending overseas to other battalions of the
Regiment no less than 600 officers and 47,000 other ranks.

The 4th Battalion was mobilised on the 4th August, and as soon
as its reserve unit was raised became known as the 1st/4th Battalion
and was, in October 1914, sent to India to replace regular troops.
The 1st/4th were later to relieve the 1st Battalion in Burma. They
met only briefly, their trains being halted side by side for twenty
minutes in the middle of India.

2nd/4th Battalion was raised on the 24th October, 1914 and
supplied many for the 1st/4th on their departure for India. They were
stationed first at Kendal and later at Blackpool, where they were
called upon to patrol the coastline on the look-out for German sub-
marines. Incidentally, later there was raised a third battalion for the
4th, and second and third battalions for the 5th. These were purely
training units.

5th Battalion. Mobilised at Workington and later moved to its war
station at Barrow. On 23rd October they entrained for Southampton
and embarked on S.S. *Manchester Engineer* for France, where they

were at first employed on guard duties and as escorts for German prisoners of war.

6th (Service) Battalion. This was the first of the service battalions of the Border Regiment to be raised under Army Order No. 324 of the 21st August, which sanctioned the addition to the army of a further six divisions. The following letter from a volunteer to the 6th Battalion gives an indication of the spirit in which the service battalions were raised:

At the outbreak of war, in August 1914, I felt a great longing to rejoin the Army, so I wrote to the Depot, Border Regiment, at Carlisle offering my services. I had been discharged from this Depot about 14 months previously after having served 21 years in the Army, retiring with the rank of Colour-Sergeant. My services were eagerly accepted, so I at once packed up my old – now very old – kit-bag and made tracks for Carlisle. On arrival at the Depot I met Colonel Broadrick, who, of course, knew me well. He informed me that he had been given command of the 6th Battalion, the first formed battalion of the Border Regiment in the New Army, that he would have me in his Battalion and that I was not to allow anyone else to claim me. He had several appointments to fill and would consider what would suit me best; in the meantime I was to go on drilling squads. Next morning I *did* take over a squad – and ye gods, what a squad! There were at least 150 of them, and this number increased every five minutes. Here were old men, young men, men of varying degrees of fatness, ex-soldiers, ex-militia men, ex-volunteers, tramps and a sprinkling of sleek-looking individuals who looked like shopkeepers. However, they were all keen and attentive, and although many of them had never been in the army before, they were all the stuff of which soldiers were made.

The dear old Depot became very much overcrowded. Cumberland must have answered this first call splendidly, and we all felt like real comrades to each other. At this time I met many dear old friends of the Border Regiment. We used to love to stand at the barrack gate to see who 'rolled up' but whoever came our remarks were usually complimentary and full of welcome. The training was intensive, and between drilling, taking men to the doctor, getting them to sign attestation papers, taking them to meals in relays, and finding a place where they might rest their weary heads at nightfall, we ex-soldiers who had returned to the fold certainly worked very hard. However, the 1914 spirit was strong within us, and we soon learned to love these new-comers and to let them have the advantage of our experience. . .

After their initial training the 6th Battalion became part of the 33rd Brigade of the 11th (Northern) Division.

7th (Service) Battalion. Raised on the 7th September 1914 and at first stationed at Wool in Dorset. They became part of the 51st Brigade of the 17th (Northern) Division.

8th (Service) Battalion. Raised at the same time as the 7th Battalion and composed entirely of men from the towns and villages of Cumberland and Westmorland – mainly Keswick, Kendal and Windermere. They spent their first winter training at Boscombe near Bournemouth, where they were part of the 75th Brigade of the 25th Division.

9th (Service) Battalion was raised on the 14th September 1914 at Carlisle and sent to Lewes, without any officers. It was three days after their arrival before a commanding officer could be found. They became part of the 66th Brigade of the 22nd Division.

10th (Reserve) Battalion. Raised in October 1914 and first stationed in Essex. They were eventually made a reserve training battalion and, in 1915, became a Young Soldiers Battalion.

11th (Service) Battalion (Lonsdale). The circumstances of the raising of this battalion have already been recorded. The officers were all selected by Lord Lonsdale who appointed a retired army captain, P. W. Machell, C.M.G., late of the Essex Regiment, to command. To begin with there were no regular officers at all, and not even an adjutant until Captain P. G. W. Biggle was appointed two months after formation. They were first stationed at Blackhall Racecourse under very severe conditions, which Lord Lonsdale sougĥt to relieve by sending them, at his own expense, 1,000 blankets and 1,000 greatcoats. They were brigaded in the 124th Brigade of the 41st Division of the 5th New Army.

12th (Reserve) Battalion. Originally raised solely as a reserve battalion for the 11th, it later amalgamated with the 12th Battalion the East Lancashire Regiment to form the 75th Reserve Training Battalion. In February 1918 it became a Young Soldiers Battalion.

The outbreak of war found the 1st Battalion in Upper Burma and, having been abroad for a period of eight years, confidently awaiting a home posting. Instead, they were immediately placed on a war footing in preparation for being sent on active service. In all there were 52 battalions in India and Burma at the outbreak of the Great War. Most of them were seasoned troops, urgently required at home to meet the crisis while the New Army was being trained.

In fact, the 1st Battalion did not sail for home until December. They went by way of Aden, Suez, Port Said and Malta, and spent four days at Gibraltar before finally arriving in England on the 10th January 1915. They joined the 87th Brigade which included, besides 1st Border, the 2nd Battalion South Wales Borderers, 1st Battalion King's Own Scottish Borderers and the 1st Battalion Royal Irish Fusiliers. They were stationed in billets in Rugby awaiting orders for an overseas posting. The Division to which they belonged, the 29th, consisted almost entirely of experienced soldiers withdrawn from Indian or colonial service, and it was obvious they would not long be kept out of things.

On the 17th March the 29th Division embarked at Avonmouth for 'an unknown destination'. It was not long, however, before it was discovered that they were bound for the Dardanelles.

The expedition to the Dardanelles was commanded by General Sir Ian Hamilton, its purpose being to force a passage through the Straits in the hope of bringing about the collapse of Turkey, who had thrown in her lot with Germany. It was hoped that the whole operation could be carried out without putting troops ashore at all, and great reliance was placed on the presence of a strong British fleet. It was soon decided, however, by the commanders on the spot that a landing would be necessary and the 29th Division, with some units of the Naval Division, were selected for the task.

The shore of the Gallipoli peninsula where the landing was to take place consists of steep sandy cliffs, broken at intervals by ravines where streams find their way down to the sea. It was an uninviting prospect, and one which was not underestimated by Major-General Hunter-Weston, commanding the Division. On the eve of the landing he issued the following messages to all ranks:

> The Major-General Commanding congratulates the Division on being selected for an enterprise the success of which will have a decisive effect on the war. The eyes of the world are upon us and your deeds will live in history.
>
> To us now is given an opportunity of avenging our friends and relatives who have fallen in France and Flanders. Our comrades there willingly gave their lives in thousands and tens of thousands for our King and Country, and by their glorious courage and dogged tenacity they defeated the invaders and broke the German offensive.
>
> We must also be prepared to suffer hardships, privations, thirst and heavy losses by bullets, by shells, by mines, by drowning. But if each man feels, as is true, that on him individually, however small or however great his task, rests the success or failure of the expedition, and

therefore the honour of the Empire and the welfare of his own folk at home, we are certain to win through to a glorious victory.

In Nelson's time it was England, now it is the whole British Empire, which expects that each of us will do his duty.

At 5 a.m. on the 25th April the attack started with a naval bombardment, and two hours later the Border Regiment landed without much opposition on 'X' Beach. The Royal Fusiliers on the neighbouring beach fared less well and were driven back from the cliff top. To assist them, the Border Regiment charged the enemy lines with the bayonet, pushing them back some 600 yards. By the end of the day's fighting only 'X' Beach was tolerably secure, landings on the other beaches having either failed or just managed to retain a foothold. At midnight on the first day the Turks counter-attacked and were driven back. Battle was now truly joined and the operation which was to cost so many brave lives well underway. In the days which followed the Border Regiment suffered heavy losses, including their commanding officer, Lieutenant-Colonel R. C. C. Hume, until, a week later, they were pulled out of the line to form part of the Brigade Reserve. It was a month before they moved forward into the trenches again, and almost immediately another attack was ordered. The objective allotted to the battalion was a strongly defended fort known as Boomerang Redoubt, which was strongly-held and protected by barbed wire entanglements. General Hamilton described their attack in the following words:

> After a special bombardment by trench mortars, and while the bombardment of the surrounding trenches was at its height, part of the Border Regiment at the exact moment prescribed leapt from their trenches as one man, like a pack of hounds, and, pouring out of cover, raced across and took the work most brilliantly.

It was part of a successful day for the whole Division, and it caused General Hamilton to publish the following Special Force Order:

> The General Commanding feels he voices the sentiments of every soldier serving with this Army when he congratulates the incomparable 29th Division upon yesterday's splendid attack, carried out, as it was, in a manner more than upholding the best traditions of the distinguished regiments of which it is composed.

The 29th Division suffered cruel losses at the first landing. Since then they have never been made up to strength, and they have remained under fire every hour of the day and night for two months on end. Opposed to them were fresh troops holding line upon line of entrenchments flanked by redoubts and machine guns.

But when yesterday the 29th Division was called upon to advance, they dashed forward as eagerly as if this were only their baptism of fire. Through the entanglements they swept northwards, clearing our left of the enemy for a full thousand yards. Heavily counter-attacked at night, they killed or captured every Turk who had penetrated their incomplete defences, and today stand possessed of every yard they had so hardly gained.

Casualties at Gallipoli were so heavy that reinforcements had to be constantly sent from home. By the beginning of 1915 there were only five of the original officers of the 1st Battalion who had not been killed nor wounded. With the heavy reinforcements also required by the 2nd Battalion quite a considerable strain was put on the Depot. In the meantime the other battalions of the regiment were reaching a point in their training when they could be sent to war. One of the first of the service battalions – the 6th – was sent to Gallipoli. They embarked on 1st July and duly arrived at Mudros Harbour, where they found the 1st Battalion in rest camp. Within a few days they were sent up to relieve front-line troops, and had their first experience of battle. One officer recorded of his unseasoned troops:

When dawn broke we looked about and found ourselves on a flat plain about 3 miles from Achi Baba in some shallow dug-outs very much exposed to view. Orders were at once issued to the men not to show themselves, but, like so many rabbits, first one and then another kept bobbing up; they had not yet learnt what fire was like, nor had even some of the officers who had seen much service realized the power of modern artillery.

The battle for the peninsula now entered another stage, with General Sir Ian Hamilton's decision to reinforce the Australian and New Zealand Army Corps at Anzac Cove and to effect a landing at Suvla Bay, with a view to gripping the peninsula at its narrowest part and cutting the Turkish army off from communication with Constantinople.

For this task a series of landings were planned. One force consisting of the 29th, 42nd, and 52nd Divisions embarked for

Suvla from Helles while the 11th Division, which included 6th Border, was to attack at Imbros. The 6th Battalion were first of all in the divisional reserve but, the first wave of the attack being unsuccessful, they were soon ordered up to reinforce the attack on Chocolate Hill, the first objective. This was achieved after a brief struggle and the Battalion, with their tails very much up, found themselves sitting comfortably on the objective while scouts were sent forward to reconnoitre a further advance. Much to their disappointment, they were then ordered back to the reserve. They were now, however, to be given a far more difficult task.

Within twelve hours of their retiral orders were received to attack the Turkish position of Ismali Oglu Tepe before dawn on the following morning. The story is soon told. At dawn, the leading company ran into such heavy fire that every officer except one was killed. Worse was to come. The line on the left collapsed, leaving the regiment's flank in the air. By 11 a.m. the position was desperate. One officer reported; 'We had about thirty rifles capable of use and on the right were two machine guns out in the open with no one serving them.' Still they held on through the long day. The battalion had gone into action on the morning of the 9th with 22 officers and 696 other ranks. When the roll call was taken at dawn on the 10th all that remained were 5 officers and 120 other ranks.

There followed a short period of rest for the shattered battalion before they were again committed, this time losing their C.O., Lt-Col. Broadrick, and two other officers. Then came a protracted period of trench duty, during which time they were reinforced from home. Then, at the end of the year, they were sent to the Island of Imbros for a well-earned rest.

At the same time as the 6th Battalion were involved in their disastrous battle, the 1st Battalion were also in the thick of things. They were required to attack an objective known as Hill 70, where they met with equally determined opposition. By early morning of the second day there was only one officer with thirty-three men of the Battalion left holding the left of the position. As the position on either flank crumbled, he was ordered to retire, which he did bringing out with him about 50 other men from various regiments. In all, the Battalion lost 14 officers and almost 400 men killed, wounded or missing, and there was nothing for it but to go into reserve until reinforcements should become available.

By now the authorities in England were beginning to realise that this expedition, so immensely expensive in men's lives, was achieving very little. On the 16th October General Sir Ian Hamilton was called home for consultation, and General Sir Charles Munro took over. As the weather grew steadily worse, the rains flooding the trenches and dug-outs, the perilous withdrawal commenced. The 1st Battalion were amongst the last to leave, arriving in Suez in late January. So ended one of the most bravely-fought campaigns of the war – yet one which must go down in history as one of the most disastrous.

Whilst the bitter battle was being fought for the Gallipoli Peninsula, the war in the main theatre was being contested no less vigorously; one by one the other service battalions of the Regiment were becoming involved.

In the autumn of 1915 the 2nd Battalion were involved in the Battle of Loos. They were part of the main attack and fought with great dash, reaching their objective and capturing a number of German guns, which they then held against a determined counter-attack. In the meantime, the 5th Battalion had been sent to France and were engaged in fighting further north which, although not part of the main attack, had a diversionary value and kept large numbers of the enemy occupied.

The 7th Battalion embarked for France on the 14th July with a strength of 31 officers and 932 other ranks. They were engaged in an attack on Hooge towards the end of September, during which they suffered slight casualties. By the time they had spent another month in the Ypres salient, however, their overall strength had been reduced to 18 officers and 393 other ranks. The 8th Battalion followed the 7th to France in September. The 9th Battalion also went to France in September, but they had scarcely settled into billets before the course of the war dictated a further move.

The attitude of the Bulgarians and the Greeks and the isolation of our allies, the Serbians, caused the British Government to decide to send a force to Salonika and the 9th Battalion was amongst the units selected for the task. Accordingly they proceeded to Marseilles and set sail in the *Egra* on the 29th October.

The last of the Service Battalions to leave England were the 11th (Lonsdale) Battalion. They arrived in France at the end of the year and Christmas found them billetted at Aveluy, close behind the front line.

At the beginning of 1916 there were no less than seven battalions of the Border Regiment serving in France, the 1st and the 6th both having arrived there after a period of rehabilitation and training in Egypt. At the beginning of April the 2nd Battalion found themselves, as part of the 91st Brigade, holding a particularly sticky part of the line at Bray. They had just taken over the sector known as Blood Alley when the Germans attacked in great force, and were only driven back at heavy cost. For many days they suffered heavy bombardment and repeated attacks, but their spirit never faltered. On one occasion the Brigade Commander came across Captain Kerr M.C. of the Border Regiment standing on the parapet with a revolver in one hand and a Mills bomb in the other, gaily singing 'John Peel' as he encouraged his men to ignore the shells which were falling all about them. They were finally pulled out of the line after a particularly heavy bombardment: Brigadier-General Minshull-Ford marked the occasion with the following personal letter to Colonel Thorpe, commanding the 2nd.

Dear Thorpe,

I cannot let your Regiment leave without writing to tell you how splendidly I think they have done. You took over a very bad piece of the line, and held it under exceptionally trying circumstances. I consider that all your arrangements for defence were excellent and worked as well as they possibly could and that nothing could have prevented the loss which occurred.

From my own personal observation I know how bravely all ranks did their duty, and thank you for defending the line so well – and for all they did for England.

I consider it a great honour to have had your fine Regiment under my command, and I wish you and it the best of luck. I was personally 'subjected' as they say to an intense bombardment in a very cramped area yesterday, as you know, and it made me most fully realise a little of what you officers and men had to put up with ; my dose lasted eight minutes, theirs an hour and a half.

I shall be very pleased to forward the names of your officers and men who specially distinguished themselves. Among them I hope you will send in Kerr's and Drake-Brockman's and I am writing to General Deverill to express my admiration of the conduct displayed by all ranks of your Regiment. I am very sorry indeed for the brave men who have gone – they died at their posts.

Yours sincerely,

M. Minshull-Ford.

The great battle of 1916 was, of course, the Battle of the Somme. It had been decided by the Allies, early in that year, that an all-out offensive should be launched by both the French and the British; to this end immense amounts of ammunition of all kinds were accumulated during the first part of the year and the British force alone was increased from 450,000 to 660,000 men.

The battle which followed lasted from the 1st July until the 17th November. So many battalions of the Border Regiment were engaged, in various parts of the line, during this long-sustained offensive that it is an almost impossible task to do full justice to all the units concerned. It will probably be easier for the reader if only the general outline is given, with a few details of those actions in which the battalions were engaged.

The Battle of the Somme may be divided into four phases, the first from the 1st to the 14th July, the second from the 23rd July to the 9th September, the third from the 15th September until the 9th November and the final stage from the 13th November until the 17th. During the first phase the 1st, 2nd, 7th, 8th and 11th Battalions were involved. Of them all the 11th (Lonsdale) Battalion had the worst time. They were part of X Corps holding the middle of the British sector. On the 30th June they moved from dug-outs at Crucifix Corner in Authmille Wood to assembly trenches, in preparation for an attack on Mouquet Farm. It necessitated a most complicated manoeuvre, including a ninety-degree swing in the middle of the attack which had to be carried out under heavy fire, exactly to time. In fact, when the moment came to scramble over the parapet, the enemy fire, which was expected to be heavy, proved to be overwhelming. Here is a description of the action given in an interview by one of the survivors to a reporter who took it down verbatim:

Aye, it was half-past seven when we started, sir. 'Twas kind of a bit of a wood, you know sir. We were third line like B and C Company being afore us. Ye see we could see them moving in the open like, past the wood, till the fire caught them and they went down like grass. I was beside the Colonel in the front trench. I carried the bombs, ye see. The Colonel was to go with the last line after us. But when he sees the second line cut down that way an' our time come, 'O damn!' he says – just like that – an' he ups an' over the parapet. 'Come on, lads' he said – like that – an' just at that moment he was hit an' kind of staggered back, an' before we could get to him like, he fell backwards into the trench again. I doubt it killed him. But we had to go on. I had me bombs you see. We were singing 'John Peel' like mad and cheering to raise the dead. . . .

I got a bullet in me arm directly I was on the parapet and somehow it made me stumble like and I fell. But I went on as quickly as I could ; me having the bombs. But ye'd have wondered to hear how loud our lads were singin' and cheerin' like at a football match. . . .

Twenty-five officers and eight hundred men went into action that morning. Within a few minutes they had withered away to only three officers and three hundred men. Colonel Machell was killed instantly. He was to have been promoted to command a Brigade the following week.

Later in the same action 8th Border came up in support, and they too suffered heavily. They reached their objective but, when both flanks gave way, they were forced to retire again. The 1st Battalion were in action for the first time in France with VIII Corps towards the north of the line while the 2nd and 7th were part of XV Corps towards the south, and met with mixed fortunes. By the end of the first phase of the battle the heavily fortified enemy position had been dented, but not broken. He was now to throw in fresh troops as the second and third phases got underway. The position is best described in the words of Sir Douglas Haig, the British Commander-in-Chief:

> There was strong evidence that the enemy forces engaged on the battle front had been severely shaken by the repeated successes gained by ourselves and our Allies ; but the great strength and depth of his defences had secured for him sufficient time to bring up fresh troops, and he still had many powerful fortifications, trenches, villages and woods, to which to cling on our front and on our flanks. We had indeed secured a footing on the main ridge, but only on a front of 6,000 yards ; and desirous though I was to follow up quickly the successes we had won it was first necessary to widen the front.

In the operations which were to follow only two of the battalions of the Border Regiment were actively involved although the other battalions were occupied in other parts of the long line, and by their presence helped the combatants. The two battalions were the 7th and the 2nd. The 7th were the first in action. They were holding Delville Wood, forming a sharp salient which the Germans, by repeated counter-attacks, seemed determined to iron out. On the 7th August the Battalion received orders to make an attack themselves on the German trenches – only 70 yards away. The operation was carried through with great gallantry, but the enemy fire was so heavy that it was quite impossible to succeed. On the 9th they were withdrawn to St. Amand to rest and await reinforcements. In the meantime, the 2nd Battalion, which had suffered so heavily, had been made up to strength again with remarkable speed. By the beginning of September both battalions were ready once again for action. During most of September the 2nd Battalion were in action in the area of Ginchy, largely in support of the 2nd Gordons and the 9th Devons. During this time they sustained about a hundred casualties before once again being withdrawn.

With the beginning of the third phase of the battle, which consisted of a resumption of the main attack, most of the remaining battalions of the Border Regiment were once again involved.

The 5th Battalion were in the line at Bécourt Wood, from where they were ordered to advance and link up with the forward positions of the 6th and 9th Battalions of the Durham Light Infantry. The opposition was so stiff, however, and the state of the ground so sodden that two attempts failed to achieve the main objective. Shortly afterwards A Company had to be withdrawn due to a heavy epidemic of dysentry, so that the next attack took place with only three companies. This time the attack was from Flers and was completely successful, the 5th advancing so rapidly that the Germans were taken completely by surprise.

The 6th Battalion left the Arras area where it had been ever since its arrival from the Dardanelles early in September, and went into the trenches near Ovillers. On 26 September, as part of 33rd Brigade, they were ordered to attack towards the village and chateau of Thiepval. The War Diary records:

> The waves left in grand style all along the line, Joseph and Schwaben Trenches being carried by 12.45 p.m., the attack of the Border Regiment being led by Captain Carr and Second-Lieutenant Fulton who, though both wounded before the objective was reached, 'carried on' and saw their men established ; the captures amounted to 2 machine guns and 191 prisoners, while nearly a hundred enemy were killed.

The Battalion remained in position under heavy shell-fire for a week before being relieved.

The 7th Battalion underwent many moves before they were finally ordered up with the 17th Division, to relieve the 8th in the front line. The Battalion faced the German-occupied Zenith Trench, and they were asked to attack if they felt they could do so with an element of surprise. After careful reconnaissance it was decided to make the attempt, which succeeded with comparatively small losses. Of their tour of duty the Divisional Commander wrote:

> The G.O.C. wishes to place on records his appreciation of the gallant manner in which the Zenith Trench was captured and held against all counter-attacks by the 7th Border and 7th Lincolnshire Regiments. The fact that the 7th Border had already done 48 hours in close support and were completing their tour of 48 hours in the front line makes their performance all the finer. The G.O.C. is particularly pleased with the initiative displayed by the Battalion and Company Commanders concerned. The dash and determination displayed despite bad weather and most trying conditions reflect the greatest credit on all ranks concerned and will still further enhance the good name gained by the 17th Division in the Battle of the Somme.

The 8th Battalion were also involved in operations around Ovillers, taking part in a highly successful attack on Regina Trench. They suffered 162 casualties and were highly commended by the Army Commander. They were part of the 25th Division, which saw more active service than any other division during the Battle of the Somme.

By the end of the third phase of the battle much had been achieved. Not only had Verdun been relieved, but the whole German army had been very considerably worn down. As the C-in-C wrote:

> Among all the long role of victories borne on the Colours of our regiments, there never has been a higher test of the endurance and resolution of our infantry. They have shown themselves worthy of the highest traditions of our race and of the proud record of former wars.

In the final phase of the battle there was to be more fighting by battalions of the Regiment, notably the 6th and the 11th. By the end of the year there were rumours that the Kaiser was ready to sue for peace. Although they came to nothing, few could have imagined that Christmas of 1916 that the struggle was to go on for two more weary years.

CHAPTER XI

EARLY IN 1917 the 1st, 2nd and 11th Battalions were engaged in operations around Ancre, and each suffered a considerable number of casualties in minor but costly actions. The 2nd Battalion in particular also suffered from sickness, and during March had to evacuate no less than 124 other ranks.

On the 8th April the Arras offensive commenced. It found the 1st Battalion in a hutted camp at Bavincourt, but soon afterwards they were ordered forward to the front line near the Arras-Cambrai road. On the way up they passed through Monchy, the scene of one of the few and one of the most disastrous cavalry charges of the war. The Diary laconically remarks 'we saw where the Cavalry had taken it in the neck.' There followed some heavy scrapping round the village of Monchy-le-Preux during which the Battalion H.Q. came under heavy fire, killing the Regimental Sergeant-Major and wounding the Adjutant. Shortly afterwards there was a direct hit on the H.Q. dug-out which buried the Commanding Officer; he was sent to hospital, but happily survived. After almost a week of constant action the Battalion was finally relieved, though they were not to stay out of things for long. The following month they took over the line at Monchy-Pelves, from which they were ordered to launch an attack. Largely due to a failure by the artillery to bombard the enemy strong-holds until too late, they landed their shells on our own troops. As a result, the attack was blunted and just failed to reach the objective. Shortly afterwards the Battalion was relieved because of the heavy casualties they had sustained.

This action was typical of many which were fought during the war. Because of heavy bombardment, telephonic communication was constantly being broken by cut wires, and the units had to rely on runners to keep in touch. The mortality amongst these brave men, who unquestioningly faced shot and shell to deliver their message, was very high and this often resulted in forward Companies being cut off for a considerable time from their H.Q.'s. To add to the confusion communications to the rear were not always good, and the greatest difficulty was often experienced in directing artillery fire and in calling up reinforcements. Thus a great responsibility fell upon the senior officer on the spot – frequently only a very newly-arrived subaltern – to do the correct thing without knowing how the general pattern of the action was developing.

While the 1st Battalion were busily engaged around Monchy, the 2nd Battalion were also moved up, but they were not to be actively engaged until the second week in May, when they took part in an action at Bullecourt aimed at reinforcing a foothold in the Hindenberg Line gained by the Australians. Rather earlier in the proceedings the 5th Battalion were also committed to the Battle of Arras, taking part in two successful attacks before returning for a period in billets near St Amand. The 7th Battalion fought a bitter battle in front of Monchy-le-Preux, suffering killed, wounded and missing a casualty roll of 15 officers and 404 men. They were relieved on the 25th April, but by the 3rd May they were again made up to strength and returned to the trenches until the end of the battle.

The Battle of Arras lasted a month, during which time nearly 20,000 prisoners were taken as well as a great number of guns. The number of casualties inflicted was estimated at 350,000. It was scarcely over before General Sir Douglas Haig switched his attention to the development of operations in the north. This resulted in the Battle of Messines, in which the 6th, 8th and 11th Battalions were involved, and the third Battle of Ypres where the 1st, 2nd, 5th, 6th, 7th and 8th Battalions played an active part. The month of May saw the 6th Battalion at Le Transloy where, the War Diary reports:

> This tour of duty in the line was most peaceful, the total casualties of the Battalion being 2 other ranks killed and 4 wounded. The moral effect on the men of the wanton destruction of trees, houses, roads and wells by retreating Germans will, it is confidently anticipated bear fruit in the next operations undertaken by the Battalion. Their feelings have undoubtedly turned to anger, and the local grindstones have been busy; the men, entirely on their own initiative, have sharpened their bayonets.

Early the following month they had an opportunity of venting their spleen. They fought a long, arduous battle in the glare of

an unusually hot sun, arriving exhausted at the objective. At once
the artillery opened up on the new enemy positions, with such
effect that it started a further retreat. 'Then,' records the Diary,
'our men and the Vickers and Lewis gunners had the time of their
lives!' The 8th Battalion also played a prominent part in the Battle
of Messines, while the 11th were in a part of the line known as
'the "C" subsector' of the Nieuport-Lombartzyde Sector. This was
right up on the coast and their presence there seems to have caused
the Germans some alarm, for they went to some pains to dislodge
them, which resulted in a very sticky action.

The Germans launched an extremely heavy bombardment, but
the Brigade orders were unmistakeable. *'The front line must be held
whether demolished or not!'* Indeed the demolition of the line seemed
imminent. In the middle of the afternoon C Company reported:

> Front line very badly smashed now, right half completely wiped
> out. Second line very badly knocked about ; parts non-existent. Third
> line receiving particular attention and badly knocked about. Com-
> munication trenches, many blown in and always shelled. Approximate
> casualties 40. The shelling is very heavy throughout and continuous
> on first, second and third lines and communication trenches. I have
> two officers in the line now and have arranged with Rowsell to signal
> from first to second line where I have my signaller on the look-out.
> My signal lamp is still O.K. and I shall keep in touch with your O.P.
> Cook, Grey and two of my runners left for B.H.Q. about three p.m.
> I shall be glad to get any news. The shelling is the 'bally limit' and
> I do not like it. We are lying low and I hope all will be well. I hope
> it will finish soon.

The bombardment did not cease until late in the evening when
the enemy rushed the position. The remnant of the 11th were driven
back, at one time holding a support trench only a few yards from
the Germans with a total strength of two officers and five men.
Incredibly, the line held and the enemy were even forced to retire.
By the time the 11th were pulled out they had lost 8 officers and
350 other ranks.

In July came the third Battle of Ypres. Unlike June the weather
was appalling, and movement was severely restricted by the
constant rainfall, which turned the heavily shell-holed ground into
a morass. Coming soon after Arras, the battle imposed a big strain
on the Battalions involved, the 7th Battalion in particular being

able to muster only 13 officers and 335 other ranks, in spite of having received a draft of 7 officers just before the battle. The long drawn-out offensive did not come to an end until 10th November, by which time the troops were suffering almost as much from exposure as from the efforts of the enemy.

The close of the battle was not, however, to be the end of operations for the year. On the 20th November there opened the Battle of Cambrai, which involved both the 1st and the 7th Battalions. Cambrai has gone down in military history as the first battle where tanks were used, but the fighting qualities of the infantry were still the decisive factor. The fighting lasted three weeks, with mixed fortunes on both sides. Writing of the importance of the Battle afterwards Sir Douglas Haig noted:

> There is little doubt that our operations were of considerable indirect assistance to the Allied forces in Italy. Large demands were made upon the available German reserves at the time when a great concentration of German divisions was still being maintained in Flanders. There is evidence that the German divisions intended for the Italian theatre were diverted to the Cambrai front, and it is probable that the further concentration of German forces against Italy was suspended for at least two weeks at a most critical period, when our allies were making their first stand on the Piave Line.

Activity on the Italian front was, in fact, increasing, and late in October the War Cabinet approved the sending of several British divisions to help their allies. Amongst these was the 7th Division; November therefore saw the 2nd Battalion the Border Regiment fitting out for a campaign in a very different climate. It is an indication of the service the 7th Division had done since 7th October 1914 that, at the time of their entraining for Italy on the 18th November 1917, they had lost a total of 2,327 officers and 53,091 other ranks.

At first the 7th Division was part of the reserve to those Italian and French forces engaged on the line of the Rivers Brenta and Piave. The first Military Cross in the B.E.F. in Italy was awarded to a Border officer, attached to the Durham Light Infantry, on the 21st December. By Christmas the whole regiment were in the line, as attacks became more frequent and severe. Later they took over the Montello Sector which, as described by the Divisional commander, General Sir H. Plumer:

> is a feature by itself and an important one. It acts as a hinge to the

whole Italian line, joining as it does that portion facing North from Monte Tomba to Lake Garda, with the defensive line of the Piave covering Venice, which was held by the third Italian Army.

With the opening of the year 1918 several new elements were introduced to the Western Front. The previous year the British Government had become increasingly worried about the dwindling supplies of manpower and, for the first time, introduced conscription to fill the thinning ranks of the army. Now the conscripts were starting to arrive in France, and were greeted somewhat warily by the Regulars and the volunteers who had already been through so much. They were not to be given much time, however, to shake down before the battle was resumed with even greater intensity.

For some time it had been obvious that the Germans were building up for a big offensive. With Russia dropping out of the war they were able to send new divisions from the Eastern to the Western Front. By the end of March the German overall strength had risen by forty-six divisions compared with the previous November, and air reconnaissance showed that a great deal of work was going on in the improvement of rail and road communications. In order to meet the impending threat considerable reorganisation was being undertaken amongst the British forces. Some battalions were disbanded to make up the strength of others, and amongst these casualties was 6th Border. Following the third Battle of Ypres they had suffered further losses in the line and at the beginning of the year were well below strength. The decision was made known on the 1st February and shortly afterwards they were split up amongst the 7th and 8th Battalions. It was a sad end to a gallant battalion, but at least the survivors remained to fight with other battalions of their own regiment.

At the same time the 5th Battalion was reorganised as a Pioneer Battalion, and for much of the coming conflict saw service as divisional troops.

On the 21st March the Germans launched their great offensive on a front of 54 miles. Later, on the 28th March, it spread northwards until there was fierce fighting along some 63 miles. At first sight it appeared an unequal contest. The Germans threw in 73 divisions and were opposed in the first place with 22 British front line divisions, with 12 infantry divisions and 3 cavalry divisions in reserve.

The Border Battalions engaged in this last battle of the

Somme were the 5th, 7th, 8th and 11th. They performed various tasks with the bravery and tenacity for which they had become known.

The main attack was confidently expected to be launched in the sector defended by the Third Army. It came instead on the front of the 6th Division, which included the 5th Battalion. Although the Battalion were not front line troops they rapidly became involved in the battle. As the tide of the attack swept forward they were almost cut off in the village of Roisel, and had to fight their way out, their total casualties being 487.

The 7th Battalion were part of the 51st Brigade of the 17th Division. This, in turn, was part of General Fanshawe's Fifth Corps, charged with the defence of the Cambrai salient. The salient was an extremely vulnerable position, representing as it did the ground gained during the battle of Cambrai, which formed a bulge in the main line. From the 26th March until the 29th the 7th Battalion were in the thick of the battle, being gradually forced to withdraw as the German attack pressed forward. On the 29th they carried out a successful counter-attack, just before being relieved and withdrawn to divisional reserve.

The 8th Battalion became part of the 16th Brigade, being held in readiness to counter-attack to the north of Vaulx Wood which had come under heavy pressure on the first day of the German offensive. The attack was duly delivered and the enemy driven back. By evening, however, it became obvious that one of the weak points in the Corps line was Vaulx Wood, for here the enemy still had pockets of men. They counter-attacked at 7.30 a.m. on the morning of the 22nd and almost immediately the 8th Battalion found itself surrounded on three sides. Eventually they were forced to retire, although two officers and twenty-four men resolutely refused to give up their positions and were never seen again. Of this action by the 8th Battalion, the Divisional history records:

Good work was done by Sergeant Macdonald, Lance-Corporal Stee, Privates Varty and Westbrooke with the Lewis guns. Sergeant Taylor, when all the officers of 'B' Company had become casualties, took command of 'B' Company, reorganised them, and during lulls in the battle produced a piccolo on which he played popular tunes to put new life into the weary men.

The Battalion was relieved on the 23rd March and went back for a brief rest at Savoy Camp.

The 11th Battalion were only marginally involved in this battle, being engaged on a course of training when the attack was launched. Within a few days, however, they were moved into the front line to the north-west of Arras. Here they endured shelling and sniping, although not in the main line of the attack. Shortly after this the Battalion was again withdrawn and given a completely new role. The bulk of the Battalion amalgamated with the 5th, leaving a cadre of ten officers and fifty-one other ranks charged with the training of the American troops now beginning to reach France. This arrangement continued until mid-summer, when orders were given for the cadre also to join the 5th Battalion and for the 11th Battalion to be disbanded. A sad end for the colourful 'Lonsdales' who had served their country so well.

The spring of 1918 saw a crisis in the fortunes of the Allies. The Germans had been halted on the Somme, although much ground had been lost. There had been a pressing danger during the fighting that they would manage to separate the French and British Forces. To make this less likely, General Foch, was appointed to command both armies and bring about a closer co-operation. At the same time, however, there was a continued shortage of manpower. To counteract this, the British Government now raised the age for military service to 50, extended conscription to Ireland and cancelled many classes who had hitherto been exempt. By these means another 355,000 men were sent out to France by the end of April, but still many divisions in the front line were exhausted by the recent fighting and weakened in manpower.

It was while the British army was recovering its breath that the Germans launched another, more limited offensive, which became known as the Battle of the Lys. This took place in the sector from the La Bassée Canal northwards and included the Ploegsteert Sector held by the 25th Division, in which was the 8th Battalion the Border Regiment. The 1st Battalion were with the 29th Division in reserve at Poperinghe.

The main German attack was launched on the right flank near Armentières, but the following day it spread to the left, where the 8th Battalion became heavily engaged. There followed some days of desperate fighting as the 25th Division were steadily forced back. The Battalion were under constant bombardment from both shells and gas, as well as being subject to repeated infantry attacks. How well the Battalion acquitted itself under these trying circumstances can be judged by the number of decorations they were awarded. The Commanding Officer won a bar to his D.S.O. for outstanding bravery and leadership, three other officers were awarded the Military Cross and there were seven awards of the Military Medal. Three of these were to two cooks and a sanitary man who captured a German aeroplane which had been forced to land, but would have managed to take off again had it not been for their efforts.

After the first retirement there was a short pause before the attack was resumed, and again the 8th Battalion were in the thick of it, winning three more Military Medals. The Battalion remained under fire or in action against the enemy for almost three weeks, by which time the Division had been driven back to the line of Kemmel Beek. Casualties were heavy, particularly amongst officers, of whom the Battalion lost 26.

In the meantime the 1st Battalion had also become engaged. The Germans, on the evening of the 10th April, had forced their way, after repeated attacks, into Estaires, thus bringing themselves into a position opposite the 50th Division, of which the 1st Battalion formed a part. The casualties in the forward battalions had been formidable and the position was altogether very shaky. Perhaps the part played by the 1st Battalion during the next few days is best described by quoting the citation whereby their Commanding Officer, Captain (acting Lieutenant-Colonel) J. R. Forbes-Robertson, D.S.O., M.C., was awarded the Victoria Cross. It read as follows:

For the most conspicuous bravery while commanding his Battalion during the heavy fighting. Through his quick judgment, resource, untiring energy and magnificent example Lieutenant-Colonel Forbes-Robertson on four separate occasions saved the line from breaking and averted a situation which might have had the most serious and far-reaching results.

On the first occasion when the troops in front were falling back, he made a rapid reconnaissance on horseback, in full view of the enemy, under heavy machine-gun fire and close-range shell-fire. He then organised and, still mounted, led a counter-attack which was completely successful in re-establishing our line. When his horse was shot from under him he continued on foot. Later in the same day, when troops to the left of his line were giving way, he went to that flank and checked and steadied the line, inspiring confidence by his splendid coolness and disregard for personal danger. His horse was wounded three times and he was thrown five times.

The following day when the troops on both his flanks were forced to retire, he formed a post at Battalion Headquarters, and with his Battalion still held his ground, thereby covering the retreat of troops on his flanks.

Under the heaviest fire this gallant officer fearlessly exposed himself when collecting parties, organising and encouraging.

On a subsequent occasion, when troops were retiring to his left and the condition of things on his right was obscure, he again saved the situation by his magnificent example and cool judgment. Losing a second horse, he continued alone on foot until he had established a line to which his own troops could withdraw and so conformed to the general situation.

The line referred to in the last paragraph of the citation was a ragged affair indeed. The Border Regiment were reduced to a strength of 8 officers and 195 other ranks, but they were not nearly so badly off as the two regiments with whom they were brigaded. The King's Own Scottish Borderers had 47 other ranks fit for action, while the South Wales Borderers were reduced to twenty-four. In spite of their cruelly reduced numbers, however, the order was to hold the line at all costs to give the Australians, who were detraining behind the lines, time to effect a relief. Time after time the enemy threw themselves against the valiant defenders, but they were up against men who were determined to fight to the last thrust of the bayonet. Through their superhuman efforts the line was held.

For a time after their withdrawal from the Battle of the Lys, the 8th Battalion were rested in the Poperinghe area. Like all the Battalions in the 25th Division they had had a severe battle and badly needed time to re-equip and train their reinforcements. Within three weeks of their coming out of the line, however, they were on the move again. As part of the 9th Corps they were entrained for the French sector near Soissons under an arrangement whereby they were to be loaned to Marshal Foch to reinforce his line. In view of the battle weariness of some of the Divisions they were allotted a sector north of Rheims in the Champagne country, which Marshal Foch himself described as 'a quiet place on the Aisne.' It was generally considered that the position was so impregnable that the enemy would not dare to attack it. In fact it was an extremely poor defensive position, being on the watershed between the Aisne and the Ailette, and being too narrow to obtain any defensive depth.

The position occupied by the 21st, 8th, 50th and 25th Divisions was generally regarded as a rest area and, as they settled in, divisional training schools were opened and courses of training for the new recruits initiated. This had not been long underway, however, before intelligence reports made it tolerably certain that all the ideas about the area had been wrong and that the Germans were preparing to attack. On the 26th May definite information was received that the attack would take place the following day, and the 25th Division, which had been in reserve, moved up in close support. At 1 a.m. the bombardment started with the massed fire of over a thousand German guns, against which the Allies could muster scarcely three hundred. The second Battle of the Aisne had begun.

The weakness of the position soon became apparent. By the end of the first day's fighting the main line had crumbled and the 8th Battalion, in their position on the Ventelay-Roucy Road, found themselves practically surrounded. At 1.30 a.m. the following morning it was decided to try and fight a way out in the dark. This was successfully accomplished but, on the days which followed, considerable reorganisation took place within the 25th Division, 8th Border becoming part of what was known as the 1st/25th Divisional Composite Battalion. The retreat ended on 6th June, eleven days after the battle had started. The British troops had played a vital part in containing the German advance, as is reflected in a letter to their Commander, Lieutenant-General Hamilton Gordon from the Commander of the 6th French Army:

> With a tenacity, permit me to say, wholly British, you have reformed the remnants of your divisions, submerged in the hostile flood, the new reinforcements which you have thrown into the fight, and which nave finally allowed us to build a dam against which the German flood has beaten itself in vain. All this no French witness can ever forget.

This was the last action in which the 8th Battalion were to be engaged as a unit. The infantry of the 25th Division were now broken up and the service battalions used to reinforce other units. Under this arrangement 12 officers and 306 other ranks of the Battalion were sent to join the 9th Loyal (North Lancashire) Regiment.

In the meantime the spell of service during which the 5th Battalion had been a Pioneer Battalion had not lasted very long. According to an entry in the War Diary on the 9th of May, when the Battalion had joined the 32nd Division, (thus replacing the 11th Battalion): 'the Battalion once more takes its place amongst the fighting units after working for a short time as a Pioneer Battalion.' On the 6th August they were inspected by the King, and shortly afterwards were again in action, taking part in the Battle of Amiens. On the 27th they were in the attack on Ablaincourt as the centre battalion, brigaded with the 2nd Manchesters on the right and the 1st Dorsets on the left. The action was most successful, as is shown by the following letter to the Commanding Officer of the 5th from Brigadier Minshull-Ford:

> We are all very proud of what the Borders have been and are doing. Please give them all our best wishes and congratulations. I am sorry that you are away from us (they were transferred to the 97th Brigade immediately after the battle) but I hope that you will be back very soon. I very much regret your casualties, of which we only know the bare facts at present.
>
> The very best of luck.

The 7th Battalion were also involved in the second Battle of the Somme, during which the enemy were slowly pushed back. On one occasion, when the Battalion took possession of trenches recently vacated by the Germans, a note was found pinned to the door of the dugout. It read:

> Dear Tommy, When you are coming we are gone, hoping you have many pleasures in our cottages. Why you send us so many iron postcards, eat some yourself. Make peace next time, have you not enough?

By the time the battle was over on the 6th September the Germans had been pushed back a considerable distance and the end of the war was already in sight. There was still the breaking of the Hindenburg Line, in which the 5th and the 7th Battalions took part, and the great final advance in which the 1st Battalion joined them. For days before the end prisoners were pouring in and the daily advances were being measured in miles when, on 11th November, came the sudden news that the Armistice had been signed.

*   *   *

The last year of the war proved to be a comparatively quiet time for the 2nd Battalion, fighting with the 7th Division in Italy. They were involved in odd skirmishes with the enemy, largely of their own making. Whilst they sat on the line of the Piave River, they occupied themselves sending forward patrols to investigate the strength of the enemy – an activity to which the enemy strongly objected, intermittently shelling the British positions by way of retaliation.

In May of 1918 there occurred a most unlucky incident, as a result of the enemy's habit of spasmodic shelling. On 2nd May they scored a direct hit on the Battalion headquarters hut, killing the Commanding Officer, Lieutenant-Colonel W. Kerr, D.S.O., M.C., and wounding four others. Lieutenant-Colonel Kerr was one of the outstanding officers produced by the Regiment during the Great War. At the outbreak of hostilities he was a company sergeant-major with the 2nd Battalion which, step by step, he rose to command.

It was only shortly before the Armistice was signed that 2nd Border finally went into attack. On the night of the 24th-25th October the 7th Division was ordered to force a passage over the Piave. The 20th Brigade, consisting of the 2nd Gordons, the 8th Devons and 2nd Border, led the attack on the right of the line. The attack was completely successful and the advance continued steadily against a demoralised enemy, until the news of the armistice was received. It was a grand finale for the 7th Division, whose record throughout the war had been second to none. One writer describes it thus:

And so at 3 p.m. on November 4th by the waters of the Tagliamento the part played by the 7th Division in the war came to an end. They ended, as their record deserved, in the front line of the advance, and the history of the last ten days made a fitting climax to their four

years of toil. In these ten days the Division had advanced 92 kilo-
meters, crossed five rivers, and captured prisoners far in excess of
its own entire strength. . . . The 7th Division had to all intents fought
until exterminated on five separate occasions in the war ; first at Ypres
in 1914 where they had earned immortality by holding the flower of
the German Army at bay for three weeks ; secondly in the offensives
of 1915, when, with a childlike faith by no means barren of results,
we had hoped to break through the German line ; thirdly on the
Somme in 1916, when after terrific fighting, the entire Division gained
its objective at every point both on the 1st and again on July 14th ;
fourthly in 1917 in following up the German retirement to the
Hindenburg Line where they sacrificed themselves without stint in the
bloody Battle of Bullecourt ; finally in an attack on the Passchendaele
Ridge, when they captured Broodseinde and Reutel, and fought themselves to a standstill in the pitiless mud which alone baulked them of
the capture of Gheluvelt. It was a record of which every man was
justly proud, and light as had been the tasks they were called upon
to bear in Italy, it is beyond question that if it had proved necessary
in October 1918 to sacrifice themselves again, the Division would once
have done so with unhesitating loyalty.

There is little to report of 9th Border, whom we last left on
the Macedonian front in 1917. The war in Salonika was a cat
and mouse affair, with the Greeks watching the fortunes of war
in the main theatres in order to decide which way to jump, while
hostilities between the Bulgarians and the British were sporadic.
During their time in Salonika the 9th Battalion were divisional
troops performing the onerous and demanding work of a Pioneer
Battalion. It was only towards the end of the campaign that part
of the Battalion were engaged in active warfare. They took part
in the final offensive against the Bulgarians which resulted, on the
4th October 1918, in the abdication of King Ferdinand and the
signing of the peace.

Lest it be thought, however, that this extremely arduous and
unpleasant campaign, where the men suffered as much from disease
as from the efforts of the enemy, was an unimportant one, it should
be put in its correct perspective by quoting General Ludendorff
when he wrote about the great Allied offensive of 1918 :

August 8th was the blackest day for the German Army in the history
of the war. This was the worst experience I had to go through except
for the events that, from September 15th onwards, took place on the
Bulgarian front and sealed the fate of the quadruple alliance.

Before finally finishing the account of the activities of the Border Regiment during the Great War, brief mention should be made of the services rendered by the 1st/4th and 2nd/4th Battalions, the two Territorial Battalions which were sent to serve in India in order to release Regular Battalions for active service. One can do no better than to quote the words of the Commander-in-Chief in India, General Sir Charles Munro, on the occasion of their return home.

On your departure from India, I desire to place on record my high appreciation of your services to the Empire during the period of the Great War.

Many of you previous to the outbreak of war had, by joining the Territorial Force, already given proof of that patriotism and public spirit from which the Force has rendered itself so conspicuous. On the declaration of war your ranks were quickly filled by eager young volunteers, animated by the same spirit of self-sacrifice ; when called upon to undertake the further obligation of service overseas your response was immediate and unanimous. By doing so you set free a large number of Regular units for service in the main theatres of war, at a time when every trained soldier was of the greatest value. I share with you the disappointment, which I know you all feel so keenly, that it has not been your luck to fight the enemy in Europe. Many of you, however, have seen service on the Indian frontier and by your conduct and bearing have added to the reputation of the famous regiments whose name you bear.

For the greater portion of your service in India you have been engaged in the somewhat dull routine of garrison duty. The standard of efficiency which you attained, both in training for war and in discipline, reflects the highest credit on you all.

Since the termination of active fighting in all the theatres of war you have been subjected to the further strain of waiting for your relief. That you have appreciated the difficulties which the authorities have to face in this respect is clear from the patience with which you have borne this trying period.

You are now returning to your homes in the United Kingdom and I bid you good-bye, Godspeed and a happy homecoming. As an old commander of a Territorial Division at home, I am proud to have again been associated with this Force in India.

CHAPTER XII

ANY ACCOUNT of the holocaust through which the Border Regiment, like so many others, passed during the years 1914-1918 must necessarily be an inadequate one. All that can possibly be attempted is to give an account of the major battles in which various battalions took part, though to do so is to ignore many gallant actions where great deeds were done and brave men lost their lives. An idea of how much has been omitted may be gained from studying the battle honours gained. There are eighty-four in all, of which ten are emblazoned on the King's Colour.

After the peace had been signed, the 1st Battalion had the satisfaction of taking part in the march to the Rhine. For a time they were stationed at Hilgen on the outskirts of Cologne until, in the beginning of April 1919, they returned to England and took up their quarters at Dettingen Barracks, Blackdown. The 2nd Battalion had left France a month earlier and had made a triumphal return to their Depot town of Carlisle, where the townsfolk had lined the streets to cheer them and they had been accorded a civic reception.

Now the anxiety was to get the country back onto a peacetime footing as soon as possible. One by one the remaining Service Battalions were disbanded and the men returned to civilian life, to take up the threads of their lives which had been so dramatically interrupted. After a few months in Carlisle the 2nd Battalion joined the 3rd at Claremorris in Ireland where the personnel of the two battalions merged. The 3rd had acted as a special reserve Battalion throughout the war. Now personnel of both battalions were selected to return to Carlisle to complete the establishment of the Regimental Depot. What then remained of the 2nd Battalion stayed in Ireland during the troublous period which ended in 1922 when the Irish Free State was created. It was the final chapter in the unhappy history of that country with which the Border Regiment had been so closely associated during those times in its history when it was not serving abroad. By one of those anomalies peculiar to the British, and perhaps particularly to the Irish, the country had been for some two hundred years both a fertile recruiting ground for the British Army and one of its most troublesome responsibilities.

The last two battalions of the Border Regiment to be disbanded were those of the Territorial Force, soon to be renamed the Territorial Army. The 1st/4th and the 2nd/4th were both delayed in India to deal with new troubles in Afghanistan. Of the two battalions the 2nd/4th had seen the most action during the war years and it was now the same battalion which became the most actively engaged.

The 2nd/4th, early on during their Indian service, had been made part of the 10th (Peshawar) Division and had won high praise by their behaviour. Major-General Woodyatt, commanding the Division, had this to say about them:

> The men of this unit were of fine physique and as keen as mustard. It was a great pleasure to deal with them, and to have a chat to individual N.C.O.'s and men in the blockhouses. On one occasion a picquet of this unit, put out to protect the Viceroy on his visit, was threatened and heavily sniped at by Mohmands. On withdrawal it was followed up by the enemy with some determination. I happened to be present as the picquet was approaching our nearest blockhouse, and noted the extreme reluctance with which the men withdrew under orders. I saw that their eyes were blazing, and that they were full of suppressed excitement. Quite the right fighting spirit. About a month later I added a hundred men of the 2nd/4th Border Regiment to a column I was taking out to destroy some villages. The start was at 4 a.m. and the men returned to camp at 7 p.m., having marched 26 miles and helped to destroy two villages. It is not exactly child's play, pushing over strong mud walls, blowing up towers and burning houses. I thought the day a good test of endurance and all ranks were very cheery at the finish.

The campaign to discipline the Afghans was an uncomfortable one in that it was conducted in extreme heat, but it was a one-sided affair. The enemy showed little inclination to stand and fight, particularly as the British troops were supported by a flight of aeroplanes which struck terror into the hearts of the tribesmen. By the end of June the Ameer had sued for peace and the part played by the 2nd/4th Battalion was over. During the three and a half years that they had been employed on the North-West Frontier they had the proud record of not having lost a single rifle or round

22. Presentation of new Colours by HM King George V on 11 June, 1924 in the gymnasium, Aldershot, to the 2nd Battalion, The Border Regiment.

23. Officers relaxing outside the Columbia Country Club, Shanghai, May, 1927.

24. Manning a boundary post, Tien Tsin, June, 1928.

of ammunition. By the end of the year both battalions were on their way back to England to be dispersed.

By 1920 the Regiment was back once more on a peacetime footing and playing its part in the multifarious duties which fell to the army charged with maintaining the peace in those many areas of the world which were still painted red on the map. The original intention of the Army Council, that one battalion of a regiment should serve at home while the other did overseas duty, soon had to be abandoned in order to meet the emergencies which continually arose in various parts of the world.

The two Territorial battalions had scarcely shaken the dust of India from their feet before the 1st Battalion was sent out there for a tour of duty. Late in 1919 they sailed for Karachi where they remained for two years before joining a punitive force which was sent against the troublesome Mahsud Waziris.

Waziristan, situated on the Afghan frontier, had long been a thorn in the flesh of the British administration. Many valuable lives had been lost over the years in attempting to maintain order in the rugged country occupied by the Darwesh Khal Wazirs and the Mahsuds. Now, in 1922, trouble threatened again and the 1st Border Regiment were amongst the troops sent to Kohat in case the emergency got worse.

It was whilst they were at Kohat that a tragic occurrence took place which horrified the world. The circumstances were that the acting Commanding Officer, Major A. J. Ellis, was away from the Battalion on a course, leaving behind his wife and daughter. During his absence a raid was made on the cantonments and Ellis's wife and daughter were seized by the raiders. Mrs. Ellis was brutally murdered before the daughter's eyes and the young girl was carried back to the hills.

The Battalion naturally wanted to set off in instant pursuit but it was considered that military action would endanger the life of the child. Under these circumstances the wife of a medical missionary, Mrs. Stair, volunteered to act as an emissary. This brave woman managed to bring the girl out safely but the incident serves to illustrate that service in India could, at times, be far from pleasant.

The Regiment was now part of the 7th Indian Infantry Brigade which also included the 1st/3rd Madras Regiment, 2nd/3rd Gurkha Rifles and 1st/9th Gurkha Rifles. The object of the operation was to enter Afghanistan and destroy the villages occupied by the insurgents as a way of 'showing the flag'. It would not have been a difficult task were it not for the mountainous nature of the country, which gave ample cover for snipers, and the severe weather conditions which caused the rivers to rise in sudden spates which made them difficult to negotiate. Lord Rawlinson, the commander of the expedition, gives some idea of the rigours of the approach march undertaken by the 7th Brigade:

> The advance up the track, which had a gradient of 1 in 9 and a width of only six feet, took place in a blinding snowstorm, and the passage over the Naria of some 1,500 camels and 1,100 mules which accompanied the column, was a fine performance. The march commenced at dawn, and, though the distance to be covered was only six miles, the last camel did not reach camp until 10.45 p.m.

For several months the Regiment was active in both fortifying its own position at various camps and in devastating the positions of the enemy. By the middle of March, 1923 most of the villages in the Makin area had been destroyed and the Mahsuds were ready for peace. Shortly afterwards the Regiment was relieved by the 1st Bn the Welch Regiment and returned to the comparative luxury of Peshawar with its polo, tennis and constant round of cocktail parties. They were not allowed to stay there long. A year later they sailed for Aden, a desolate station where they put in another year's overseas service before returning home.

The 2nd Battalion, after their return from Ireland, were stationed at Aldershot where, in 1924, new Colours were presented by His Majesty the King. The old Colours, which were now laid up in Carlisle Cathedral, had been carried since 1888. Shortly after this impressive ceremony, the Battalion again went abroad – first to Malta, then on to Khartoum for a year and then back to Malta.

It was whilst the Regiment was thus disposed – the 1st at home and the 2nd in Malta – that another emergency arose – this time in China. Civil war broke out and British property in Shanghai was threatened. At midnight on 21st January orders were received for the mobilisation of the 13th Brigade of which the 1st Battalion formed a part. So great was the urgency of the situation that the mobilisation was completed in eight days – six days less than the normal time. By the 29th January the Battalion was aboard the *S.S. Karmala* and on its way to China.

At this time the 1st Battalion was commanded by one of the most remarkable regimental officers ever to serve in The Border Regiment, Lieutenant-Colonel G. Hyde Harrison, D.S.O.

Both his father and his step-father had served in the 55th and Harrison could remember the formation of the Border Regiment in 1881. He joined the 1st Battalion in 1899 and apart from two short breaks, when he commanded a battalion of the Royal Sussex Regiment during the 1914-18 War and when he was instructor at the Staff College just after that war, he served continuously with the Regiment until his promotion to Brigadier General in May, 1927. He was appointed Colonel of The Border Regiment in 1936 and held this appointment until 1947.

'Georgy' Harrison's influence was felt throughout the Regiment during a span of nearly fifty years and the reason why this was so is probably best explained in a letter written to him by Lieutenant General Sir Charles H. Harrington, Commander-in-Chief Northern Command, on the occasion of the 1st Battalion's departure from York to China. In this letter the C-in-C said:

> I have watched with much interest the way in which you have commanded (the battalion), and the way in which every officer, NCO and man looks to you and is inspired by your leadership, and will answer any call of yours. The thorough way in which everything is done – your training, musketry, games, etc – have all impressed me very much . . . the way in which your officers play in with your men is the secret of leadership.

At the same time the 14th Brigade which contained the 2nd Battalion were given similar orders and sailed on *S.S. Megantic* to become part of the Shanghai Defence Force. They were the first to arrive and were posted to various points around the perimeter of the International Settlement. When a few days later the 1st Battalion disembarked the band of the 2nd Battalion played them into camp.

This situation, whereby two battalions of the same regiment served in a foreign station side by side, was almost unique in the history of any regiment of the British Army, and both battalions made much of it. Inter-battalion sports were arranged and a good time generally had by all.

In the event the tension in China soon eased without the active involvement of British troops and, at the end of the year, the 1st Battalion were sent home again. In the meantime the 2nd Battalion had sailed for Chinwangtao and proceeded from there by rail to

Tientsin, where they provided the Legation Guard. Those companies not on duty were employed in training or resting at Shanhaikuan, a pleasant seaside resort at the eastern end of the Great Wall of China. They remained in this not uncomfortable station for just over two years, and then moved to India and occupied various stations there right up to 1939.

During this period the 1st Battalion served at home, spending four years at Holywood in Northern Ireland during which time they were called out to aid the civil power in quelling the riots in Belfast. In January, 1937 they were sent to Catterick Camp where they were incorporated as a rifle battalion under the new army reorganisation. Then, in November of the same year, they were sent for a short tour of duty to Palestine where the situation was extremely tense due to the activities of Arab gangs. For almost two years the Regiment was engaged in a running fight with the Arab terrorists culminating in a highly successful action which is described in a message to the Regiment from the Brigadier Commander, Brigadier A. R. Godwin-Austen, O.B.E., M.C.:

The Brigade Commander, on behalf of all ranks in the Brigade warmly congratulates 1st Battalion The Border Regiment on killing in battle the chief leader of the rebellion in Palestine, Abdul Nahim El Haj Mohd, and so seriously wounding Salieman Abu Khalifa, a notorious sub-leader, that he subsequently died of his wounds.

In April, 1939 they embarked for England, arriving at Southampton on the 8th May, whence they proceeded to Aldershot.

While the Border Regiment was being deployed on its various duties in the outposts of the British Empire, danger was lurking much nearer home. In 1934 Field-Marshal Hindenberg, President of the German Republic, had died and a new ruler had emerged, Adolf Hitler, who at once started to violate the Treaty of Versailles clause by clause. Some years earlier another unknown, Benito Mussolini, had grabbed power in Italy and turned it into a Fascist state. As the League of Nations stood helplessly by he marched into Abyssinia and annexed the country. The following year he added Albania to his empire.

Hitler was no less active, increasing the size of his army far beyond the agreed limits and taking over the Sudetenland. In Spain General Franco led the Fascists in a bloody conflict with the Communists which ended with the establishment of a new Fascist régime. Each year brought new acts of aggression by the Fascist powers – the march into Austria, the violation of Czechoslovakia – until it was obvious to everyone that a stand had to be made and that the outcome would probably be another world war. Hope for a peaceful settlement flickered briefly when Neville Chamberlain negotiated a pact with Hitler in Munich in 1938, which at least gained for Britain a short breathing space in which to put herself on a more warlike footing.

In April, 1939 the British Government decided to double the strength of the Territorial Army and the order was given to start recruitment at once. The two Territorial battalions of the Border Regiment set to their task with a will. The 4th Battalion were, in fact, the first unit in the whole of Britain to reach the required target and the 5th Battalion were not far behind. At the same time the National Service Act was brought into being which required all young men to carry out six months' training with the Regular Army. Then they could opt whether to join the Regular Army or serve four years with a Territorial unit. The first of the new Militia started to arrive at the depots in July 1939. Less than two months later, at 11 a.m. on the 3rd September, Great Britain and France once more declared war on Germany.

At the outbreak of the 2nd World War the 1st Battalion was still stationed at Aldershot and was immediately mobilised under the command of Lieutenant-Colonel W. H. Chambers, M.C. and formed part of the 4th Brigade in the 2nd Division, which in turn was part of 1st Corps commanded by General Sir John Dill. The 2nd Battalion was in Calcutta under command of Lieutenant-Colonel G. Tarleton, M.C., the 4th and 5th mobilised in their own areas and then moved to an area in Northumberland for training as part of the 42nd Division T.A. The 6th and 7th Battalions were concentrated in the areas of Kendal and West Cumberland respectively where they devoted themselves to training so far as was possible in view of the shortage of arms and equipment. They were part of the 66th Division T.A. which was commanded by Major-General Alan Cunningham, D.S.O., M.C., who afterwards became General Sir Alan Cunningham and who commanded the army in the brilliant campaign which ended in the liberation of Abyssinia. Finally there was the 8th Battalion, later renumbered the 30th, which consisted of old soldiers who were given the role of defending strong points in their area.

The atmosphere which prevailed in the country in the early days of the 1939-45 war was very different from that at the outset of First World War. There was no hysterical patriotism, rather the mood was grim and determined. Memories of the earlier conflict were still fresh and people knew better what to expect. In fact the unexpected happened, or rather the expected did not happen. After the initial excitement of the mobilisation period there began a period of brooding quiet. For several months neither side made any offensive moves. A position of stalemate seemed to prevail which was a welcome respite for those engaged in the training of new recruits for the conflict which was bound to come.

The 1st Battalion, being highly trained, was amongst the first to go to France, landing at Cherbourg on 21st September scarcely three weeks after the outbreak of war. Early in October they were at Orchies employed, like all the other units in the vicinity, in digging defences along the Belgian frontier. On Christmas Day they moved by rail to the Saar where they were one of the first British units to take over part of the French sector in front of the Maginot Line. They remained there for three months before moving to Rumages where they joined the recently arrived 42nd Division. Just over a week later the period of the phoney war came to a sudden end with the simultaneous German invasion of Belgium and Holland.

Anyone who expected, when battle was joined, that it would be a static affair with each side digging in as in 1914, was in for a rude awakening. The German 'Blitzkrieg' methods, however, took by surprise even those whose thinking was a bit more up to date. They moved their armour forward at great speed, ignoring what the text books had to say about extended lines of communication. Soon they were pouring through the Ardennes and across the Meuse. Further north the Belgian defences had failed to hold and on the 15th May news came that Holland had surrendered.

The 1st Battalion had been charged with holding vulnerable points on the Franco-Belgian frontier near Comines. Although they were not in the direct line of attack they were kept busy trying to regulate the streams of refugees pouring out of Belgium, as well as straggling columns of French soldiers. By the morning of the 17th the situation had become grave in the south with the Germans reported as having crossed the Oise and threatening G.H.Q. The 42nd Division was now ordered to cover the crossings of the Scarpe. By the 19th May the

1st Battalion was defending a front three and a half miles long with the other two regiments in reserve. It was a difficult position on the west bank of the Escaut with unbridged canals to the rear which made communications with H.Q. extremely difficult. The Germans attacked this position on the 20th and again the following day and succeeded in infiltrating the areas occupied by B and C Companies. The carrier platoon launched a gallant but unsuccessful counter-attack, the platoon commander, 2nd Lieutenant D. K. Fitzgerald being killed.

On the third day of the fighting the Germans succeeded in crossing the Escaut and the whole Division was forced to withdraw. Now followed a period of extreme difficulty. The roads were jammed with disorganised French troops and their transport which made any movement chaotic with a grave risk of the various companies losing touch with each other. For a short time 1st Border found themselves fighting alongside the 5th Battalion. The Battalion arrived at Loos on the 27th where they heard the news that Belgium had surrendered, leaving the British left flank completely in the air. Now orders came to withdraw to the Dunkirk perimeter, blowing the bridges behind them. By the 29th May most of the Battalion, less H.Q. which had become detached, reached the beaches and were quickly taken off. Battalion H.Q. followed the next day having managed to collect about sixty stragglers who had lost their companies in the confusion. The period of the withdrawal had proved a heavy drain on man-power. Between the 17th and the 30th May the Battalion lost about 250 all ranks, killed, wounded, or taken prisoner. France had fallen.

The embodiment of the Territorial Army had been ordered on the 1st September, 1939 and on that date the 4th Battalion the Border Regiment started to mobilise as part of the 126th Infantry Brigade, which in turn was part of 42nd Division T.A. As has already been mentioned they had been charged a few months earlier with forming a duplicate battalion. This they now cast off to become the 6th Battalion.

For a short month the battalion went to train in Northumberland; then they were withdrawn from the 42nd Division and, together with 4th Battalion the Buffs and 5th Battalion The Sherwood Foresters, they were sent to France. They landed on the 17th November scarcely a month after the 1st Battalion, and thus were one of the very first of the Territorial Army to be sent overseas. They were stationed around Morlaix in Brittany where they resumed training as well as carrying out guard duties on the lines of communication in that area.

When the German invasion started on the 10th May it was realised that they would soon be plunged into a more active role. By the 16th matters had become grave and it was becoming increasingly difficult to get accurate information as to what was happening at the front. The Battalion received orders to proceed to Rouen where they arrived on the 18th – the day the Germans reached Amiens. At Rouen they were joined by No. 5 Reserve Motor Transport Company, R.A.S.C. and became a motorised battalion. In this role they took up positions guarding bridges over the Seine. On the 23rd May they were ordered forward to come under command of the 2nd Armoured Brigade, situated just west of Amiens, and were at once put into the attack with orders to take the three bridges over the Somme at Saveuse, Ailly and Picquigny.

All three attacks met with heavy opposition. A Company attacked Saveuse and captured the village but were unable to reach the bridge. At Ailly C Company succeeded in crossing the bridge but there came under such heavy artillery fire that they were forced to withdraw again. D Company at Picquigny succeeded in clearing out the woods but could get no further and by nightfall they too were forced to retire. Eventually all companies rallied with H.Q. near the main Amiens-Rouen road. There they were given orders to move out to Aumale to protect the right flank of the 51st Highland Division and two armoured brigades who had been cut off from the main B.E.F. during their retreat from the Saar. Communications were virtually non-existent so it was with joy that D Company found a wireless set in a house near Conteville. On it they heard Mr. Churchill deliver his famous 'backs to the wall' speech and learned that the Germans had captured Boulogne and that the rest of the B.E.F. had been evacuated from Dunkirk.

On the 5th June the Battalion were relieved by the 6th East Surreys and ordered to make for the coast at Sept-Meules. On the way they were harassed by enemy aircraft but arrived virtually unscathed, only to learn that the 51st Division's attack on Abbeville had failed and that they were falling back. The Germans were believed to have crossed the River Bresle and to be in the Forest of Eu. The Battalion was ordered to clear the enemy out of the forest to relieve the pressure on the 51st and this was accomplished by D Company, who crossed the river and occupied Beauchamps on the north side. The rest of the Battalion, however, could make no progress and D Company were eventually ordered to withdraw to Incheville which was to be held at all costs. Held at all costs it was. Early in the action some of the wounded were successfully evacuated from the position. After that they held the enemy at bay for six days until they were all either killed or captured. Eric Linklater, in his book *The Highland Division*, described the action of the 4th Battalion:

> When at last the Battalion was ordered to withdraw, one of the companies, surrounded near the river bank, could not be extricated. It remained, and continued to fight. Beyond all hope of relief it went on fighting, and five days later there was still a nest of wrathful, indomitable Englishmen maintaining their cause in the Incheville wood.

The Battalion C.O., Lieutenant-Colonel Tomlinson, was awarded the D.S.O. in recognition of the fine efforts of the whole Battalion.

Now the Battalion withdrew to a line just north of Dieppe, but the position proved untenable and they withdrew further to the coast at Fécamp where they found the Germans already in the outskirts. Some sharp fighting followed. Then they withdrew again. This time half the Battalion were transported successfully to Havre while the other half under Lieutenant-Colonel Tomlinson were attacked and found their route blocked. After a hard fight Lieutenant-Colonel Tomlinson extricated his men, who made their way twenty miles to Havre on foot.

Time was now running out as the German troops surged forward on all sides. Orders were given to move into the docks, destroy their vehicles and embark. As they marched through the empty streets, they were illuminated by burning oil storage tanks while much of the town itself was also on fire. However, the embarkation was carried out in perfect order and the exhausted men lay on the docks to sleep.

It might have been expected that this was an end of their ordeal, but it was not. Their ship put into Cherbourg harbour and they finished up in a château about ten miles inland. The following day half the Battalion, under Captain J. L. Burgess, were ordered to entrain immediately for an unknown destination. The train duly steamed out and, after a night of conjecture as to its destination, the party finally arrived at Brest. From there they embarked in the *Yorktown* and later docked in Southampton. The other half of the Battalion afterwards embarked in a small cargo boat which took them to Poole. Then, after a few days of one half of the Battalion not knowing the whereabouts of the other, they were reunited in Sheffield.

The third battalion of the Border Regiment to be involved in the French fiasco was the 5th. At the outbreak of war, they were in camp at Halton near Lancaster under command of Lieutenant-Colonel H. F. d'A. S. Law, M.C. As was the case with other Territorial Battalions it had doubled in strength in the spring of 1939 but had not yet split into two. This now had to be accomplished in a hurry, an operation which was made the more difficult because many of them had been sent off immediately war had broken out to guard strong points in the district. Within a few days, however, the reorganisation was accomplished and two separate Battalions, the 5th and the 7th, came into being. The latter remained at Halton whilst the 5th joined the 42nd Division and concentrated in the Wooler area in Northumberland.

The training programme of the 5th Battalion was beset with difficulties. In the first place practically no transport was available. What there was had to be hired locally and was in such poor mechanical condition that two-thirds of it were almost permanently off the road. The water supply also presented problems. The only water available was from a nearby pond from which it had to be pumped daily into an improvised water truck and delivered to the companies. On top of it all came the coldest winter that anyone had known for many years. Thick snow restricted training and the treacherous conditions of the roads made the transport position even more acute.

On the 15th January the Battalion moved south to Swindon, where they commenced to mobilise for overseas service. They also underwent a strenuous course on co-operation with tanks which culminated in the Battalion giving a demonstration with the 7th Tanks to the three divisions in the area. This was followed by a course in trench warfare and, at the end of March, all units were given forty-eight hours embarkation leave. They embarked at Southampton on the 17th April and the following day landed at Havre.

Their first duties were in the Lille area where they were required to construct defences along the Franco-Belgian border. Whilst carrying out this duty they unearthed many old pill-boxes which had been constructed during the 1914-18 war and incorporated them into the general scheme of defence.

The Battalion were not left long in peace. On 10th May, as has already been recorded, the Germans started their invasion of Holland, Belgium and Luxembourg. At first the plan was for the 42nd Division to remain static until the situation had developed considerably further. The speed of the attack was such, however, that on May 16th the 126th Brigade, which included the 5th Battalion, was ordered forward to straddle the Escaut and hold the line against the enemy who had broken through at Arras. The march to Tournai, on an exceedingly hot day, proved something of a nightmare. The roads were packed with refugees of every sort who poured through in a never-ending stream. Every form of transport from cars to farm carts had been pressed into service and so great were the numbers that control by the civil authorities was virtually impossible.

In Tournai itself conditions were even more chaotic. In addition to the thousands of refugees, the town was being heavily bombed and blazing fiercely. The 1st and 2nd Corps were falling back and the task of the 125th Brigade was to keep the lines of communication as clear as possible and to be responsible for blowing the bridges as soon as withdrawal over the Escaut had been completed. It proved a difficult responsibility as the stream of refugees increased. Realising that he would only receive the shortest notice to blow the bridges Lieutenant-Colonel Law, commanding the 5th Battalion, ordered both the forward companies to load up all their transport and, with the exception of one 15 cwt and one 8 cwt truck, sent everything back to the west side of the river. In fact the notice received was only one hour. By going forward himself to contact his companies the C.O. managed to have the bridges blown within the allotted time.

There now followed a period of confused withdrawal with very little information being available as to what was happening elsewhere. The Battalion first fell back to Cysoing where they spent three days under almost constant shell fire. Meantime the enemy had by-passed Cambrai and had taken Amiens, Abbeville, Boulogne and Calais in quick succession, thus severing the lines of communication with the B.E.F.

On the night of the 26th May the 5th Battalion were ordered to retreat further and to hold the line at Lesquins. Within a few hours, however, orders came for a further withdrawal to Bizet just north of Armentières. Here they were joined by some eighty other ranks of the 1st Battalion who had become detached from their main body. Two days later they moved again, this time to Mousbrugge-Harringhe, where they dug in. At nightfall firing was heard from their right rear and there was some further fear that they might be cut off. At 10 p.m., however, a motor-cyclist got through with orders that they were to withdraw to the perimeter of Dunkirk. They were also ordered to immobilise all their transport and leave behind any kit which could not be carried.

By 8 a.m. the following morning the final withdrawal had been accomplished along roads littered with discarded guns, equipment and stores, and a defensive position was taken up along the line of the Canal des Chats. From there that evening a detachment of men not urgently required to man the defences was sent down to the beaches and the next night the rest of the Battalion followed. A rearguard under Major H. T. Thompson remained all the following day, dug in and under heavy bombing, but fortunately suffered few casualties. They finally embarked at 11 p.m. that night and, early on the 3rd June, set sail for England – one of the last parties to leave the beaches. Eventually the whole Battalion was re-united at Spennymoor, Co. Durham. The war had not got off to a good start.

CHAPTER XIII

Aᴏᴛᴇʀ ᴛʜᴇ debacle in France the whole nation, as it were, tightened its belt. With the long period of inactivity after the declaration of war had come a feeling of growing security, a feeling that Hitler had bitten off more than he could chew. Now everybody knew different. With the invasion of Britain imminent, vigilance on the beaches redoubled and training was entered into with greater enthusiasm whilst in the factories every nerve was strained in an effort to supply much needed arms and ammunition as quickly as possible. For a time the only weapons available to the Home Guard were pikes. It was a measure of the determination of the country to fight to the last ditch.

By the beginning of 1941 there were eight battalions of the Border Regiment in Britain, including the recently formed 30th Battalion. Only the 2nd Battalion were abroad in India.

After their return from France the 1st Battalion went first for a short time to Welwyn Garden City and then moved to Crickhowell in Wales where, in addition to an anti-parachutist operational role, they became involved in a strenuous training programme which involved the use of mules and horses. Whatever secret role the powers that be had for the Battalion was so secret that even they themselves did not know about it. Nevertheless for a year and a half they struggled up and down hills and across country with their recalcitrant charges with great enthusiasm. Then, quite suddenly the mules were taken away and they were told that they were amongst the first to be selected to train as airborne troops.

The 4th Battalion were also given an anti-parachute role after being made up to strength from the Infantry Training Centre in Carlisle. They, too, were stationed in Wales but in the south while the 1st Battalion were in the north. In spite of a lamentable shortage of vehicles and equipment, they were also involved in a heavy training programme with the rest of their Brigade, the 25th, which included the 4th Buffs and the 2nd Essex. Their training was punctuated by several false alarms that they were again to be sent on active service until, on the 19th March, 1941, they finally entrained for Avonmouth. There they embarked on H.M.T. *Orontes* and made the long journey via the Cape for Egypt.

The 5th Battalion, after their return from France, were reunited at Spennymoor in Co. Durham. In the months which followed they underwent several moves. First they went to Northallerton where they were made up to strength by a draft of 250 Seaforth Highlanders. Then they moved for a time to Gloucestershire and later to Henley-on-Thames. In December their whole Division was sent to Beccles and Lowestoft to take over beach defences, and in the second half of May the following year they went into camp in Colchester for weapon training. Finally, they moved to Shrubland Park near Ipswich to carry out guard duties on aerodromes and to build defences.

It was while the Battalion was at Shrubland Park that the decision was made to convert the 42nd Division to armour. It was news which was enthusiastically received by all ranks. After a period at Barnard Castle, the Battalion moved to Skipton where, in November, the 5th Battalion the Border Regiment was redesignated the 110th Regiment R.A.C. (Border Regiment). At first they were issued with Covenanter tanks, and were just becoming accustomed to them when they were withdrawn from the 42nd Division and the 126th Brigade became the 11th Independent Tank Brigade equipped with Churchills. This was not so well received as it indicated that they would not be called upon early for overseas service. The depression was further intensified when two months later the brigade was ordered to supply overseas drafts and it became obvious that there was little prospect of their going overseas as a unit. In January, 1943 the future of the brigade became clearer when they were transferred to the 77th Reserve Division at Catterick. For many it must have spelt the end of any hope of active service. The blow fell in November when the news was received that they were to be disbanded. It was a sad end to a battalion with a fine territorial record, but one which had to be accepted.

The 6th Battalion, as has already been recounted, was born out of the 4th Battalion. When the split came one battalion became known as the 4th (Westmorland) Battalion and the other as the 6th (East Cumberland) Battalion. The 6th was commanded by

Lieutenant-Colonel Sir Fergus Graham, Bt., and formed part of the 198th Brigade of the 66th (Lancs and Border) Division.

As was the case with other Battalions which came into being at the beginning of the war the amount of equipment and transport was minimal. In fact, in its early days the 6th Battalion had only one 15-cwt. truck and very few rifles. To begin with they were billeted in their own homes and reported each day to the nearest drill hall for training. Their progress was further handicapped by the demands made on them for drafts to other units. When the 4th Battalion went to France they took with them over a hundred men of the 6th Battalion whilst smaller parties were sent all over the country.

In April 1940 the 66th Division moved to the Malton area of Yorkshire, the 198th Brigade consisting of the 6th and 7th Battalions The Border Regiment and the 8th Battalion The King's Regiment. It was hoped that now they would be able to concentrate on training although their equipment was still primitive. Shortly after platoon and Company training had started, however, there came the disaster of Dunkirk which at once put a different complexion on matters. As far as the 6th Battalion was concerned this meant taking anti-parachute measures which involved standing to every night between 10 and 11 o'clock and again from 3.30 to 4.30 in the morning. There was also an inlying picquet standing by to be rushed to any threatened area in assorted furniture vans. General Shears in his book on the Border Regiment during the 1939-45 war gives a good idea of the situation in the following passage:

> From time immemorial the British Army has trained with impro-vised weapons and equipment, and in the end made a success of things. The 6th Battalion was no exception to the rule. Early in June the first Brigade scheme was held.The general idea was that the Brigade was to move as a flying column to intercept paratroops who had landed twenty miles north of Hull. One company of the 6th Battalion formed the rear guard. Some eighteen-pounders drawn by red coal lorries, to which they were attached by ropes, moved in rear of the column, protected by a platoon of D Company in a bright red omnibus, built in 1923, and the sole carrier the Battalion possessed, commanded by 2nd Lieutenant G. Carruthers.

There followed several moves and a variety of tactical roles until the Brigade, having been withdrawn from the 66th Division, was

sent first on embarkation leave and then found their role changed
once again. This time they were employed on beach defence and
were allotted the stretch of coast from Hythe to Ramsgate. They
were at first accommodated in the peace-time training camp of the
Buffs but the C.O., Lieutenant-Colonel Warren, considered the white
building and paths too obvious a target and insisted on moving to a
less distinctive site. The day after they moved out a lone German
plane dropped four bombs on their old camp. Weapons were still in
deplorably short supply and the existing defences of the coast
extremely scanty. There followed a period of industrious trench digging, interrupted by periodical parachute landing scares to relieve
the monotony.

With the coming of summer, enemy air activity was considerably
stepped up and one of their chief targets was Manston Aerodrome,
soon to gain the reputation of being the most bombed in Britain,
which was guarded by A Company whose Bren gunners were constantly in action. One of them, Private Lister, when he was severely
hit by a cannon shell went on firing his gun. He later had his leg
amputated and was awarded the Military Medal, one of the few
people to receive the award for an action which took place on English
soil.

The Germans not only bombed the aerodrome frequently but often
returned afterwards to machine-gun the repair parties from the Battalion whose job it was to fill in the craters on the runway, making it
altogether a very hazardous situation. As the Battle of Britain
became more and more intense, the Battalion was almost constantly
in action in one way or another. If they were not attempting to shoot
the Germans out of the sky, they were engaged on the less popular
work of guarding the wreckage of planes which had come down in
their area. This eventually became a very onerous duty, each 'plane
requiring a guard of an N.C.O. and six men until it was collected
by the R.A.F. which often took several days. On one day when
180 German 'planes were shot down, no less than five crashed in the
Battalion area within half an hour.

In the midst of all this activity was the constant tactical role of
guarding the beaches. The most secret word in Britain at that time
was 'Cromwell'. The receipt of this code word meant that the German
invasion had started and everyone must rush to action stations. Early
in September of that year the C.O. of the Battalion who had an over-

25 & 26.   Day and night uniforms, Palestine, winter 1937-38.

27.   Boy drummers of 1st Border (1931) – dressed in uniforms of 1811
with the Arroyo Drums.

28.   Recruiting 1940.

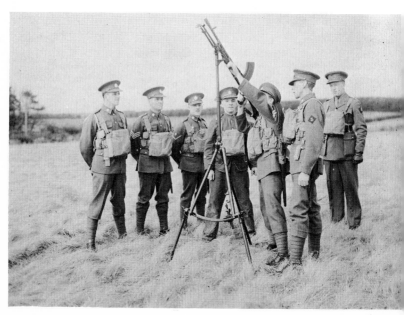

29.   Learning to use the Bren for Ack-Ack defence.

all command of the area received the dreaded word. At once he rushed across to the billet of the officer commanding the air station. Bursting in at his door he shouted 'Cromwell!' 'Good show,' replied the Air Force officer, turning over in bed, 'I'm Boadicea!' Nonetheless the whole battalion, in common with all troops throughout the country, spent the whole night standing to. It proved, however, to be a false alarm. It was not until after the war that the Prime Minister, Mr. Attlee, explained that the British Chiefs of Staff had been misled by reports of unusual shipping activity between Ostend and Havre and by information gained from four captured spies.

In the middle of November the Battalion were relieved of their guard duties and moved to Ashford in Kent. Shortly afterwards they ceased to be an independent brigade and replaced the 161st Brigade in the 54th (East Anglia) Division. Just before Christmas they moved to Haltwhistle in Northumberland which proved popular with the men, many of whom found themselves only a few miles from their homes. At last equipment was beginning to be in plentiful supply and training could be undertaken with more realism. It was altogether a happy time for the Battalion and it was with great regret that they once again left the hospitable north, to be stationed first in the Cotswolds and then, early in August, scattered in billets in the town of Watford, in the north of London. They took part in the giant 'Exercise Bumper', and spirits were high with the knowledge that, as a trained Battalion, they could hope soon to be sent overseas.

It was not to be. Instead, the division was sent to relieve the 15th (Scottish) Division on the Suffolk coast and immediately became subject to demands for drafts to reinforce battalions who were suffering heavy losses in the North African campaign. It was a bitter blow, for it now seemed certain that they were not destined to fight together as a unit. This drafting, which lasted all through 1942 and into the early months of 1943, proved a sore trial to morale. It was only when the drafting ceased and the numbers were again being made up to strength that there was renewed hope that they would finally see action as an operation unit.

In August, 1943, the C.O., Lieutenant-Colonel Cooper and certain selected personnel were sent on a training course in Scotland to learn about Beach Groups, and shortly afterwards the battalion were sent to Gailes Camp in Ayrshire to train in their new role.

The Beach Groups which came into being in preparation for the

Second Front were composed of units or sub-units from every group in the Army, with Navy and R.A.F. representation. Their task was to land with the assault troops, organise the beaches and establish dumps for supplies and reinforcements. The whole group would be under command of the C.O. of the infantry battalion.

Once training started, it moved fast. They were particularly fortunate when, after being in some bad billets, they took over Ayr Race Course. Here they were able to establish a central officers' mess which enabled the members of all the various forces to get to know each other – a very important consideration. Several elaborate exercises followed culminating, in February, 1944, with one at Gullane near Edinburgh which lasted for eight days. Later there was a divisional parade and General Eisenhower carried out an inspection. Now all ranks knew that the long awaited day was at hand.

On D-Day all the Beach Groups got ashore exactly as planned. Enemy resistance was at first stiff but by the second day everything was running smoothly, with the Groups carrying out the tasks for which they had trained so hard. This continued for six or seven weeks while the main question under discussion was what would be the future of the beach battalions after their formations were broken up. There was still hope that they would become combatant units in the main advance.

The answer came on Sunday, 16th July in a personal letter from Field-Marshal Montgomery to Colonel Cooper:

> By the end of this month we shall be running short of infantry reinforcements, and there are not sufficient in sight for some time to come. At the same time the battle will have reached a crucial phase during which it will be essential to keep the battalions in the divisions up to strength.
>
> No one is more fully aware than I of the magnitude of the contribution made by you, and the officers and men under your command, to the success of this operation, or of the outstanding efforts which you and they have made during training. It is therefore with the very greatest regret that I have to decide that, when the time comes, drafts shall have to be taken from the battalion under your command to make good deficiencies in divisional units.
>
> I have given orders that, in carrying out this drafting, every regard possible in the circumstances shall be paid to regimental affiliations, and that where possible officers and men will be posted together in units in parties approximating to a platoon in size. In effecting this you will be consulted.

Please convey to all your officers and men my thanks for their splendid work which they performed during the assault and in the days which followed, and my regret at the necessity for having to draft so many from your battalion.

So the drafting started once more and it could only lead to one conclusion. On 5th August, heavy drafts having been sent to more than half a dozen fighting battalions, orders came for disbandment. The epitaph of the 6th Battalion is perhaps best expressed in a letter from Major-General C. M. Barber, C.B., D.S.O., commanding the 15th (Scottish) Division, to the Colonel of the Regiment. Writing in April, 1946, he said:

Now that my old division, the 15th Scottish, is practically disbanded, I would like you to know how well the many reinforcements of your Regiment did.

As you will remember, when the 6th Battalion was disbanded after its work on the beaches in August 1944, practically the whole battalion came to the 15th Division as reinforcements; twenty-five officers and over 550 men. Right up to our own disbandment we have had some of the 6th Border men in every one of our nine battalions.

Twelve of the twenty-five officers were wounded and the other rank casualties ran into three figures. Your honours were one M.C., one M.B.E., two Military Medals and over six Mentions.

It may be easier for Border men to join Scottish regiments than for others, but I know that all my old C.O.'s, will testify to the way the ex-Border men accepted loyalty to their new regiments.

Beyond the officers and men of your 6th Battalion, we also received some six officers and 200 men of other Border battalions so that we had almost a complete battalion of yours serving with us.

It is probable that the 6th Battalion cannot write a corporate battle history of its own, and I certainly hope in our Divisional History to make some mention of all your men did for us.

The 7th Battalion, as has already been stated, grew out of the 5th Battalion and, when the two battalions became separate entities, the 7th stayed at Halton while the 5th Battalion moved to Northumberland.

The 7th Battalion became part of the 198th Brigade together with 6th Battalion The Border Regiment and 8th Battalion the King's Regiment. Thus, until the end of 1942, their history is much the same as that of the 6th Battalion which has already been told. There were the same frustrations over lack of equipment, the same training difficulties and the same disappointments over the practice of drafting from the Battalion.

In September, 1942 the Battalion was selected to arrange and take part in a demonstration on the Orford Battle Area entitled *The breaching of a highly organised defensive position including Minefields and Obstacles*. It was a great success and showed the Battalion to be up to a high standard of fitness and training. They had been made up to strength after the drafting and it was hoped that they would now be sent overseas. At the end of the year, however, hopes were extinguished when the Battalion was withdrawn from the 198th Brigade and transferred to the 22nd Brigade of the 76th Reserve Division.

The role of their new division, the 76th, was to give corps training to new recruits and for this purpose they spent most of 1943 at Hopton near Great Yarmouth. In November the 222nd Brigade was disbanded and the 7th Battalion were transferred to the 220th Brigade to carry on the the same task. As has been described earlier the 5th Battalion were disbanded at the end of 1943. Now, in April, 1944, the 7th Battalion became the 5th. It was as the 5th Battalion that they undertook further training duties. One of their tasks was to train all the specialists, signallers, anti-tank gunners, mortar and carrier teams, for the 38th Division. They were then stationed at Dalton-in-Furness near their home counties and many visits were made to Cumberland and Westmorland to 'show the flag'. The Border Regiment have always been well known for the high standard of their drummers and the 7th Battalion had an exceptionally good corps under Sergeant Drummer Cooker. They played in various towns and in the home counties and took part in the ceremony of the presentation of the Freedom of the City of Carlisle to the Regiment.

When the end of the war came they were declared redundant and put into suspended animation pending the re-establishment of the Territorial Army. Although they had seen no active service they could be proud of a tedious job well done, and of the fact that members of the original Battalion and men they had trained had acquitted themselves well in almost every theatre of war.

During the summer of 1939 instructions were issued to the Territorial Army Association to enrol old soldiers over the age of 45 to form a National Defence Corps. Group 100 of National Defence companies consisted of one company drawn from Westmorland, one from Cumberland and three from Lancashire. Their task was to guard vulnerable points and, after the outbreak of war, this became a most onerous duty. Group Headquarters was at Kendal and the surrounding points to be guarded consisted of Vickers Armstrong's Works, the Docks and a petrol depot, two aerodromes and an ammunition depot. It necessitated the men being on guard duty for two hours, with four hours off, under conditions of great hardship. During the exceptionally hard winter there were no greatcoats and the accommodation available was of a very poor standard. All ranks, however, set a fine example of cheerfulness and devotion to duty and there was surprisingly little sickness.

In December 1939, 100 Group was reorganised into a battalion which at first it was intended should be part of the King's Own Royal Regiment. It was later decided, however, as most of the old soldiers were from the Border Regiment that the unit should be known as the 8th (H.D.) Battalion the Border Regiment. In June, 1940 the strength of the Battalion was greatly increased, there being ten companies in all. New recruits were found amongst seventeen-year old volunteers.

The guard at Jarrow, in particular, came in for a bad time with frequent bombing raids to contend with. Fortunately they suffered no casualties. Later, three young soldier companies were withdrawn and formed the nucleus of the 70th (Young Soldiers) Battalion the Border Regiment. In December, 1941 the 8th Battalion was renumbered the 30th (H.D.) Battalion the Border Regiment. In March 1942 the role of the Battalion changed and it became a field unit at the disposal of the District Commander, with a counter-attack role. They were brought up to scale with weapons and transport and carried out their training from Aspatria, Wigtown and Hadrian's Camp. By June, 1942 they were concentrated at Greystoke Castle, sending their lower medical grade officers and men to the 30th Battalion the Manchester Regiment and receiving a smaller number of A1 personnel in return.

By September, the authorities decided to reduce the number of infantry battalions, and the 30th Border was one of those selected for disbandment. It was distressing coming so soon after their appointment as a field unit, but perhaps inevitable in the circumstances. Disbandment took place at Ulverston from where personnel were transferred to a number of other units to carry on useful work until the end of the war.

The 9th Battalion came into being at Workington on the 9th October, 1940. It was created out of what had been a 'holding battalion' – that is to say a battalion of trained men waiting to be sent as reinforcements to their units. It was brought up to strength with drafts from the I.T.C. at Carlisle and consisted largely of men of the 23-27 age groups. The first commanding officer was Lieutenant-Colonel T. W. MacDonald, D.S.O., who had previously commanded both the 5th and the 7th Battalions of the Regiment.

The Battalion was made part of the 225th Infantry Brigade and remained in training with Western Command until February, 1941. Then a general reorganisation took place by which twelve special divisions became known as 'County Divisions', each being named after a county and being responsible for coast defence. Under this arrangement the 9th Battalion became part of the Northumberland County Division and took up the defence of a sector of beach from just south of Berwick to Bamburgh. They carried out the duties which had become familiar to other battalions of the Regiment – the construction of defences and the constant patrolling of the beaches.

The tedium of this static role was broken by a training period from April to September during which they took part in large scale exercises designed to fit them for war. Then a further reorganisation caused another change in plan. It had long been felt that the army required more armoured battalions and the only way to get them was to convert infantry battalions from the County Divisions. Every battalion in the Northumberland County Division was scheduled for conversion with the exception of 9th Border and the 9th Gordon Highlanders. They were both earmarked for service in India.

There followed a further period of coast defence while the 15th Scottish Division took over from the Northumberland County Division, which had broken up. Then, on the 28th February, 1942 mobilisation was ordered and their role at home came to an end. On the 28th May the Battalion entrained for Glasgow and there embarked on H.M.T. *Orcades*, which sailed two days later with a heavily escorted convoy.

CHAPTER XIV

W E NOW TAKE up the story of the 1st Battalion, whom we left rather bewildered in early 1942 at their sudden change of role from training with mules to being airborne troops.

The metamorphosis was not, as might be expected, greeted with universal enthusiasm. There were some, particularly amongst the longer service N.C.O.s, who felt that it was too late for them to change their spots. There were also some soldiers who were obviously unsuited to the new role. So there began a period of pruning and reinforcement. In all some forty per cent of the Battalion either dropped out or were discarded. Reinforcements were sought in the first place from other battalions of the Regiment, who were justly incensed at having large numbers of their best men arbitrarily transferred to the 1st.

While the first orders for gliders were being placed in September 1942, their enthusiasm and *espirit de corps* started to grow. The issue of their distinctive red berets did much to boost morale so that when training in the unknown art of gliding commenced everyone was as keen as mustard—a keenness which did not deteriorate when an unfortunate accident killed three of the earliest experimenters. At first it was all a matter of trial and error as tactics were worked out and proper equipment began, bit by bit, to arrive. The pilots were also getting their training at the same time so that they were all in the same boat together.

It was not until the spring of 1943 that the 1st Air Landing Brigade could be said to be ready for action, and even then they required making up to strength with such auxiliary services as engineers, signallers and medical staff. However the need was pressing and the Brigade embarked for Africa in May, landing at Oran in June. The 1st Parachute Brigade had gone ahead of them and had been in time to play an important part in the great victory gained by the 1st and 6th Armies in Tunisia. It was an encouraging start.

Immediately after their arrival the 1st Battalion moved to Mascara and at once set about preparing for a landing in Sicily. At once difficulties began to appear, not the least of them being the shortage of aircraft. This was overcome by a generous gesture from the Americans, who loaned a large number of Dakotas and Waco gliders. Unfortunately, the Brigade had been trained in a different sort of glider, the Horsa, which carried thirty-two men as opposed to the eighteen carried by the Waco. This caused organisational difficulties which were aggravated further by the fact that the Waco could not carry both a jeep and an anti-tank gun, as the Horsa could. Added to this most of the British pilots had never flown a Waco.

For these very sound reasons it was decided that it was imperative to get a few more Horsas from Britain, but how? They were most uneconomical, in terms of space, to ship and shipping space was at a premium. The difficulty was overcome by two R.A.F. officers who experimented by towing Horsas behind Halifax aircraft round Britain and proved that they could just make the necessary 1,400 miles without running out of fuel. Accordingly, the operation was undertaken and successfully carried out. They flew them to Sousse over, or rather through, the Atlas mountains as they could not get the necessary height. The aircraft arrived in North Africa a few days before they were due to go into action.

On the night of 9th/10th July an airborne attack on Sicily got underway. There were 137 gliders employed on the operation, though all the new Horsas were allotted to the South Staffordshire Regiment. The main point of the attack was to secure the Ponte Grande, a vital bridge near Syracuse, so as to assist the task of the seaborne troops, with a secondary role of creating a diversion by attacking the western outskirts of the city.

The whole essence of the attack was surprise. The towing aircraft were not to approach nearer than 3,000 yards from the coast and were to release their gliders between 21.10 hours and 22.30 hours. To avoid being picked up by radio locaters they flew an extremely devious route close to the waves. Their task was made infinitely more difficult by a gale which sprang up and at times reached a force of 45 m.p.h. This drove many of the combinations off course. One glider was released off Malta and, thinking they had arrived in Sicily, leaped out of their craft and took up battle stations. It was with the greatest chagrin that they discovered they had landed on the wrong island!

Fortunately for the rest the wind moderated to 30 m.p.h., which enabled the rest of the aircraft to reach their destination but, here, for one reason or another, more troubles occurred. The offshore wind, the intense darkness of the night, made even darker by the thick dust clouds stirred up by the wind, and the inexperience of the pilots were all contributory factors in causing many of the gliders to be parted too early from their tugs. The result was that over sixty per cent landed in the sea.

This was a bitter blow, coming as it did after long months of training and careful planning. Both the C.O.'s glider and that of his second-in-command were dumped in the water, but Lieutenant-Colonel Britten and Major T. Haddon managed to swim ashore with their crews. Others were not so lucky, landing much further out. Non-swimmers were in a particularly dangerous situation. They clung to the wings and were later, fortunately, picked up by invasion craft. An example of the fine discipline maintained by these men is demonstrated by the action of C.S.M. Pope. When about to be picked up by a landing craft he and his crew were standing on the wings of their glider in about four feet of water. Nonetheless, he saluted the officer commanding the craft smartly and reported his men present and correct before being taken aboard.

The Adjutant of the Battalion also found himself in an awkward situation. He had wrapped round his body the Union Jack which he intended to hoist when they made their landing. Thus encumbered he was unable to swim and so unwrapped the flag. The last that was seen of it was as it floated away out to sea.

Out of the whole Brigade only about thirty men managed to reach the objective of Ponte Grande. This party, commanded by Lieutenant Welch of the 1st Battalion, at once set about removing the demolition charges and gallantly defended the bridge throughout the night while other small parties started to straggle in. Apart from their small arms their only weapons were one 3-inch mortar, one 2-inch mortar and four Bren guns. By 3 p.m. the following day, as a result of heavy shelling, only about fifteen of the party remained unwounded and, their ammunition being exhausted, the position was overrun. Lieutenant Welch and seven men managed to avoid the enemy and soon afterwards met patrols of the 17th Infantry Brigade. A counter-attack was organised and the bridge re-taken intact. Thus the main objective was achieved in spite of all the difficulties. Later General Montgomery was to send this message to the Brigade: 'For those responsible for this particular operation, I am filled with admiration. Had it not been for the skill and gallantry of the Air Landing Brigade, the port of Syracuse would not have fallen until very much later.' All, therefore, had not been in vain.

Later the 1st Battalion, having collected as many men as possible, formed up and marched into Syracuse a hundred and fifty strong. Others managed to join up with the main body, but the casualties amounted to about two hundred and fifty all ranks. A week later they were withdrawn to North Africa and, almost at once, preparations began for the next operation.

By August Italy began to show signs of giving in and the Air Landing Brigade was given orders to prepare for a seaborne landing in Italy. They arrived too late, landing after the Italian capitulation, at Taranto where they joined with an armoured brigade and a regiment of artillery and formed the infantry base of the mobile party. With the 1st Battalion in the lead they pressed on northwards and were the first British troops to enter Foggia.

The Italian campaign was almost at an end but, just before the 1st Battalion were relieved and sent back to North Africa, there is a nice gesture to record. A former officer of the Regiment, Brigadier Darwell, sent a gift of his hunting horn to the Commanding Officer (now Lieutenant-Colonel Haddon vice Lieutenant-Colonel Britten) for the purpose of rallying his troops in battle. Sadly, the Brigadier died on the day his gift arrived with the battalion. The Division returned to England in 1943.

The High Command was now more than ever convinced that the projected operations in Europe could not be undertaken without the help of airborne troops. Steps were taken to increase the strength of the Air Landing Troops by the addition of another division and the bringing up to strength of the 1st Division by the inclusion of the 7th Battalion King's Own Scottish Borderers. The new Corps was commanded by Lieutenant-General F. A. M. Browning. Later, in March, 1944, the force was increased to an Army by the addition of an American Corps, the whole being under the command of General Brereton.

Morale was now at a high pitch and the men of the Battalion

were all on tiptoe to take part in further operations. It was a bitter disappointment when D-Day in Europe came and went without their being allotted a role.

Shortly after D-Day, the 1st Airborne Division moved to the Andover area and held itself in readiness to co-operate with the ground forces now advancing through France. There were no less than sixteen occasions when airborne operations were planned, but all of them were cancelled at the eleventh hour. The main reason for these cancellations was that the ground troops had advanced faster than had been anticipated so that no great advantage could be gained by putting airborne troops onto an objective whose capture was anyway imminent. In the end, however, it was the very speediness of the advance which gave the airborne troops their opportunity.

By the middle of September, 1944 the British Second Army had already penetrated into Holland but was still being supplied from the artificial landing port of Arromanches —a distance of some two hundred and fifty miles. This put such a strain on the supply transport that one corps had to be completely frozen and all available vehicles used to supply the leading troops. With lines of communication becoming ever more stretched the whole advance was brought to a standstill.

Two courses were now open to Field-Marshal Montgomery. He could either remain where he was until the supply position was improved and so allow the Germans to reorganise and consolidate their defences, or he could by some means continue the forward surge and turn the end of the Siegfried Line, thus taking advantage of the chaos into which the enemy had been thrown by the rapid advance He had the means of maintaing the impetus to hand – the airborne troops – and he decided to use them.

The main defensive position of the Germans where the Siegfried Line ended in the Reichswald Forest was a high ridge of ground from which an extended view could be obtained on all sides and which was protected along the western and southern sides of the rivers Waal and Maas. Montgomery's plan was to give the Airborne Divisions the task of securing the bridges in this area and of forming a corridor down which the ground troops could race through the last defences before the Rhine itself. The vital areas were pinpointed as Nijmegen and Arnhem. The tasks given to the three divisions under his command were for the 101st American Division to create a corridor from Eindhoven to just south of Graves, for the 81st American Division to make it secure from Graves to Nijmegen and for the 1st British Airborne Division to capture the road bridge over the Lower Rhine at Arnhem.

Now came the usual technical difficulties. There were not sufficient aircraft to transport all three divisions in one lift. Moreover, the aircraft which were available were not entirely suitable for the task. The Dakotas were slow and unarmed and not fitted with self-sealing petrol tanks. The Stirlings and Halifaxes were not designed to fly at low levels in daylight (it was to be entirely a daylight operation) over territory which was known to be heavily protected by anti-aircraft guns. It was also known that, assuming the landing could be carried out successfully, the airborne troops could not remain self-sufficient for more than two days and could not hope to survive without the prompt arrival of heavy artillery and tanks – and this could not be achieved unless all three of the main bridges were in our hands.

On the other hand the prospect which success held out was that the war would be over by Christmas; it was therefore decided that the calculated risks must be taken.

The day chosen for the launching of this hazardous operation was Sunday, 17th September. Because of the shortage of aircraft the plan for the Arnhem operation was for a first wave, consisting of 1st Parachute Brigade and 1st Air Landing Brigade (less half of the South Staffords), to lead the way, followed the next day by the rest of the Division. The first wave, which included 1st Battalion the Border Regiment, emplaned at 9 a.m., and the greatest airborne operation ever conceived was underway. Few of the hundreds of thousands in the south of England who saw this vast airborne armada pass over their heads that fine Sunday morning will ever forget the sight. In addition to the gliders and their towing aircraft there was fantastically strong fighter support in the ratio of two fighters to every glider, so that the sky was filled with aircraft as far as the eye could see all making their purposeful way to the very heart of the enemy defences.

As for the troops themselves, there was not a man who would willingly have given up his place in the great enterprise. Some of the officers had voluntarily dropped a rank in order to take part. They knew they were in for at least two days of bitter fighting. Now they were to be once again in the thick of things and their only anxiety was to get there – and here must be recorded one of the saddest hard-luck stories of the war.

Shortly after the glider containing the C.O. of the Battalion, Lieutenant-Colonel Haddon, had taken off, it broke its tow-rope over Oxford and had to make a forced landing. Fortunately no one was hurt. They returned to Andover and the following day set off again with the second lift. This time the tug-aircraft was destroyed by anti-aircraft fire over Antwerp and one wing of the glider was shot off. They crash-landed and again no-one was hurt. Colonel Haddon, whose only thought was to reach his Battalion, crossed the Rhine with a battalion of the Dorsets and when they were held up, made his own way forward alone through enemy lines. After a perilous journey he finally managed to reach Oosterbeek only a few hours before they were due to be evacuated. He was then, by the greatest of ill-fortune, made a prisoner while still trying to find the shrunken perimeter of the remnants of the Division.

To return to the battle. Ahead of the main force was the 21st Independent Parachute Company who were to act as a marker force and this task was perfectly carried out. Behind them came the Parachute Brigade and the gliders and they too made an almost perfect landing, ninety-five per cent of the troops reaching their rendezvous at the right place and the right time. Then the parachute battalions set out on their task of seizing the bridge at Arnhem, while the Border Regiment and the K.O.S.B. moved to take up their positions to cover the landing grounds. This they did successfully, the Germans being taken completely by surprise by the suddenness of the attack. Although the parachute battalions were involved in some heavy fighting all remained quiet in the Battalion's area for the rest of the day.

The landing of the second wave was due to take place early the following morning but it was delayed by mist in England and they did not arrive until between 3 and 4 p.m. – an unfortunate delay for it allowed the Germans time to bring up reinforcements and largely wiped out the element of surprise which had been gained. Nonetheless, the defence of the landing ground was successful and the second wave landed without any difficulty. By now, however, the position at the bridge had become serious. The northern end of the bridge had been taken but all our efforts could not dislodge the enemy from the southern end. Moreover, the opposition had stiffened to such an extent that the 1st and 3rd Battalions of the Parachute Brigade could not get through to reinforce their 2nd Battalion, who were the forward troops. Accordingly the Divisional Commander, Major-General Urquhart sent part of the second wave to assist in the operation. The opposition, however, was hourly growing stronger and the attempt to reach the bridge again failed. Eventually the relieving troops had to be withdrawn with heavy losses and take refuge in the woods to the west of the position. In the meantime the 4th Parachute Brigade, whose task had been to hold the northern perimeter of the approaches to Arnhem, had failed to gain their objective and had been reduced to an overall strength of two hundred and fifty all ranks. The Border Regiment and the King's Own Scottish Borderers succeeded in reaching approximately the positions originally chosen for them but they too became involved in heavy fighting and suffered many casualties. By the end of the third day there was no sign of relief by the Second Army, now twenty-four hours overdue, and it was obvious that the object of the operation was now impossible of achievement.

It was under these circumstances that Major-General Urquhart was forced to take the decision to abandon all the troops at the north end of the bridge and form a perimeter round the suburb of Oosterbeek, where he would try to hold out with the remainder of his sorely-depleted force until such time as the Second Army should arrive. Now it became a matter of grim endurance as they fought on day after day against enormous odds. Their weapons were pitifully inadequate against the giant Tiger tanks and the powerful self-propelled guns of the Germans, yet they continued to attack them, often with nothing more than PIATS and Gammon bombs. Food and ammunition ran desperately short until there was scarcely any of either left. With little or no sleep they fought on for eight days and nine nights, where the maximum time it had been considered they could last without reinforcements had been two days. Then, on Monday, 25th September the order came to retire and it was carried out that night. At the end water was almost exhausted and food completely so, whilst many of the houses in which they sought refuge had been set on fire by phosphorous bombs.

The only route open for evacuation was across the fast-running Lower Rhine. B and H.Q. Companies of 1st Border led the way, taking with them all the walking wounded, while A and C Companies held off the enemy. Major Breese commanded the rear party, and collected all the remaining wounded into the last boat. Then the rest, under Sergeant Clark, swam across. On the 27th September they reached Nijmegen and safety. Of all the units involved, 1st Border was the only one to go in and march out as a battalion. The Division had started out 10,095 men strong and returned with only 2,400 survivors. They had failed in their objective but they had achieved much. They had put out of action some seventy tanks and s.p. guns and they had killed 7,000 of the enemy. They had kept a large force, including portions of two Panzer divisions, thoroughly occupied, thus making the task of capturing the bridges at Garve and Nijmegen an easier one for the American Divisions. Field-Marshal Montgomery summed up the whole heroic action in these words:

In the annals of the British Army there are many glorious deeds. In our Army we have always drawn great strength and inspiration from past traditions, and endeavoured to live up to the high standard of those who have gone before.

But there can be few episodes more glorious than the epic of Arnhem, and those that follow after will find it hard to live up to the standards that you have set.

So long as we have in our armies of the British Empire, officers and men who will do as you have done, then we can indeed look forward with complete confidence to the future.

In years to come it will be a great thing for a man to be able to say, 'I fought at Arnhem'.

After Arnhem, the 1st Battalion did not go into action again. Before they could refit, 21st Army Group had crossed the Rhine and by May, 1945 the war in Europe was over. Instead the Battalion, now commanded by Lieutenant-Colonel C. F. O. Breese, proceeded to Norway and was later part of the Army of Occupation in Germany. In October, 1945 their role as an airborne unit came to an end and the occasion was marked by the following message from Brigadier R. H. Bower, C.B.E., commanding the 1st Air Landing Brigade:

It is almost exactly four years since the 1st Battalion The Border Regiment became an airborne unit. At that time the fortunes of this country were not very bright and the Army was somewhat indifferently trained and equipped. However, even in those days preparations for offensive operations were being started and the 1st Airborne Division came into being.

For the succeeding fourteen months I had the honour of commanding the 1st Battalion, and I shall always remember your splendid and cheerful response to our efforts to carry out the experimental and sometimes hazardous glider training of those early days. Many of you will remember the day early in 1942 when B Company carried out the first glider exercise ever undertaken by the British Army, and Mr. Churchill was present to see it.

Based on long regimental traditions and on unsurpassed *esprit de corps,* the 1st Battalion has lived up to the high standard of courage, discipline and military training which it has set itself. As a result of this, the Battalion has acquitted itself with honour and distinction in the battles of Sicily, Italy and finally at Arnhem.

You have now finished with great credit the airborne role that was assigned to you, and you can hang up your red berets on the peg at home with the knowledge that your duty was well and truly done, and that you have added a worthy chapter to the famous history of your Regiment.

CHAPTER XV

W E MUST now return once more to the 4th Battalion. After their long journey round the Cape, they disembarked at Suez and moved to a staging camp sixty miles from Cairo. They were now brigaded with the 1st Buffs and a Czechoslovak battalion as part of the 23rd Brigade of the 4th Indian Division.

In September the previous year six Italian divisions had marched across the Egyptian frontier from Libya. In December General Sir Archibald Wavell had counter-attacked with two divisions and had thrown them back over the frontier to Bardia. A month later he had followed up this success and driven the Italians further back, capturing a great number of prisoners. Benghazi was captured and the enemy pursued along the coast to Tobruk, in spite of the need for rest and consolidation. At this stage many British troops were siphoned off to meet the German threat to Greece while the Germans, in contrast, strongly reinforced their troops in the desert. Under these circumstances the British were forced to fall back leaving a garrison beleaguered in Tobruk.

This was the situation which prevailed when the 4th Battalion arrived in the Western Desert. Early in June an attack was planned to relieve Tobruk and the 23rd Brigade were given the role of the defence of certain forward airfields, with the object of later relieving one of the forward brigades. The attack went as planned, but the Germans counter-attacked in such strength that the operation had to be temporarily suspended. Before the 23rd Brigade could again be committed to battle there came news of a serious threat to the French mandated territory in Syria and they were switched to that theatre.

For some time the Battalion was employed in operations against the Vichy French Forces, largely devoted to the unenviable duty of carrying out patrol work on bare hillsides where the slightest move-ment by day was apt to call down the enemy's fire. During this operation the 4th Battalion found themselves fighting alongside the

Cheshire Yeomanry who, to everyone's surprise, were still equipped with one squadron of cavalry.

By the beginning of July, the Vichy French resistance started to ebb and the 4th Battalion were amongst the troops employed in the advance against them – an advance which was considerably slowed down by the number of road blocks and booby-trapped positions they encountered. A week after the advance started, the French asked for an armistice, which was granted and signed on the 14th July.

The Battalion then spent a short time on the border at Aleppo where one of their jobs was to search the trains for Germans seeking to escape back to friendly territory. They did not find any Germans, but they were compensated by finding a number of British soldiers making their way back from being stranded in Greece.

During this interlude the position in the desert had remained more or less static while both armies reorganised. By September, however, the Australian Government was getting impatient for the relief of their troops in Tobruk and it was decided to mount an operation to relieve them by sea. The task was given to the 70th Division which consisted of the 14th, 16th and 23rd Brigades. The relief was carried out at night, the ships, packed with troops, skilfully negotiating the wreck-strewn harbour. The 4th Battalion were part of the second wave, which arrived in October, when they took up guard duties on the perimeter of the Tobruk-El Adem road.

For sometime General Auchinleck, who had succeeded General Wavell as Commander-in-Chief, had been planning a big offensive to retake Libya, and this included a break out by the garrison at Tobruk. As part of the preparations intensive patrol work was carried out after dark in which the Battalion played a prominent part. This night patrolling was exciting work and required good leadership and coolness. The art of moving across the desert at night is a difficult one made more difficult by the problem of keeping direction; it must all be done by the stars or by compass. So complete was the British mastery of no-man's land that it was only on rare occasions that the patrols were disturbed, and even then they usually brought it on themselves by deciding to 'tickle up the enemy'.

The main offensive started on 18th November, 1941 when the Eighth Army crossed the Egyptian frontier and advanced towards El Adem, where it was planned they would meet with the Tobruk forces. Two days later came the break out from Tobruk but it was not until the night of the 3rd/4th of December that the 4th Battalion left the perimeter on a feature known as El Duda, about twelve miles south east of Tobruk and about three miles north of the famous battlefield of Sidi Rezegh. Daylight found the Battalion within a few hundred yards of the enemy and their supporting tanks reported that the German positions were strongly held.

That afternoon a decision was taken to remove the enemy from their position and an attack was launched by one company supported by artillery. It did not succeed immediately but the enemy were so severely shaken that they withdrew after dark leaving behind them all their guns and equipment.

The following night the Brigade was ordered to advance along the top of the escarpment to El Adem. The Durhams led the way, closely followed by the Border Regiment in trucks, leading the tanks. It was not long before the Durhams made contact. With the help of the tanks they finished off the enemy. Then the Border Regiment dismounted from their trucks and took up the advance. For the remainder of the night the Battalion made its way silently along the escarpment. On both sides they could hear the enemy shouting and starting up their transport, but they showed no fight and the objective was reached without incident.

The Battalion knew they had penetrated deep into the enemy's territory but few expected the extraordinary sight which greeted them when the dawn broke. Below them on the flat desert plain hundreds of Italians were fleeing across the desert, casting away their equipment as they ran. On the other side of the escarpment the enemy could be seen walking about their positions only a few hundred yards away, quite unaware that the British were upon them. There followed a day of shelling and counter shelling but by nightfall the enemy had had enough. Surprise had been complete and for many of them it was then end of the war, 5,600 Italians were captured.

Shortly afterwards the 70th Division were denuded of their transport and were ordered back to Egypt to refit. That Christmas they all had five days' leave in Cairo.

In the New Year orders were received for the Durham Light Infantry and the 4th Border Regiment to leave for Malta. The D.L.I. set sail but, before the 4th Battalion could follow, the orders were cancelled. Instead, with the rest of 70th Division they boarded H.M.T. *Mauretania* and were eventually landed in Bombay.

CHAPTER XVI

On the 7th December, 1941 the Japanese launched their surprise attack on Pearl Harbour and the war suddenly escalated to involve the whole world. The Americans declared war against the Axis. Soon, early in 1942, the Japanese land forces were sweeping into Burma and a new front was opened against the Allies. The sudden switch of the 4th Battalion, with the rest of 70th Division, to India was to rush them to the defence of Burma, but the Japanese had moved too fast and the country had fallen by the time they arrived. Now the problem was not the saving of Burma but the saving of India itself. The difficulties were added to by serious disturbances in India. After a short period in Poona, followed by another period at Ranchi with the role of repelling any enemy landing on the eastern seaboard, the 4th Battalion were switched to one of the main trouble spots, Patna, where they were engaged in restoring law and order.

It will be remembered that the 2nd Battalion had, during the early stages of the war, remained in India. In the first days of the war they had been employed in building internment camps for enemy nationals rounded up by the Calcutta police, and in seizing any enemy ships which happened to be lying in the harbour.

For the rest, however, life for the troops in India had continued very much on a peacetime basis. They still had their families with them and life would have been quite pleasant but for the constant worry for relatives at home and for Britain's fortunes. They had to stand by impotently while France fell and the Germans swept across the desert. After Pearl Harbour, however, their period of waiting was at an end and they were immediately mobilised to go to the defence of Burma. They were actually embarked and lying at the mouth of the Hoogly when the news came, as it had come to the 4th Battalion, that they were too late and Rangoon had fallen. Instead they were sent to Calcutta. Their families were sent to Kailana while the Battalion moved to Horana in Ceylon, where they underwent an intensive period of battalion and divisional training. Then they were moved to Kurunegela where they were to spend seven months studying the new science of jungle warfare in all its aspects. January, 1943 saw them in Kandy and there, in June, a reorganisation took place with the formation of the 100th Brigade, which consisted of 2nd Border, 14th/13th Frontier Force Rifles and the 4th/10th Gurkha Rifles. The 100th Brigade became part of the 20th Indian Division under Major-General D. D. Gracey, O.B.E., M.C. Finally, in October, 1943, they moved into Burma at a camp near Imphal.

This rigorous period of training, which included all ranks, even the cooks, marching sixty miles a week, resulted in a highly competent battalion. However, it had hardly been completed before, by one of those strange decisions of higher authority, large numbers of the Battalion were repatriated to England. It was with dismay that the Battalion saw first a party of 104 men, including senior N.C.O.s, trained in the art of jungle fighting, being sent out of the theatre, followed, during the next four months, by further large parties as the qualifying period for repatriation was further reduced. The vacancies were made up from other units, but many of the intake were untrained.

In the meantime, on the 13th August, 1943, the 9th Battalion had also arrived in India. Thus, in the deadly conflict which was to come, The Border Regiment had three battalions involved – more than any other regiment in the British Army.

By this time all the British forces had been driven back across the Chindwin as the Japanese had advanced down the Sittang and Irrawaddy Rivers. But now there came a pause, forced on the Japanese by the necessity to catch up administratively with the speed of their own advance to which was added the impossibility of their operating during the monsoon period. It was a heaven-sent respite for Generals Wavell and Stilwell, giving them time to reorganise their forces to save India and reconquer Burma.

February, 1943 had seen the first Chindit operations carried out by Brigadier Orde Wingate, but it was not until the autumn that the 14th Army was considered strong enough to take the offensive. Even then it was on a limited scale. The first objectives were:

1. To clear the enemy out of the Arakan.
2. To aid General Stilwell's drive to Myitkyina by dropping airborne troops (the Chindits) in the enemy's rear.

3. To draw off as many enemy divisions as possible from General Stilwell by strong but limited attacks across the Chindwin.

The last of these objectives became the task of the 2nd Battalion as part of the 20th Division.

In November, 1943, the 2nd Battalion dug themselves in south of Moreh on the main road through the Kabaw valley, at a site they had appropriately named Carlisle Camp. From there they carried out a series of patrols deep into enemy-occupied territory. It was rigorous and dangerous work, the patrols often being out for as much as ten days at a time. Later they moved further down the valley to Hollywood Camp where the arduous task continued, patrols of platoon strength sometimes undertaking round trips of 150 miles. Some of them were sent as far south as the Chindwin where they operated with Colonel Bill Williams (Elephant Bill) and elephants were used. It was D Company who first drew blood, encountering a Japanese patrol and killing them for the loss of one man. Later A Company captured some prisoners and gained useful information as to the Japanese defences.

On another patrol Corporal D. George came across a staff car containing three Japanese officers. Telling the rest of his patrol to remain hidden, he dashed forward, killed the three officers and before the escort knew what was happening, scooped up operational papers from the car and disappeared once more into the jungle. The papers proved of immense intelligence value and confirmed what was already suspected, that the Japanese were on the point of invading India. One of the officers killed was the chief administration officer of the attacking force. Corporal George was given the immediate award of the D.C.M. for his bravery and quick-wittedness.

The enemy were now bringing up tanks and artillery, the Battalion being shelled most of the night of the 13th/14th March. Shortly afterwards, with the Japanese advancing across the Chindwin from Homalin, it was expedient to withdraw the 17th Division, in which the 9th Battalion was, and the 20th Division as their stretched lines of communication made them extremely vulnerable. It was as they 2nd Battalion and the 4th/10th Gurkhas were ambushed and, before Battalion and the 4th/10th Gurkhas were ambushed and, before defensive action could be taken, the mules had panicked and scattered in all directions. In the resulting confusion order was only restored by one of the Battalion buglers, Private Lennon, sounding the regimental call followed by the 'Charge', which rallied the men to counter-attack.

It was 2 a.m. before the wounded had been treated and the march could be continued, but they were not long left in peace. The Japanese opened up with mortars and rifles at close range. The mules, or what few were left of them stampeded again and both battalions got broken up into small parties. It was four or five days before they were all assembled again, having made their way independently back to Brigade H.Q. Fortunately, it was found that casualties had not been as heavy as they might have been.

On the 23rd March, 1944 the 100th Brigade moved back and took up positions on the Shenam Ridge, sixty miles south of Imphal. These hills were in fact very steep wooded mountains, with bare peaks linked by narrow ridges which were often only wide enough to take two men abreast. All water had to be taken up along these ridges. The Battalion took up various positions on hills overlooking the road. On the night following their arrival the forward platoon of A Company, who occupied a position called Nippon Hill, was attacked and suffered severe casualties. The Japanese took over the position and repeated counter-attacks as well as heavy artillery fire failed to dislodge them. The attacks went on until the Battalion was relieved on the 4th April, but the position was not finally retaken until July when the siege of Imphal was raised, and then only as the result of a brigade attack.

While the 20th Indian Division continued to hold their main positions successfully, the situation became much more fluid elsewhere. The Japanese succeeded in seizing the high ground at Ukhrul and from there advanced north, to cut off Kohima and south-west to cut the Kohima-Imphal road. This manoeuvre not only threatened Imphal from the north but also threatened to cut the Bengal-Assam railway, the main supply line for General Stilwell's force, now a hundred miles into Burma. Kohima was eventually relieved by the intervention of the 2nd Division brought from India, but Imphal remained under heavy siege, the whole of the 4th Corps being supplied by air.

The Japanese were desperate to gain Imphal before the monsoon set in, but the 20th Indian Division stood firm across their easiest line of approach in spite of anything the attackers could bring against them. By the 10th May the Battalion was in a forward position and subjected to heavy and accurate artillery fire, which caused constant casualties among all the companies.

On the 14th May the Division was relieved by the 23rd Indian Division and moved to a sector by the 16th Milestone on the Imphal-Ukhrul road. It turned out to be a move to even heavier fighting as the Japanese made a last all-out effort to reach Imphal. For fifteen days A Company was completely cut off and had to be supplied by air, but once again the Division stood firm and all attacks failed.

It was during this operation that Sergeant Hunter of the 2nd Battalion volunteered to lead in the relief company to get out the wounded and get the Frontier Force Rifles into position. Sergeant Hunter, who had previously patrolled the area, later led in C Company to assist in the evacuations but was seriously wounded. He was awarded the D.C.M. for his conduct. It was also the only occasion when the Battalion came across the use of flame-throwers by the Japanese. Then came the monsoon, which lasts from May until August and which put an end for the time being to the Japanese attacks.

It was at about this time that 2nd Border met with 4th Border on the Ukhrul Road, the latter being on a long range sortie from Diampur to Imphal. The two battalions had short talks and many of the troops had the opportunity of 'brewing-up' together sharing their tea rations and swopping experiences. 2nd Border looked rather enviously at the Special Force rifles with which their comrades had been equipped.

Early in June, despite the rains, General Slim decided that the time had come to counter-attack. The plan was to attack from Kohima towards Imphal, throwing out one division to catch the enemy as they fell back towards Ukhrul, while 4th Corps tried to break out of Imphal and link up with 33rd Corps. The role of the 20th Indian Division was to carry out a flanking move to the east directed at Ukhrul. The plan worked perfectly and the Japanese found themselves attacked on all sides at once. Particularly they were caught in a cross-fire from the 7th and 20th Indian Divisions while the survivors ran into the 23rd British Brigade, which included 4th Border, coming in from the east. Thus the siege of Imphal was raised and the Japanese attempt to invade India utterly smashed.

30. Major Jock Neill, DSO, and Captain McCartney at Arnhem, September, 1944.

31. Private O'Dowd of 1st Border with a radio set at Arnhem.

32. Men of the 4th Border Regiment crossing a river close to Kohima, 26 June, 1944.

33. Muleteer Little gets wet feet.

34. 9th Border Regiment in Meiktila, shortly after its capture, 1945. (*Imperial War Museum*).

35. 9th Border Regiment occupy Pegu, 1945. (*Imperial War Museum*).

36. Three former Colonels of the Regiment, *from left to right*, Major-General P. J. Shears, CB (1947-52); Major-General V. Blomfield, CB, DSO (1951-59); Brigadier-General G. H. Harrison, DSO (1936-47).

37. Men of the Regiment on parade outside Carlisle Castle.

General Sir William Slim, commanding the 14th Army, issued the following Order of the Day:

In my last Order of the Day, I told you you had defeated the Jap Armies opposing you and that it remained to destroy them. The extent to which you have done this is shown by the 50,000 Japanese dead on the soil of India and Northern Burma, the great quantities of equipment and guns captured, the prisoners you have taken, the advances you have made, and the flight of the remnants you are still pursuing. To the 15th Corps in the Arakan fell the unique honour of being the first British-Indian formation to hold, break, and decisively hurl back the major Japanese offensive. Their was an example of tenacity and courage which inspired the whole army . . .

There is not a division or brigade in the 14th Army which has not proved its superiority over the enemy, and knows it.

The 20th Indian Division early proved its superioty over the Jap by several well-staged and successful small actions in the Kabaw Valley. When the major Jap offensive came, you made an invaluable contribution to success by your stubborn and gallant defence of the Padel area. Your reward came later when you took the offensive against the Jap 15th Division, with such excellent results.

To the officers and men of the 20th Indian Division I send my congratulations. The 14th Army has inflicted on the Japanese the greatest defeat his army has yet suffered. He is busy trying to build up again and reinforce his broken divisions. He will fight again, and viciously, but we have paid him something of what we owe. There still remains the interest. He will get it.

We must now return to the 4th Battalion, whom we left in 1942 in Patna concerned with the local Indian disturbances.

Later in the year the Battalion undertook a period of training with tanks, the 23rd Brigade and the 50th Tank Brigade being linked together for the purpose. Early in 1943 they were sent to Chittagong to cover the withdrawal of the 26th Indian Division, but the Japanese did not follow up and there was no fighting. Instead, the Brigade got caught up in the monsoons and had a bad time bivouacking in the open, which brought on an epidemic of malaria. Out of 800 men almost 600 caught the fever. Things would have been much worse but for the Mepachrine, which became a universal issue to the forces. The Japanese did not have this drug and in consequence suffered a great deal more from this scourge than our troops. After their return to Bangalore they were due to start training in combined operations and senior officers of the Battalion, including the C.O., Lieutenant-Colonel J. Burgess, were sent on a preliminary course to Bombay. No sooner had they returned, however, than the role of the Battalion was again changed.

The previous year Brigadier Wingate's newly-formed Chindits had cut deep into enemy territory and had suffered severe casualties. On the other hand they had achieved much, sufficient anyway to persuade the authorities that there was a future for such operations carried out on a large scale. In consequence Wingate was given the 70th Division as a special corps. These new Chindits were one of the most multi-racial forces ever to face an enemy together. Supported by the U.S.A.A.F. they consisted of Gurkhas, West Africans, Burmese and British. It was a proud moment for the 4th Battalion when they learned they were selected to be part of a force which had already won undying fame for their fighting ability.

Consequently, a reorganisation of the Division took place, whereby each Brigade was to consist of four battalions and each battalion was to be split into two columns. The 23rd Brigade was now made up with 1st Essex, 2nd Duke of Wellington's Regiment, 4th Border and the 60th Regiment R.A. operating as infantry. The two columns of the Border Regiment were numbered 34 and 55 and commanded by Lieutenant-Colonel J. Burgess and Major A. W. Thompson, M.C. respectively. Shortly afterwards Major Thompson got a command and his place as column commander was taken by Major G. B. Harker.

Immediately the reorganisation was completed the Division moved to the Central Provinces for intensive jungle training. This consisted of learning to cross rivers without boats and living off supplies dropped by air, as well as undertaking long and arduous marches through the jungle. The first Chindit operations had been undertaken by the troops marching into the jungle. This time it was planned to fly them in.

The object of the Chindit operations was to harrass the enemy's lines of communication and to stop supplies being brought up for the Japanese opposing General Stilwell's force on the Chindwin. All the brigades under General Wingate's command were flown into makeshift airstrips in the area except the 23rd. They were given the special role of proceeding to the Naga Hills to attack the supply lines of the Japanese 31st Division, then making a right-hand hook attack on Kohima. While the Brigade was moving up by train they heard the tragic news that General Wingate had been killed in an air crash.

The Naga Hills are between 5,000 and 7,000 feet high, their flanks covered with thick jungle and with the little Naga villages perched on the hilltops. It was intensely difficult country in which to operate, but the Battalion soon found that one of the compensations was the total loyalty of the head-hunting Naga tribesmen. Their conception of the British Empire could not extend further than the British planters with whom they had come in contact – indeed they believed that the monarch's head on a coin was the profile of the District Commissioner – but their devotion was in no way impaired by these limitations. They carried messages in the traditional way in a cleft stick and performed much useful work in spying on the Japanese.

Their good sense was shown in an amusing incident which occurred when the column commanded by Lieutenant-Colonel Burgess found themselves one night in a comfortable camp recently deserted by the Japanese. Amongst the amenities was a bath which the Colonel immediately appropriated for his personal use. He was in the middle of enjoying this unaccustomed luxury when he found himself surrounded by Naga tribesmen. They had come, it transpired, from some Japanese nearby who, knowing of the bath, had sent them to bring it back. The Colonel was justly incensed and let it be known that under no circumstances would he give up his prize. The Naga thought about this for some time and then pointed out that they could not go back and say they could not take the bath otherwise they would know of the presence of the British. Eventually it was decided that they would report that the bath could not be found. The Colonel then completed his ablutions at his leisure and was later able to lead his column in a surprise attack on the avaricious Japanese.

By early April, 1944 the two columns were making their way in dense country on parallel courses. The 34th were the first to make contact with the enemy, surprising an enemy patrol and killing all except two who were made prisoners – some of the first Japanese prisoners to be taken. Shortly afterwards the 55th column also successfully engaged the enemy. Both columns now converged close to one of the main supply routes where they continued their harrassing tactics.

The situation of the Japanese 31st Division was now becoming desperate. Around Kohima they were attacked by the 33rd Corps who inflicted severe casualties, whilst at the same time they were suffering from lack of supplies and disease. Overcome by these difficulties they started to retire and fell into the trap which had been set for them. They fell easy prey to the 4th Battalion, who took full advantage of the opportunity. At the same time attempts by other Japanese formations to break through to Imphal were frustrated and, by the end of May, General Slim was in a position to launch his counter offensive. The strategy worked brilliantly and operations in which the 2nd Battalion had taken part were complementary to those in which the 4th had been engaged. As already mentioned, the two battalions met briefly as the 4th went back to refit and the 2nd were moving up to play a new part.

It is worth noting that through all the operations of the 4th Battalion, involving as it did their being cut off for weeks on end, they never went short of supplies. The air drops were immensely efficient and the attention to supply detail magnificent. One point will emphasise this. Before setting out, each man had left behind him a broken-in pair of boots. When they were required they were sent for by a code word allotted to each man and arrived by the next drop.

The new task allotted to the 23rd Brigade was to move against Ukhrul and to trap the Japanese trying to escape from the pincer caused by the 33rd and the 4th Corps moving together. Whilst the 1st Essex and the 60th R.A. of the 23rd Brigade moved down to the south of Ukhrul, 4th Border and the 2nd Duke of Wellington's made straight for the town and covered all other exits while the 20th Indian Division attacked. The town fell without much opposition and the task of the 23rd Brigade was over.

The campaign which they had just completed had been an onerous one indeed. For three months they had operated in the Naga Hills, supplied by air and sometimes carrying as much as five days rations on their backs. To appreciate what this meant in terms of physical endurance it is necessary to realise that the marching was through some of the worst country in the world and that movement from one point to another almost always meant descending and climbing hills up to 7,000 feet high. Part of the campaign was carried out during the monsoon which greatly added to the difficulties and discomforts. It was not surprising that, after their efforts, a period of recuperation was required, as many men were suffering from malaria and dysentry. Late in October orders were received to repatriate all ranks with over three years and eight months service. This affected over two thirds of the personnel and reduced the strength of the Battalion to under 400.

The 9th Battalion landed in India on the 13th August, 1942. They had lingered for a time in Durban where there had been a rumour that their destination was to be changed to North Africa and, as a result of the subsequent flurry of training activity, had missed much of the famous Durban hospitality.

Everyone was keyed up for active service when they eventually arrived in Calcutta, but they were to be disappointed. They were immediately assigned to internal security duties, providing guards and pickets over a wide area. There was also training in such new skills as crossing rivers without the use of boats or bridges – a task made particularly difficult by the fact that many of the troops could not swim.

Christmas came and went with the usual celebrations which the Army seem to manage where ever they are but, in the New Year, there came bad news. Reinforcements were required in the Arakan and the Battalion was required to send thirty of their best men from each company to join their new regiments at forty-eight hours' notice. Worse still, General Irwin let it be known that the 9th Battalion were low on the priority list and could not expect to see action as a unit for many months.

Just when morale was at a low ebb, however, the whole picture changed with dramatic suddenness. Orders were received for the Battalion to join the 17th Division, who had taken part in the long fighting retreat from Burma. Better still, the men they had lost as Arakan reinforcemens were to be returned to them and they were to be brigaded with the 2/5th and the 1/7th Gurkha Rifles, some of the finest fighting troops in the world, to make up the 48th Light Indian Brigade. Thus 9th Border became the only 'Light' British battalion and the only one brigaded in a Light Division.

A long and tiresome journey was now undertaken by rail, river and road before they arrived at Happy Valley, Shillong in Assam where there followed a period of arduous training to accustom them to their new role.

It will be remembered that part of the task laid down by General Slim for the 14th Army offensive was to clear the enemy out of the Arakan and to draw off as many troops as possible from General Stilwell's front by making limited attacks in strength across the Chindwin. This was the operation in which the 48th Brigade were to be involved – the same operation, but from a different aspect, which was occupying the 2nd Battalion.

Early in November, 1943 the 48th Brigade with the H.Q. of 17th Division moved into Burma, passed through Imphal and finally reached the Tiddim area, 5,000 feet above sea level. Here they practised on assault courses which many of the troops believed to be worse than facing the Japanese. At the same time there was a certain amount of recreation with swimming, gymkhanas and rugby matches, and Arroyo Day was celebrated in unusual surroundings which did nothing to quench high spirits.

This comparatively pleasant interlude was, however, cut short as a result of a surprise enemy attack on the 63rd Brigade. They were moved south of Tiddim where the patrol work they had been practising suddenly became a reality. It was like being suddenly thrown in at the deep end, with a five mile move taking anything up to ten hours of hard marching up and down the vast *khuds*. They were now in the Chin Hills which had long been the battle ground of the 17th Division, faced by their old enemies, the crack Japanese 33rd Division. Now, while the 14th Army prepared their counter-attack, the Japanese were equally busy with their plans to invade India.

The Battalion was positioned on Kennedy Peak, estimated as being 10,000 feet high. They came into their first contact with the Japanese on the 24th January when Captain Hetherington was hit and killed by an enemy sniper. Thereafter they were constantly on the alert, listening through the long cold nights for the crack of a twig which might give warning of a surprise attack.

On the 1st March heavy Japanese shelling marked the beginning of their attempt to invade India, and shortly afterwards they started a strong thrust down the Arakan which ended in complete defeat of the enemy as already recounted in the history of the 2nd Battalion. The attack on Homalin, however, seriously menaced the long lines of communication of the 17th and 24th Divisions and they were forced to withdraw. The Battalion, after a few days of heavy shelling at Tiddim, acted as the rearguard to the Division. The way back to Imphal was a hard one, with the Japs threatening to cut off the line of retreat. It was accomplished, however, in three weeks and at small cost. Many acts of gallantry were carried out by the Battalion during the retreat, in one action alone, which took place above the village of Sakawng, four N.C.O.'s were awarded the Military Medal.

For their operations in the Chin Hills the Battalion had been equipped with mules. It was surprising how soon the men got used to this new form of load-carrying and how fond they became of their not always tractable animals – and how much they missed their load-carrying ability if one became a casualty.

By the beginning of May the 48th Brigade were concentrated at Wensing and in close contact with the Japanese. Here, as a change from the everlasting patrol work, they were given the task of carrying out a set-piece attack against a Japanese position which was threatening a vital airstrip – vital because, it must be remembered, at this time all supplies were coming in by air. This time, fortunately, they caught the Japs facing the wrong way and cleared the whole area for a cost of only six killed, fourteen wounded and two missing.

Soon afterwards they took part in another attack, being ordered to take the village of Potsangbam. This was achieved after a bitter struggle at a loss of nineteen killed and forty-five wounded.

This was a severe loss, but it must not be imagined that the long period of patrolling and ambushing the enemy was a one-sided affair. Although an ambush contained the element of surprise the Japanese did not give up easily and a sharp skirmish usually followed in which the casualties were not confined to one side. Patrolling, which had been such a feature of life in the Chin Hills, was also a tricky matter. Sometimes a fighting patrol was one platoon strong, and sometimes consisted of only an officer and his orderly – and often there was somebody lying out alone in the shade to watch a jungle track by day or moving silently by the stars at night. When there was no definite reconnaisance on hand the favourite and most usual was a 'Tiger Patrol' of two men who, armed with tommy guns and grenades, would try to catch the Japanese in the open and spread as much consternation and destruction as possible before disappearing into the jungle. The trouble was that the Japanese seldom stirred out of their main positions and it took plenty of nerve for two men to attack in country where even a broken ankle might mean starvation in the jungle or capture by an enemy who was governed by no rules in his treatment of prisoners.

Another aspect of life in the jungle which has not perhaps been adequately covered in the short account of the activities of the other two battalions was the hazards produced by the jungle itself. It is true that in some parts the country was fairly open, with the added compensation of passing through acres of beautiful flowering rhododendrons but for the most part it was quite the opposite. Apart from the natural difficulties of the terrain there were special hazards; for instance, tough creepers in which it was easy to get entangled without noticing, only for it to pull a man backwards as if he had been attached to a piece of very strong elastic. There was also a species of prickly fern which removed water bottle covers, extracted bayonets from scabbards and whisked cap comforters from heads, while the long-suffering troops grimly muttered through their teeth the 14th Army slogan – *The Jungle is your Friend.*

As spring turned into summer the role of the Battalion became more and more an attacking one with fixed objectives as the Japanese began to retire, sorely beset by their enemies, and by disease. After the battle for Potsangbam there were several days of confused fighting as the Brigade concentrated on harassing the Japanese lines of communication. Then they started to move south from Kwa Sipahi where they had had their headquarters, leaving behind their B Echelon in the administrative area. For some reason the Battalion H.Q. department had been left outside the administrative area with a great deal of equipment, stores and mules, and it was at this point that the Japanese launched a night attack. The R.Q.M.S. was killed and a great part of the stores lost, as well as two hundred mules. It was altogether an unfortunate incident.

To add to the Battalion's troubles they were now becoming short of men and had to re-organise into three companies. Lack of food affected the men's stamina, and this was aggravated by loss of sleep due to the number of nights when a stand-to was ordered. On the night of the 8th June the Brigade was ordered to withdraw to Bishenpur where they took over defence duties. For ten days they were constantly on the move and in contact with the enemy, but their casualties were fortunately slight.

On the 17th July the Battalion moved to Imphal and in September they went back to Ranchi to refit. From November, 1943 to July, 1944 they had been in almost constant action and had lost seven officers and eighty-one other ranks killed, twelve officers and two hundred and forty-five other ranks wounded and a further twenty-nine other ranks missing. By the end of the year, however, they had again been made up to full strength and further training was being undertaken to prepare them for the advance through Burma.

We left the 2nd Battalion when they were relieved in June, 1944 and moved back to Imphal for a well-earned rest. They saw the rains out in a camp by Waithou Lake and did not move again until November. During their stay there they were visited by the Viceroy, Field-Marshal Lord Wavell, who presented many awards for gallantry. They were also visited by Admiral Lord Louis Mountbatten who afterwards wrote to the Commanding Officer, Lieutenant-Colonel Harvey:

> I am writing to tell you how glad I was to have a chance of seeing the 2nd Battalion The Border Regiment, and to find them in such good heart.
> Your Battalion have certainly done great things, and have every reason to be proud of themselves.

During their time at Waithou, the Battalion lost further drafts of trained personnel as the term of service overseas had now been reduced to only a little over four years, thus much of their time was taken up with training the new intake and digesting the lessons they had learned in the jungle. There was, however, some time for social life and sport, the Battalion winning the brigade and divisional swimming competition.

In the middle of November the 2nd Battalion became attached to the 2nd British Division as its Provost Battalion during its advance down the Kabaw Valley. It was an onerous task and at one time the Battalion was spread out along the route for a distance of eighty-five miles. At the beginning of December, however, they were relieved and rejoined the 100th Brigade and the 20th Indian Division. They were now to play a more active part in the advance through Burma. The objective given to the 20th Indian Division was the capture of Monywa, a large town on the Chindwin, near where it joined the Irawaddy. Now, for the first time, the Battalion was marching through open country as opposed to the jungle in which they had fought for more than a year, and they found the experience much more enjoyable.

It was reported, when they reached Kyauklegge, that Monywa was only lightly held and, accordingly, the 100th Brigade (who happened to be the nearest troops) were ordered to form a motorised coloumn and push forward with all speed. Known as 'Rushcol', the party consisted of A Company and one platoon of C Company, together with one troop of Field Artillery, one R.A. Troop of 3-in anti-tank mortars and one section of Sappers and Miners under command of Lieutenant-Colonel Harvey.

At the end of the first day's march, during which they covered fifty miles, they ran into strong opposition at Budalin and were held up until reinforced by 80th Brigade. Then 80th Brigade took up the advance while 'Rushcol' remained to hold Budalin until caught up by the rest of 100th Brigade. Two days later the advance was resumed, the objective being Myimmu on the north bank of the Irrawaddy. They reached it without opposition and then were presented with the problem of effecting a crossing – a considerable task as the river was 1,000 yards wide with a very strong current. The task of being the assault troops was given to the 2nd Battalion.

There followed a period of intensive training and experimentation with various types of craft on a nearby lake, while small patrols were sent across the river to gain as much information as possible about the enemy's dispositions. One patrol capsized their boat on the way back and had to swim 800 yards to safety. The current, however, carried them so far downstream that they landed in enemy territory and had the greatest difficulty in rejoining the Battalion.

On the 30th January it was found that the Japanese had occupied the villages of Wetto and Satpangan on the north bank in some strength. As these villages were the starting point of the attack it was essential that they be cleared. Wetto was soon taken but the Japanese withdrew their men to Satpangan which was a much more formidable proposition. The first attack was unsuccessful and cost the lives of one officer and eighteen other ranks. The next day a second attack was successful but was also expensive in lives, one officer and twenty-one other ranks being killed, thirty-nine wounded. The final assault across the Irawaddy took place on the night of the 13th-14th February, 1945. The method used was for three rubber boats tied together to be towed behind canvas-type assault boats fitted with outboard motors.

Certain difficulties were encountered by the leading company due to their boats swinging, and progress was very slow. On arrival at the other side, the leading troops, who had to paddle the last 100 yards with their spades as a result of engine failure, dug in, and at first light beat off a Japanese attack. The second attack did not come until that evening when the Battalion was well dug in, and it was beaten off with heavy casualties to the enemy. By this time the bridgehead containing the whole of the 100th Brigade were firmly established.

On 17th February the village of Alethaung was attacked by A Company supported by C Company and a squadron of light tanks, and captured after some brisk fighting. A few days later B Company captured Sindat further along the bank and the bridgehead was considerably extended. By the beginning of March the Japanese started to withdraw and immediately plans were made to follow up the advantage. This time the 2nd Battalion was in the rear, out to one flank. The march into enemy territory lasted some three weeks with only light opposition. A stand was finally made at Kume but it was quickly overcome, the Battalion losing only five men before the enemy once more withdrew.

It was shortly after this that the Battalion, with very much regret, left the 100th Brigade with whom they had trained and fought for over three years and joined the 36th British Division at Shwele. They were now part of a force selected to take part in a seaborne invasion of Malaya and in consequence, after the capture of Mandalay, were withdrawn to India to train in their new role. Exercises were carried out on the lakes near Poona but the operation never took place. On 14th August, 1945 the Japanese surrendered unconditionally.

The 9th Battalion were also to play an important part in the final dash across Burma which was to end with the liberation of Rangoon.

The task of the 17th Division in the new offensive was to sweep across central Burma and capture Meiktila and its airfields so as to form a firm base to support the 2nd, 19th and 20th Divisions coming down from the north.

The 9th Battalion left Ranchi on the 16th January, 1945. They travelled by railway to the Brahmaputra which they were ferried across and continued their journey to Manipur Road. There they exchanged their mules for motor transport and continued their journey through the Kabaw Valley and Kale Valley to Kan. They crossed the Irawaddy on the 21st February and commenced a swift advance to Meiktila. Within seventy-two hours the airfield was successfully taken and the battle for Meiktila itself commenced. It proved a tough struggle, the Japanese refusing to surrender and having to be killed almost to a man.

Although from now on the battle for the reconquest of Burma was against an enemy who were suffering from malnutrition and disease and often without leadership, it must not be thought that it was a rout. It was not for nothing that they had gained their reputation for fanaticism, as the following passage written by Major Cooper, the C.O. of B Company, will show:

> Almost to a man the Japs died without trying to escape. One was burning in the open, and his yellow limbs were black and shining like those of some fantastic negro ; another who had come out to fight was dead and sprawling, a bayonet, like an out-size arrow, sticking in his chest ; three more, already wounded, were running for the cover of a tall bamboo clump some thirty yards away . . .

After Meiktila, on the 8th March, the Battalion was on the move again, pressing south to Pyawbwe. There was a great deal of enemy activity but they managed, with the assistance of a squadron of tanks, to establish a firm base at the village of Yindaw. While they were there a patrol discovered that the Japanese were moving up in strength from Rangoon to the relief of Meiktila. This force ran straight on to the Battalion position and a fierce battle followed in which the enemy were driven back with heavy casualties.

For the rest of the month of March repeated actions were fought as the Japanese tried to reach Meiktila and it was not until the 15th April that an all-out effort could be made to capture Pyawbwe. The Battalion put in their attack from the west, supported by a squadron of tanks from Probyn's Horse. They had to advance over open ground and the two leading companies had considerable trouble from various strong points and from being shelled by 75mm guns. Eventually, however, all the objectives were gained. The plan had been for the town to be attacked simultaneously on all sides but the other attacks did not materialise and the Battalion was left to maintain their position for the night on their own. In the morning, however, it was found that the Japanese had had enough and had retired, leaving behind over a hundred and fifty dead.

Organised Japanese resistance was now crumbling still further and the advance towards Rangoon accelerated. The 5th Indian Division had been flown in and now took turns with the 17th Indian Division to lead. Very little trouble was encountered until 50 miles from Rangoon. At Pegu the Japanese had blown the only road bridge over the river, which was seventy yards wide. A diversion was made over a railway bridge but, after the 48th Brigade had got across, the approaches became impassable. A bailey pontoon bridge was constructed and the 63rd Brigade, less the 9th Battalion, made the crossing. Then the rains started and during the night the river rose fifteen feet and the pontoons were swept away. It was some time before a new bridge could be constructed and in the meantime it had been decided that the 17th Division would not, after all, go to Rangoon which had already been captured by an air and sea invasion. Instead they moved back to picquet the road so as not to allow the Japanese to escape eastwards over the Sittang River.

In July the Battalion was relieved by the 7/10th Baluch Regiment and were employed instead in providing road-stops on the Rangoon Road and patrolling the foothills of the Pegu Yomas. It was while they were thus employed that information was received that the Japanese were planning a break out by their 28th Army H.Q. and their 53rd Division. Thus the 63rd Brigade were ready for them when the attempt was made on the night of the 20th July. After a small initial success the attempt failed and the Battalion were kept busy mopping up parties of Japanese trying to escape. During the period 20th July to the 5th August, the 17th Indian Division killed some 5,000 Japanese and captured a further 5,000, while over a 1,000 bodies were counted floating down the Sittang River. From the condition of the prisoners it was obvious that the Japanese were now a shattered army.

News of the surrender was received on the 15th August but as no cease fire was ordered, patrols continued as usual. It was not until the 24th August that a request for an armistice was received and the war could be said to be over. There followed a move to Mikpalin where the Battalion was charged with the job of disarming over 2,000

Japanese. At the same time they had some trouble with dacoits who had to be rounded up – no small task as the allotted area for policing was approximately a hundred miles long by forty miles wide. While these operations were in progress, repatriation started and on the 19th October a party of four officers and 250 other ranks left for home.

Their return to England was well merited. As a battalion they had endured the longest single period in contact with the enemy and had acquitted themselves brilliantly.

The 4th Battalion, meanwhile, had also suffered through having to send large drafts home. At the beginning of 1945 they were at Dehra Dun where they were part of the 16th Special Brigade training for a role on Special Force lines. The battle, however, had got ahead of them and they eventually abandoned their Special Force role and were sent to Kalewa to undertake traffic duties on either side of the Chindwin. This vital road was in an appalling state, convoys sometimes taking as much as six hours to cover one mile. Finally they moved to Rangoon, still not reinforced, where they carried out police and guard duties. By the end of October the Battalion had sent home so many men that they could no longer carry out any operational duties.

It was at this stage that amalgamation with the 9th Battalion was decided upon. The 9th were stationed nearby and much friendly rivalry existed between the two battalions. They managed to celebrate Arroyo Day together in Rangoon, there being as many 9th present as there were 4th. The amalgamation was done in a rather curious way. All the personnel of the 4th were posted to the 9th and then the reinforced Battalion changed its number to the 4th.

The act of the amalgamation took place with impressive ceremony on the 1st December. The parade was addressed by the G.O.C. 17th Indian Division, Major-General H. G. Crowther, before the flag of the 9th Battalion was lowered for the last time and that of the 4th Battalion hoisted in its place. As General Crowther pointed out in his address, battalion numbers did not matter very much. What was important was that the Border Regiment should continue its existence.

For a time the newly constituted Battalion became operational again with the role of suppressing the large bands of dacoits which infested the area. Daily patrols were sent out and some successes marked up against an enemy which it was always hard to locate. These activities continued until the end of the year when a memorandum was received from the Chief Secretary of the Government of Burma expressing the extreme gratitude of the Government for the very able assistance to the Civil Authority. At the beginning of the following year operations were halted and the Battalion was concentrated in Rangoon in a state of 'suspended animation' prior to disbandment. The majority were then drafted to the 2nd Border Regiment, the 1st King's Regiment and the 2nd East Lancashire Regiment.

There was now only a small cadre left to return to England, soon to be reconstituted as a unit of the new Territorial Army.

CHAPTER XVII

WITH THE cessation of hostilities, there came the urgency of getting the war-time soldiers back to their peace-time jobs as soon as possible. Thus it was only a cadre of the 4th/9th Battalion which returned to England to become part of the new Territorial Army. Their territory now embraced the whole of Cumberland and Westmorland with Battalion H.Q., a support Company and A Company at Carlisle Castle, B Company at Penrith, D Company at Kendal with a headquarters for a fourth company to be decided.

Of all the battalions which had served so well in the war only the 1st Battalion was to remain on an operational footing. In fact, on VE Day they once more took to the air, this time with the role of taking the surrender of the German Army in Norway. Unfortunately, when the aircraft carrying the Battalion arrived over Oslo it was to find that landing conditions were nearly impossible. Two or three aircraft tried to land and managed to get down. Then one overshot the runway with the tragic loss of all aboard. The remainder flew back to England and did not complete the operation until the following day.

When they finally disembarked, the sight which met their eyes was an unforgettable one. The German troops who so recently had been the hated enemy now paraded smartly at the airfield to greet their conquerors with a smart salute. In Oslo the scenes of enthusiasm from the civilian population were overwhelming. The troops were cheered and mobbed wherever they went and every house was open to the liberators. Their role, however, did not allow them to stay and enjoy the fleshpots of the capital.

Within a few days they embussed for the north, their destination being Bergen. Before they reached the city, however, they encountered a blown bridge. They had to cross the river by ferry and finish the last seventy miles of the journey on foot.

At Bergen their job was to repatriate the Germans and release the Russian prisoners. The first move was to give the Russians the old German billets and house the Germans in the much inferior accommodation they had forced the Russians to occupy. The Germans, however, proved well-disciplined and orderly and the operation was carried out without incident. At the same time the Battalion had a more diverting job. They were equipped with a powerful, ex-German patrol boat which they used to search the fiords for U-boat pens. They took to the water as readily as they had taken to the air and, as British soldiers all over the world will, found plenty to keep them amused in unlikely surroundings.

The task in Norway lasted for almost five months. Then the Battalion were flown back to England to learn, with bitter regret, that they were finally to give up their red berets and distinctive smocks and be re-converted to a regular infantry battalion. It was, of course, inevitable, but it was nonetheless hard to bear for men who had become intensely proud of their place as some of the most élite fighting troops.

Almost immediately after this they were sent to Hannmünden in Germany on garrison duties. They arrived at full strength due to their recent operational role but soon became faced with the same trials and tribulations as other regiments. Constant drafts of highly-trained troops had to be sent home on demobilisation, to be replaced by raw recruits, so that a constant programme of rebuilding had to be undertaken. Nevertheless, they managed to distinguish themselves by having one of the finest football teams in the Army. They won the Corps Cup and were only defeated in the final of the 21st Army Group Championship.

There followed several moves inside Germany before, in October, 1946, they were sent to Trieste on the Yugoslavian-Italian border. Their job was to patrol the Morgan Line to stop the illegal entry of communist agitators into Italy. Trieste was also the starting point for the famous Orient Express, which has provided the background for so many romantic stories of beautiful spies and sudden death. It was part of the Battalion's job to search this train before each journey with the help of the local police, to prevent any of the romance becoming reality.

Early the following year they moved to Padua and from there went to Palestine via Venice and Egypt. They were stationed at Julis Camp, outside Gaza, from where they carried out patrols in Arab territories and escorted Jewish convoys. Britain's time in Palestine was, however, running out and a month before the final evacuation they moved again, on 28th February, 1948, to El Ballah. They only stayed there a few weeks before going to Somaliland to police the colony.

The position in Somaliland was potentially a dangerous one. The Somalis had had the use of the grazing lands during the whole of the war, but it had now been decreed that they should be handed back to Ethiopia, and it was expected that there might be considerable trouble. In the event the fears were not realised and the Battalion's six-month stay was an extremely pleasant one, unmarred by any incidents. The Battalion was then sent to Mogadishu in Italian Somaliland where the situation was even more explosive.

The move was marked by an incident straight out of Gilbert and Sullivan. When crossing the frontier the official papers were inspected by the Ethiopian guards who did not understand a word of them. They allowed the Battalion through and then, suddenly convinced that the whole thing was a trick, fired wildly after the disappearing convoy! Fortunately, no-one was hurt.

In Somaliland it was feared that the troubles between the Italians and the Somalis might well lead to a blood bath. That it never happened was largely due to the steadiness of the Battalion. The conduct of one company in quelling a riot, under command of Major John Gibbon, M.C., was for a long time afterwards taken as a model by the Staff College of how such an operation should be carried out.

It was at this time that the King awarded the 1st Battalion the Border Regiment, together with the 9th Airborne Squadron, R.E., the 2nd Battalion the South Staffordshire Regiment and the 1st Glider Pilot Regiment, the right to wear an embroidered Glider Badge. This was to mark their participation, on 9th/10th March, 1943, in the first action when British glider borne troops went into action.

The Battalion's duty in Italian Somaliland came to an end in May, 1950 when they handed over for the Italians to begin their ten-year mandate. They then returned to England where they were stationed at Barnard Castle, and here the 1st and 2nd Battalions officially amalgamated. Perhaps 'amalgamated' is not quite the right word, for the 2nd Battalion had now been run down to a small cadre of men who were simply absorbed into the 1st. The result, however, was the same whatever the correct description. The 2nd Battalion now ceased to exist. On the 7th April, 1951 there came a happier event in the Regiment's history. They were presented with their new Colours and the old ones were laid up in Carlisle Cathedral. At the time of the ceremony the Colours were the oldest in use by any regiment in the British Army, having last been renewed eighty years earlier.

The impressive ceremony had hardly been completed when it became known that King Farouk was going to revoke the Suez Canal Treaty. The Battalion was sent to join the 3rd Infantry Division, first in Cyprus and later in the Canal Zone. It was whilst they were there that the whole Regiment celebrated the 250th anniversary of their formation. Apart from the official celebrations there must have been many ex-Border officers and men all over the world who raised a silent glass to the men who had preceded them, and to their proud record since the days of Queen Anne. Little could they have known that only a few years were to pass before the name of the Regiment was to disappear forever.

The final years of the Regiment were spent with the 1st Battalion back in Germany carrying out training and patrolling the frontier at Göttingen before moving to Berlin. Then they returned to England as rumours grew that they were finally to loose their old identity.

At the end of summer, 1959 they were at Humbledon Camp at Barnard Castle. Only a mile away at Westwick Camp was the 1st Battalion of the King's Own Royal Regiment, with whom it was now known that they were going to amalgamate. It was some consolation that their name from now on was going to be linked with so fine a regiment, but it cannot be denied that, for many old soldiers, something very dear to them was passing out of their lives for ever.

The month of September was spent with The Border Regiment as host to a working party from the King's Own, working out the final details of the amalgamation. Apart from the main issues to be dealt with there were many minor but important matters for their consideration, for it was vital that both Regiments should feel that as much as possible of each other's historic traditions should be embodied in the 'new look'. The new dress, the new Regimental badges and crests and even the new stationery were all matters which had to be agreed upon.

The day fixed for the official birth of the new Regiment was the

1st October, and at reveille on that day the flag of the 1st Battalion The King's Own Royal Border Regiment was raised for the first time. At nine a.m. the Commanding Officer, Lieutenant-Colonel Robinson, addressed the Battalion, who were now wearing their new shoulder titles in the Regimental colours of royal blue, yellow and green, with the title King's Own Border, and under the title a small glider.

The Commanding Officer ended his address with the following words:

I can sum up as follows. We have a tremendous task before us, of building this new Regiment up to something we and our sons can be proud of – it is a challenging task we should find absorbing and enjoyable. Whilst drawing from the strength of the old, we must work for the new, and join in the building, with God's help, something of which we shall all be proud.

There followed the reading of a message from Her Majesty The Queen:

I sincerely thank all the ranks of the 1st Battalion the King's Own Royal Border Regiment for their loyal greetings on the day of the Regiment's formation. I send my best wishes and am sure that the Regiment will live up to the traditions of its two famous parent Regiments.

Elizabeth R.

And so, quietly and without fuss, two proud Regiments passed into history and a new Regiment was born.

For many, however, the last word was not written until the 31st October, when the final amalgamation parade was held at Barnard Castle. In a moving ceremony of great dignity both Regiments marched past for the last time with their Colours flying, while a large assembly of ex-Officers and men watched with a mixture of pride and sadness what were to them the last rites. As the Border Regiment passed the saluting block they moved into a new era, but an era in which the great traditions of the past will never be forgotten.

The badge of the new Regiment bears with pride the laurel wreath granted to the old 34th for their part in the Battle of Fontenoy. It is not inappropriate that it commemorates a gallant defeat and not a very great victory, for it is not by victories and defeats that a Regiment is remembered. It is by its devotion to its country and its determination to do its duty. That the Border Regiment has never been found lacking is its finest epitaph.

POSTSCRIPT

Little mention has been made in the account of the Border Regiment, during the last war, of individual acts of gallantry, because it would have been invidious to single out a few from among so many. Some idea, however, may be gained from cold statistics. Of all the members of the Regiment three were awarded the C.B. and four the C.B.E. There were sixteen D.S.O.s and three bars. There were twelve O.B.E.s and twenty-two M.B.E.s. Forty officers were awarded the M.C. and two were given bars. There were eight D.C.M.s and fifty-seven M.M.s with two bars and ten B.E.M.s, while no less than a hundred and ninety-six officers and men were mentioned in despatches, many of them twice and three times.

The record of the Border Regiment in the period 1939-1945 stands second to none. They fulfilled almost every role possible in the great effort which resulted in such a complete victory. Sometimes the roles were relatively humble, more often they were in the very forefront of the battle. In every situation the Border soldiers lived up to the high example of their predecessors whose history has been traced in this book. That is the highest praise that any member of the Border Regiment could wish.

APPENDIX I

The Regimental Music

Since early in their existence both the 34th and 55th Regiments have had bands (or at least musicians), as the following Annual Inspection Returns show:

    1st/34th Foot
    1.8.1771 – Have a Band of Music
    55th Foot
    9.5.1768 – 5 fifers. Band of Music
    7.5.1787 – Drummers and fifers, clothing showy

The Regimental March of the 1st Battalion is *John Peel*, an obvious choice for a regiment which recruited in that character's hunting country. The words of the song, written in the 1820's, are by John Woodcock Graves, a friend of John Peel, and are set to the old folk tune *Bonnie Annie*.

The Regimental March of the 2nd Battalion is *The Lass o' Gowrie* which was formerly the march of the 55th before they became the 2nd Border Regiment.

The Regimental Slow March, *Horn of the Hunter*, comprises three tunes; a *Chinese Air*, believed to have been adopted in commemoration of the 55th's part in the China War of 1841-42; *Horn of the Hunter*, a Cumberland tune which forms the centre portion of the March; and a tune of French origin, *La Ligne* (to which the words of *Soldier, Soldier Will You Marry Me* are normally sung); it is normally a quick march but, in this case, is played in slow time.

Rule Britannia was sometimes played before the Regimental Marches to commemorate the service of the 34th with the Fleet during the 18th century.

In 1811, at the Battle of Arroyo dos Molinos in the Peninsula, the 34th captured the whole of the French 34e Régiment, with their Eagles, drums and band. To mark this feat, in 1950 the March of the 34e Régiment was incorporated into the Regimental March. Every year, on the anniversary of the battle, a parade was held in which the captured drums were taken up by six drummer boys, in the uniform of the French regiment, and marched to the flanks and then to the centre. Three French tunes were played; *Le Réve Passe* as the drummers marched to the flanks, *La Marseillaise* as they slow-marched to the centre, and the March of the 34e Régiment as the Regiment marched off.

The March of the French 34th Regiment of Infantry was originally scored for fifes and drums, but was later scored for full military band in 1920 by Bandmaster Quick. It was re-scored by Bandmaster Owen Geary (later Lt.-Col. Geary, Director of Music, Royal Artillery), and was used in this form at the annual parade of the captured drums. Since amalgamation with the King's Own the parade is held on St. George's Day, and not on the date of the battle, 28 October.

When the band played in the Officers' Mess, *Chinese Airs* was played immediately before the Regimental Marches, followed by *A Spanish Air*, reputed to have been adopted during the Peninsular War.

There is also a song which the officers of the 4th Battalion sang in their Mess after dinner, *Joe Bowman and his Ullswater Hounds*, a song of the Ullswater Hunt. It is still included in the programme when the band plays in the ante-room.

The Cap Badges of the Regiment

by

JOHN GAYLOR

Secretary of the Military Historical Society

The adoption of the Austrian-pattern field-service cap by the British Army in the mid-1890s meant that new badges were required as the ones worn on the glengarry proved too large. The Regiment took a variation of the helmet-plate centre and placed this on a star, topped by what is usually referred to as 'Queen Victoria's Crown'. The arms of the cross carried battle-honours and rested on a laurel wreath said to have been awarded to the 34th for service at Fontenoy. In the centre a circle carried the honour 'Arroyo dos Molinos, 1811', whilst inside the circle was a dragon with 'China' above. The lower part of the centre was voided and backed by red felt: this represented the two-thirds red and one-third white shako pom-pom of the French 34th Regiment defeated at Arroyo dos Molinos. The change of monarch at the turn of the century meant a change of crown and a slightly larger badge meant that more honours could be placed on the arms of the cross. After the Queen's accession in 1952 a further change of crown necessitated another badge.

Militia battalions often wore differenced badges and 3rd Border was no exception. The arms of the cross were blank, the part-time soldiers having gained no honours whilst the Dragon in the centre of an honourless circle was not identified as a Chinese one! Oddly enough, however, the Fontenoy wreath was present.

The 4th and 5th Territorial Force Battalions wore the badges shown: they were basically of Regimental pattern but, again, the arms of the cross were bare of honours whilst the South Africa honour gained by their Volunteer predecessors were carried on the centre circle. The title scrolls indicated their respective recruiting areas.

Finally, the last badge shown is that worn by the 11th Battalion. Raised in August, 1914, by Lord Lonsdale as part of Kitchener's Army, it bore a family badge above its title spelled out in full. The first badges issued were in silver, a presentation from the Colonel but subsequent issues, by a less paternal War Office, were in brass.

The merger in 1959 with The King's Own Royal Regiment meant another new design after a brief spell of using the badge of the Lancastrian Brigade. The badge ultimately chosen was a whitemetal Lion of England from the King's Own, surrounded by a brass Fontenoy wreath and surmounted by a crown.

APPENDIX III

The Victoria Cross

CITATIONS OF AWARDS

MADE TO MEMBERS OF THE BORDER REGIMENT

34th Regt Private WILLIAM COFFEY
For having on 29th March, 1855, thrown a lighted shell that fell into the trench over the parapet.

34th Regt Private JOHN J. SIMMS
For having on 18th June, 1855, after the regiment had retired from the trenches from the assault on REDAN, gone out over the open ground under a heavy fire in broad daylight and brought in wounded soldiers outside the trenches.

55th Regt Private THOMAS BEACH
For conspicuous gallantry in the battle of INKERMAN when on picket, in attacking several Russians who were plundering Lt-Col Carpenter of the 41st Regt who was lying wounded on the ground. He killed two of the Russians and protected Lt-Col Carpenter until the arrival of some of the 41st Regt.

55th Regt Bt Major FREDERICK C. ELTON
For distinguished conduct on the night of 4th August, 1855, when in command of a working party in the advanced trenches in front of the Quarries in encouraging and inciting his men, by his example, to work under a dreadful fire, and when there was some hesitation shown in consequence of the severity of the fire, going into the open and working with a pick and shovel, thus exhibiting the best possible example to his men. In the words of one of them, 'There was not another officer in the British Army who would have done what Maj ELTON did that night'.

INDIAN MUTINY 1857

34th Regt   Sergeant GEORGE RICHARDSON

Richardson did, despite the fact that his arm was broken by
a rifle bullet and leg slashed by a sabre, rush to the aid of
his officer, who was attacked by six natives, and, that crippled
as he was, succeeded in killing five and the sixth fled.

N.B. The body of the late Sergeant Richardson is interred in
Prospect Cemetery, Toronto, Canada.

A suitable marker, with a replica of the Victoria Cross cut in
the stone, was erected by The Colonel Sydney Lambert Chapter,
Imperial Order of the Daughters of the Empire, Toronto,
Canada.

The grave will receive perpetual care by the Chapter and will
be suitably decorated each year.

THE GREAT WAR 1914-18

21 May, 1918   Captain (A/Lt-Col) JAMES FORBES ROBERTSON
DSO, MC, 1st Battn

For most conspicuous bravery whilst commanding his
battalion during the heavy fighting. Through his quick judgement, resource, untiring energy, and magnificent example,
Lt-Col FORBES ROBERTSON, on four separate occasions, saved
the line from breaking and averted a situation which might
have had the most serious and far-reaching results.

On the first occasion, when troops in front were falling back,
he made a rapid reconnaissance on horse back in full view
of the enemy, under heavy machine gun and close range shell
fire. He then organised, and, still mounted, lead a counter
attack which was completely successful in re-establishing our
line. When his horse was shot under him he continued on
foot.

Later on the same day, when troops to the left of his line
were giving way, he went to the flank and checked and steadied
the line, inspiring confidence by his splendid coolness and
disregard of personal danger.

His horse was wounded three times and he was thrown five
times.

The following day, when the troops on both his flanks were
forced to retire, he formed a post at Battalion Headquarters
and with his battalion still held his ground, thereby covering
the retreat of troops on his flanks. Under the heaviest fire

this gallant officer fearlessly exposed himself when collecting parties, organizing and encouraging.

On a subsequent occasion, when troops were retiring on his left and the condition of things on his right were obscure, he again saved the situation by his magnificent example and cool judgement. Losing a second horse, he continued alone on foot until he had established a line to which his own troops would withdraw and so conform to the general situation.

18 Feb, 1915   No 10694 Private ABRAHAM ACTON 2nd Battn
                        No 6423 Private JAMES SMITH 3rd Battn Attd 2nd

For conspicuous bravery on 21 December at ROUGES BANCS in voluntarily going from their trench and rescuing a wounded man who had been lying exposed against the enemy's trench for 75 hours, and on the same day again leaving their trench voluntarily under heavy fire, to bring into cover another wounded man. They were under fire for 60 minutes whilst conveying wounded men to safety.

9 March, 1917   No 9887 Sergeant EDWARD JOHN MOTT 1st Battn

For most conspicuous gallantry and initiative when in an attack, the company to which he belonged was held up at a strong point by machine gun fire. Although severely wounded in the eye, Sergeant MOTT made a rush for the gun, and after a fierce struggle seized the gunner and took him prisoner, capturing the gun. It was due to the dash of the Non-Commisisoned Officer that the left flank attack succeeded.

11 June, 1918   No 9522 Sergeant CHARLES EDWARD SPACKMAN
                         1st Battn

For most conspicuous bravery when in action. The leading company was checked by heavy fire of a machine gun mounted in a position which covered the approaches. The ground was absolutely devoid of cover of any description. Sergeant SPACKMAN realizing the situation, and seeing it was impossible for troops to advance, went through the fire to attack the gun. Working forward gradually, he succeeded in killing all but one of the gun crew. He then rushed the gun and captured it singlehanded, thereby enabling the company to advance. The behaviour of the Non-Commissioned Officer was gallant in the extreme and he set a fine example of courage and devotion to his men.

INDEX

Abercromby, Col the Hon Alexander, 64, 65
Abercromby, General, 39-41
Abercromby, Sir Ralph, 58
Abyssinia, 164-165
Acton, Pte Abraham, VC, 131-132
Airborne Division, The 1st, 187
Airborne Squadron, The 9th RE, 218
Airey, Lt-Col (later Sir Richard), 86-87
Aisne, Battle of the, 154
Albania, 164
Albuhera, Battle of, 65
Alma, Heights of, 97-99
Amherst, General, 41
Amiens, Battle of, 155
Amiens, Treaty of, 59
Anne, Queen, 15, 19, 25
Argyll, Duke of, 25
Armistice, The (1918), 156
Army Council, The, 127, 161
Arnhem, 187-191
Arroyo Day, 206
Arroyo dos Molinos, 66-68, 86
Attlee, C. R. (later Earl), 177
Auchinleck, Field Marshal Sir Claude, 194
Austrian Succession, War of the, 29

Badajoz, 64, 68, 70-71
Balaclava, 100, 103
Barber, Major-General C. M., 179
Barcelona, 18-20
Bartlett, Col (later Major-General), 92
Battle of Britain, The, 176
Battles of the Crimean War (see Pemberton, W. B.)
Beach, Pte, VC, 101
Beatson (*Naval and Military Memoirs*), 34, 36

Bell, George
    Rough Notes of an Old Soldier, 66-71
    Soldier's Glory, 74-75
Beresford, General Lord, 65
Bergen-op-Zoom, 80-82
Biggle, Capt P. G. W., 134
Bird, Major, 88
Bizanet, General, 81
Black Watch, The, 40
Blake, Surgeon Ethelbert, 102
Blakeney, General, 34-35
Blenheim, Battle of, 22
Boers, The, 116-119
Bonnie Banks of Loch Lomond, 31
Border Regiment, The, 38, 56, 96, 114-120, 122, 129, 131-132, 139-143, 145, 156, 159, 160, 162
    Amalgamation with King's Own Royal Regiment, 219-220
    Battle Honours, 159
    Cap badge, 86, 227-228
    Colours, 162, 219
    Freedom of City of Carlisle, 180
    Redesignated 110 Regiment RAC, 174
1st Battalion, 114, 120, 134-137, 139-140, 146, 148, 151-152, 156, 158-160
    Afghanistan, 160
    Airborne Troops, 172, 183-185
    Aldershot, 165
    Amalgamation, 218
    Arnhem, 187-191
    China, 162-163
    Cyprus, 219
    D-Day, 187
    Egypt, 217, 219
    France, 166-168, 172
    Germany, 159, 219
    Ireland, 164
    Norway, 216-217

Nijmegen, 187-191
Palestine, 164
Sicily, 184-186
Syracuse, 186
Wales, 173
2nd Battalion,
    Amalgamation with 1st Battalion, 218, 219
    Burma, 198-200, 209-211
    China, 163
    Colours, 162
    Great War Service, 123
    India, 163, 165, 173, 196, 197
    Ireland, 162
    Italy, 156
    Khartoum, 162
    Malta, 162
3rd Battalion, 132, 159
4th Battalion, 132, 158, 160-161, 165, 167-169, 173-175, 193-196, 201-205, 214, 216
5th Battalion, 132, 139, 143, 150-151, 155-156, 164-167, 169-172, 174, 179-180, 182
6th Battalion, 133, 140, 143-144, 149, 174-179
7th Battalion, 133-134, 139, 144, 147-148, 150, 155-157, 165, 170, 179-180, 182
8th Battalion, 134, 139, 144, 150-151, 153-154, 165, 179-181
9th Battalion, 134, 139, 143, 157, 182, 197
    Africa, 205
    Burma, 206-216
10th Battalion, 134
11th Battalion, 120-131, 134, 139, 144-145, 147, 150-151
12th Battalion, 134
Bouchain, 23
Bourbon, House of, 18
Bower, Brig R. H., 191
Boyne, Battle of the, 14
Brandywine, Battle of, 47
Breese, Lt-Col C. F. O., 191
Brereton, General, 186
Britten, Lt-Col, 185-186
Broadrick, Lt-Col, 138
Browning, Lt-General F. A. M., 186
Buffs, The, 16, 167, 173, 193
Buller, Sir Redvers, 116-118
Bulow, General, 80

Burgess, Captain J. L., 169
Burgess, Lt-Col J., 202-203
Burgoyne, General John, 46, 48-49
Busaco, Battle of, 64
Bushman's Kop, Battle of, The, 119
Butler, Lt, 90
Byng, Admiral, 34

Cadiz, 22
Campbell, Sir Colin, 109-110
Cambrai, Battle of, 149-150
Cambridge, Duke of (C in C), 114
Canning, Lord, 108
Cardigan, Lord, 107
Cardwell, Lord Edward, 113, 114, 127
'Cardwell System', The, 114
Carleton, Sir Guy, 48
Carlisle Castle, 17-18
Carlyle, Thomas, 54
Carpenter, Col, 101
Carruthers, 2nd Lt G., 175
Carter, Cpl, 121
Catalonia, 19
Cavendish, Lord Frederick, 36, 51
Cecill, Capt, 15
Chamberlain, Neville, 165
Chambers, Lt-Col, W. H., 165
Chapoo, 92
Charles II, 13
Charles, Archduke, 19, 20
    King of Spain, 20
Cheshire Yeomany, The, 85, 194
China, Civil War, 162-163
Cholmondeley, Col the Hon James, 27
Chudleigh, Col, 26-27
Churchill, Sir Winston, 168, 192
Clark, Sgt, 191
Clements, Cpl, 93
Clements, General, 123
Clinton, General Sir Henry, 47
Colchester, 14
Coldstream Regiment, The, 13
Colenso, Battle of, 116-118
Colville, General, 119
Connaught Rangers, The (88th Regiment), 56, 116
Cooker, Sergeant Drummer, 180
Cooper, Lt-Col, 177
Cooper, Major, 212

Cornwallis, Colonel, 27
Cornwallis, General Lord, 45
Corunna, 25
Cowan, Assistant Surgeon, 102
Crimean War, The, 96, 102-103, 105-108, 111, 114-115, 127
Crowther, Major-General H. G., 214
Cuddy, Lt (later Brevet Lt-Col), 92, 93, 105
Culloden, Battle of, 32-33
Culyer, Lt, 42
Cumberland, Duke of, 29, 32
Cumberland Volunteers, 119
Cunningham, General Sir Alan, 165

Dalzell, Capt, 42
Dannenberg, General, 100
Dare, Col, Thomas, 15
Darwell, Brigadier, 186
Daubeney, Major-General Sir H. C. E., 90-91
Davidson, Colour-Sergeant, 90
D-Day, 178, 187
de Burgh, General, 55
d'Estaing, Admiral, 47-48
de Montcalm, Marquis, 39
de Vendreuil, Marquis, 42
Devonshire Regiment, 156
Dill, General Sir John, 165
Dorset Regiment, 155, 189
Doyle, Drummer, 105
Dublin Fusiliers, 120
Duel, Ensign, 90-91
Duke of Wellington's Regiment, 202, 204
Dunkirk, 23
Durham Light Infantry, 195

East Lancashire Regiment, 215
Effingham, Earl of, 36
Eighth Army, 194
18th Regiment, 89
Eisenhower, General, 178
Elizabeth II, HM Queen, 220
Ellis, Major A. J., 161
Essex Regiment, 202, 204
Eversley Royal Commission on Recruiting, 113

Fancourt, Lt-Col, 77
Fanshawe, General, 150
Farouk, King, 219
Farquhar, George, 21
Fenwick, Lt-Col, 73
15th Regiment, 47
51st Highland Division, 168
53rd Regiment, 109
55th Foot, 38-42, 45-49, 51, 54-55, 57-60, 78, 82, 84, 89-102, 104-105, 110-112, 114-115
    Aden, 111
    Cape Town, 82, 87
    Carlisle, 112
    China, 90, 93
    Crimea, 96-97
    Gibraltar, 96, 105
    Holland, 80-81
    India, 110-111
    Ireland, 94, 105, 110
    Jamaica, 78-79
    Scotland, 53
    South Africa, 94
    Uniforms, 39
    West Indies, 48, 57
Fitzgerald, Lt D. K., 167
Flynn, Biddy, 74-76
Foch, General, 151, 153
Fontenoy, Battle of, 29
Forbes-Robertson, Lt-Col J. R., VC, 152-153
Fort du Quesne, 39
Fort, Edward, 49
Fort George, 49
Fort Land Guard, 16-17
Fort Niagara, 41
Fort St Philip, 33
41st Regiment, 100
42nd Regiment, 46-47
42nd Highlanders, 30, 84
44th Regiment, 46, 58-59
45th Regiment, 58
46th Regiment, 47
48th Regiment, 58-59
49th Regiment, 89, 92
Fowke, General, 35

Gallipoli, 135-137, 139
Garth, Major, 15
Gates, General, 48-49
Geary, Lt-Col Owen, 226

George, Cpl D., 198
George I, 25
George II, 35-36
Gibbon, Major John, 218
Gibraltar, 26
Gladstone, W. E., 113
Glider Pilot Regiment, The, 218
Gomm, Lt-Col, 57-58
Goodall, Ensign, 81
Godwin-Austen, Brigadier A. R., 164
Gordon Highlanders, 129, 156
Gordon, Lt-Col Hamilton, 154
Gortschakoff, Prince, 100
Gough, Sir Hugh, 89-90, 92-93
Gracey, Major-General D. D., 197
Graham, Lt-Col Sir Fergus, 175
Graham, General Sir Thomas, 80
Grant, Major-General James, 47, 51
Grenadier Guards, 129
Grey, General, 46
Grey, Sir Charles, 54, 57
Gurkha Rifles, 197-198, 202, 205

Haddon, Major (later Lt-Col) T.,
    185, 189
Haig, Field Marshal Earl, 142, 148
Haldane, R. B., 127
Hamilton, Lt-Col Hans, 18
Hamilton, General Sir Ian, 122, 135-
    137, 139
Harker, Major G. B., 202
Harrison, Col G. Hyde (see Hyde
    Harrison)
Hart, Major-General Fitzroy, 120
Harvey, Lt-Col, 209-210
Havannah, 36
Haviland, Col, 42
Hawley, General, 32
Hayes, Lt-Col Robert, 27
Hetherington, Capt, 206
Heyliss, Pte Thomas, 117-118
Highland Division, The (see Eric
    Linklater)
Hill, General Sir Rowland (later
    Lord), 66-68, 71, 76, 186
Hinde, Col, 118
Hindenburg Line, 155, 157
Hitler, Adolf, 165, 173
Home Guard, 173
Hong Kong, 89-90
Horse Grenadier Guards, 36

Howe, Lord George, 39
Howe, Admiral Lord Richard, 44
Howe, General Sir William, 44-49
Hubbard, Mr, 17
Hume, Col Sir Gustavus, 97
Hume, Major-General John, 97, 99
    114
Hume, General Sir Robert, 97 99,
    111, 136
Hume, Capt Walter, 97
Hunter, Sgt, 200
Hunter-Weston, Major-General, 135-
    136
Hyde Harrison, Brigadier G., 163

Indian Mutiny, 108
Inkerman, Battle of, 100-101
Inniskillings, 123
Irish Brigade (General Hart's
    Brigade), 118-119
Irwin, General, 205

Jacob, Sir John, 14
James II, 14, 25
John Peel (Regimental March), 115,
    119-120, 140, 142, 225
Johnson, Sir William, 41
Jones, Col, 17

Kaffirs, The, 87
Kaiser, 129, 144
Kelly, Col, 108-109
Kelly, Pte, 93
Kerr, Capt, 140
Kerr, Lt-Col W., 156
King's Own Border Regiment, 220-
    221
King's Own Royal Regiment (Lan-
    caster), 181, 219
King's Own Scottish Borderers, 153,
    186, 189-190
King's Regiment, 175, 179, 215
Kitchener, Lord, 129
Kitson, Capt, 15

Ladysmith, 116, 118-119
Lass O'Gowrie (Regimental March),
    115

Law, Lt-Col H. F. d'A. S., 170, 171
Lawrence, Sgt, 29
League of Nations, 164
Lechine, Capt, 15
Lennon, Pte, 199
'Light Bobs', 46
Light Brigade, Charge of the, 107
Linklater, Eric (*The Highland Division*), 169
Lister, Pte, 176
Long, Major-General, 78
'Long Peace', The, 83
Lonsdale, Earl of, 129-130, 134
'Lonsdales', The (see Border Regiment, 11th Battalion)
Loos, Battle of, 129
Loudon, Earl of, 39
Louis XIV, 14, 23
Louis XVIII, 76
Lucan, Lord, 107
Lucas, Lord Robert, 14-16, 18
Lucknow, 108-111
Ludendorff, General Erich von, 157-158
Lugard, Sir Edward, 110

Macdonald, Sgt, 150
MacDonald, Lt-Col T. W., 182
Machell, Capt P. W., 134
Machell, Col, 142
Mafeking, 120-121
Maitland, Sgt, 93
Malplaquet, Battle of, 22
Manchester Regiment, 155, 181
Marlborough, Duke of, 18, 22-24
Marmont, Marshal, 71-72
Mawood, Colonel, 45
Magaliesburg, 123
Massena, Marshal, 64
Mill, Col, 88
Minorca, 33-35
Minshull-Ford, Brigadier-General M., 140
Moira, Lord, 78
Monk, General, 13
Montgomery, Field Marshal Lord, 178, 186-187, 191
Montjuich, 19-20
Moore, General John, 59
Moro, 36

Mountbatten, Admiral Lord Louis, 209
Munro, Brigadier, 78
Munro, General Sir Charles, 139, 158
Murray, Col, 41
Mussolini, Benito, 164

Napier, Sir William, 29, 65, 76
Napoleon, 72, 76-77, 79, 81-83
National Service Act, 1939, 165
Naval and Military Memoirs (see Beatson)
Newdigate, Col, 112
New Model Army, 13
Nightingale, Florence, 102, 108
Nijmegen, 187-191
92nd Highlanders, 96
Nive, Battle of, 76
Norfolk, 14-15
North Lancashire Regiment (9th Loyal Regiment), 155

Orange, The Prince of, 57
Ormonde, Duke of, 22
Orthes, Battle of, 76

Paget, Lord George, 107
Pardon, Capt, 15
Parsons, Capt, 15
Parliament, 17
Peel, Sir Robert, 85
Pélissier, General, 104
Pemberton, W. B. (*Battles of the Crimean War*), 98
Pennefather, General, 99
Perry, Col George, 38
Peru, 25
Peterborough, Earl of, 18-19
'Peterloo Massacre', 85
Philip, Duke of Anjou, 13
Philip, King, 20
Pichegru, General, 55
Picton, Sir Thomas, 72-73
Plumer, General (later Field Marshal), Sir Herbert, 148-149
Pontevedra, 26
Pope, C. S. M., 185
Powell, Lt-Col, 32

Prideaux, Brigadier-General, 41
Probyn's Horse, 212

'Q' Authorities, 17
Quick, Bandmaster, 226

Raglan, Lord, 104
Ramillies, Battle of, 22
Rawlinson, Lord, 162
Recruiting Officer, The, 21
Redan, The, 104
Regimental Marches, 225-226
Rendell, Assistant Surgeon, 102
Richelieu, Marshal, 34-35
Ring, Ensign, 81
Roberts, General Lord, 118-120
Robinson, Lt-Col, 220
Rondondella, 26
Rooke, Sir George, 18
Rough Notes of an Old Soldier (see George Bell)
Royal Army Service Corps, 168
Royal Artillery, 93, 202, 204
Royal Fusiliers, 136
Royal Scots, 13
Russell, Dr 'Billy', 96-97, 100, 108

St Arnaud, Marshal, 97
St Leger, Col, 48
St Malo, 35
Salamanca, 72
Saratoga, Battle of, 48-49
Saxe, Marshal, 29
Schoedde, Col (later Major-General), 92
Scots Guards, 129
Scutari, 102
Seabright, Pte, 104
Seaforth Highlanders, 174
Sebastopol, 99, 103, 105
Seven Years' War, 36
17th Regiment, 45
Shadwell, Capt, 15
Shears, General, 175
Sherwood Foresters, 167
Short Service Act, 1870, 113
Shovell, Sir Cloudesley, 18
Simms, Pte, VC, 104
69th Regiment, 80-81

Skiddy, Mrs. Bridget, 74-75
Slim, Field Marshal Viscount 200-201, 204, 206
Smith-Dorrien, Sir Horace, 128
Smith, Pte James, VC, 131-132
Smith O'Brien Rebellion, 94
Soamwar Pettah, 88
Soldier's Glory (see George Bell)
Somme, Battle of the, 141, 149-151
Somme, Second Battle of the, 155
Soult, Marshal, 64, 71, 76
South African War, 115, 120, 127
South Staffordshire Regiment, 188, 218
South Wales Borderers, 153
Spain, King of, 26
Spanish Succession, War of the, 16
Spectator, The, 15
Spion Kop, 117
Stair, Mrs, 161
Starkie, Pte, 120
Stee, L/Cpl, 150
Steele, Capt (Richard Steele), 15, 17
Stilwell, General, 197-199, 202, 206
Stuart, Charles Edward, 30-32
Sussex Regiment (25th), 63
Suvla Bay, 137-138

Tarleton, Lt-Col G., 165
Tatler, The, 15
Taylor, Sgt, 150
Teesdale, Sgt (28th Foot), 28
Territorial Army, 123, 160-161, 165, 167, 180-181
Thirteenth Light Infantry, 14
30th Regiment, 99
33rd Regiment, 80
34th Regiment of Foot, The, 15-16, 63-67, 71, 73, 82, 84, 86-87, 94, 103-105, 108-110, 112, 114, 115
  Amalgamation with 55th Foot, 38
  Airey, Lt-Col, 86-87
  'Ball tuft', 86
  Canada, 48
  Cape Town, 82
  Carlisle, 112
  Culloden, 32
  Dress, 33
  Flanders, 29-30
  Fort St Philip, 33-34

Forty-Five Rebellion, 32
France, 76
Gibraltar, 26-27
George II, 35
Hawley, General, 32
India, 77-78
Ireland, 77, 85
Laurel Wreath, 30
Minorca, 33-35
Moro, 36
Nive, 76
North America, 86-87
Orthes, 76
Peninsula, 76
St Malo, 35
Seringapatam, 77
Vellone, 77
West Florida, 37
West Indies, 59
37th Madras Rifles, 89
38th Regiment, 109
Thompson, Major A. W., 202
Thompson, Major H. T., 172
Thorpe, Col, 140
Ticonderoga, 39-41, 50
Times, The, 96-97, 108
Tomlinson, Lt-Col, 169
Torres-Vedras, 64
Tortosa, 19
Toussaint L'Ouverture, 79
Tower of London, 16-17, 35
Trevelyan, 22, 24
26th Regiment, 89
28th Regiment, 64, 67
29th Regiment, 64

Urquhart, Major-General, 190
Utrecht, Peace of, 23

Valencia, 19
Varty, Pte, 150
Versailles, Treaty of, 164
Victoria, Queen, 86, 103

Victoria Crosses awarded to Regiment, 229-31
  Acton, Pte Abraham, 131-132
  Beach, Pte, 101
  Forbes-Robertson, Lt-Col J. R., 152
  Simms, Pte, 104
  Smith, Pte James, 131-132
Vigo, Port of, 26
Villars, General Claude, 23
Vittoria, Battle of, 72

Wade, General, 31
War Office, The, 130
Warren, Col, 91, 93, 98-99, 176
Warren, General, 117
Washington, George, 45-47
Waterloo, 77, 82, 84-85
Wavell, Field Marshal Lord, 193-194, 197, 209
Welch, Lt, 185
Wellesley, Sir Arthur (see Duke of Wellington)
Wellington, Duke of, 63-64, 68, 70-74, 76, 79, 82, 84, 107
Wells, H. G., 128

Westbrooke, Pte, 150
Wheel, Betty, 74
White, Major-General, 54
White Plains, Battle of the, 45
William, King, 14-15
Williams, Col Bill, 198
Wingate, Brigadier Orde, 197, 202-203
Woodyatt, Major-General, 160
Worsley, Major Henry, 73
Wyndham, General, 108-109

York, The Duke of, 54-55, 57, 59
Ypres, Battles of, 131, 147, 149

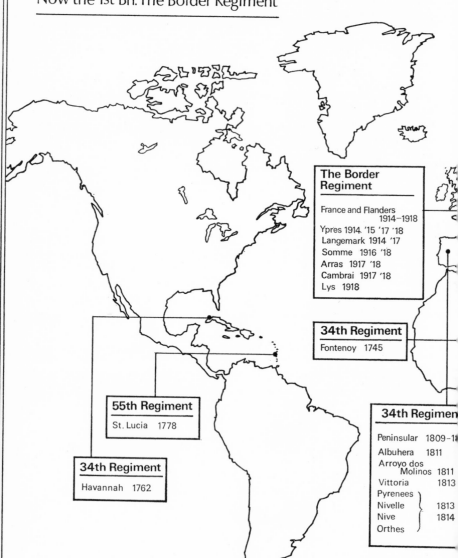

THE 34th REGIMENT OF FOOT
(Raised 1702)
Now the 1st Bn. The Border Regiment

The Border Regiment

France and Flanders
1914—1918

Ypres 1914. '15 '17 '18
Langemark 1914 '17
Somme 1916 '18
Arras 1917 '18
Cambrai 1917 '18
Lys 1918

34th Regiment

Fontenoy 1745

55th Regiment

St. Lucia 1778

34th Regiment

Havannah 1762

34th Regimen

Peninsular 1809-18

Albuhera 1811
Arroyo dos
   Molinos 1811
Vittoria 1813
Pyrenees
Nivelle } 1813
Nive 1814
Orthes